CLYMER®

SUZUKI

GS400-450 CHAIN DRIVE • 1977-1987

The world's finest publisherr of mechanical how-to manuals

CLYMER®

P.O. Box 12901, Overland Park, Kansas 66282-2901

Copyright ©1989 Penton Business Media Inc.

FIRST EDITION
First Printing July, 1978
Second Printing February, 1982

SECOND EDITION
Updated by Dave Sales to include 1981 models
First Printing February, 1982

THIRD EDITION
Updated by Dave Sales to include 1982-1983 models
First Printing March, 1984
Second Printing May, 1985
Third Printing April, 1986
Fourth Printing June, 1988

FOURTH EDITION
Updated by Ed Scott to include 1984-1987 models
First Printing August, 1989
Second Printing May, 1991
Third Printing January, 1993
Fourth Printing January, 1995
Fifth Printing November, 1997
Sixth Printing June, 2000
Seventh Printing November, 2003
Eighth Printing November, 2006
Ninth Printing March, 2012

Printed in U.S.A.

CLYMER and colophon are registered trademarks of Penton Business Media Inc.

ISBN-10: 0-89287-237-2

ISBN-13: 978-0-89287-237-4

MEMBER

*COVER: 1982 GS450T courtesy of Diane Picco of Shorewood, Il. Photographed by Dave Picco. Special thanks to the Suzuki Owners Club or Ammerica (**soc-usa.org**) and to Jason Shields, who has been a good friend and great advisor on all things GS related.*

*TOOLS AND EQUIPMENT: K & L Supply Co. at **klsupply.com**.*

CLYMER®

Publisher Ron Rogers

EDITORIAL

Editorial Director
James Grooms

Editor
Steven Thomas

Associate Editor
Rick Arens

Authors
Ed Scott
Ron Wright
Michael Morlan
George Parise
Jay Bogart

Illustrators
Bob Meyer
Steve Amos
Errol McCarthy
Mitzi McCarthy

SALES

Sales Manager–Marine/I&T
Jay Lipton

Sales Manager–Powersport
Matt Tusken

CUSTOMER SERVICE

Customer Service Manager
Terri Cannon

Customer Service Representatives
Dinah Bunnell
Suzanne Johnson
April LeBlond
Sherry Rudkin

PRODUCTION

Director of Production
Dylan Goodwin

Production Manager
Greg Araujo

Senior Production Editors
Darin Watson
Adriane Wineinger

Associate Production Editors
Ashley Bally
Samantha Collins

Penton

P.O. Box 12901, Overland Park, KS 66282-2901 • 800-262-1954 • 913-967-1719

More information available at *clymer.com*

CONTENTS

QUICK REFERENCE DATA

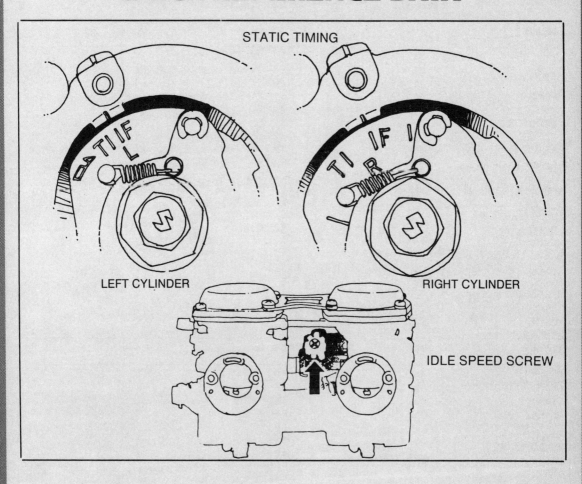

STATIC TIMING

LEFT CYLINDER

RIGHT CYLINDER

IDLE SPEED SCREW

TUNE-UP SPECIFICATIONS

Recommended spark plug	
1977-1985	NGK B8ES or ND W24ES
1986-on	NGK B8ES or ND W24ES-U
Spark plug gap	0.6-0.8 mm (0.024-0.031 in.)
Breaker point ignition (GS400, GS425)	
Point gap	0.3-0.4 mm (0.012-0.016 in.)
Dwell angle	
GS400	180°
GS425	190°
Valve clearance (cold)	0.03-0.08 mm ((0.0012-0.0031 in.)
Ignition timing *	
GS400, GS425	10° BTDC below 1,500 rpm
	40° BTDC above 3,600 rpm
GS450	10° BTDC below 1,650 rpm
	40° BTDC above 3,500 rpm
Idle speed	1,100-1,300 rpm
Carburetor air screw	
All models manufactured	
after January 1978	Pre-set @ factory (non-adjustable)
All earlier models	1 1/4 turns open

* Timing on GS450 models is pre-set. No routine timing adjustment is necessary.

CAPACITIES

Fuel tank	Liters	U.S. gal.	Imp. gal.
GS400, GS425	14	3.7	3.1
GS450L	11	2.9	2.4
GS450E, S	15	4.0	3.3
GS450ET, ST, LT, TX	14	3.7	3.1
GS450LZ	11	2.9	2.4
GS450TZ, TXZ	12	3.2	2.6
GS450EZ	14.5	3.8	3.2
All 1983 models	16	4.2	3.5
All 1985-on models	13	3.4	2.9

Engine/transmission oil	cc	U.S. qt.	Imp. qt.
Without filter change			
GS400, GS425	2100	2.2	1.8
GS450	2600	2.7	2.3
With filter change			
GS400, GS425	2400	2.5	2.1
GS450	2900	3.1	2.6
At overhaul			
GS400, GS425	2700	2.8	2.4
GS450	3000	3.2	2.6

Fork oil	cc	U.S. oz.	Imp. oz.
GS400	145	4.9	5.1
GS425L	160	5.4	5.6
GS450N, C	145	4.9	5.1
GS450LZ	189	6.4	6.7
GS450EZ	178	6.0	6.3
GS450TZ	181	6.1	6.4
GS450TXZ	143	4.8	5.0
GS450ED			
Right leg	165	5.6	5.8
Left leg	187	6.3	6.6
GS450TXD	155	5.2	5.5
GS450LD, LF, LG, LH	277	9.4	9.8

Fork oil level *	mm	in.
GS400	187	7.1
GS425LZ	173	6.8
GS425E	187	7.1
GS450LZ	117	4.6
GS450EZ	131	5.6
GS450TZ	125	4.9
GS450TXZ, TXD	208	8.2
GS450ED	190	7.5
GS450LD, LF, LG, LH	118.5	4.7

* Measure the oil level from the top of the fork leg with the fork leg held vertical, the spring removed and the fork leg completely compressed.

INTRODUCTION

This detailed, comprehensive manual covers the Suzuki 400-450 series twins from 1977-1987.

The expert text gives complete information on maintenance, tune-up, repair and overhaul. Hundreds of photos and drawings guide you through every step. The book includes all you will need to know to keep your Suzuki running right. Throughout this book where differences occur among the models, they are clearly identified.

A shop manual is a reference. You want to be able to find information fast. As in all Clymer books, this one is designed with you in mind. All chapters are thumb tabbed. Important items are extensively indexed at the rear of the book. All procedures, tables, photos, etc., in this manual are for the reader who may be working on the bike for the first time or using this manual for the first time. All the most frequently used specifications and capacities are summarized in the *Quick Reference Data* pages at the front of the book.

Keep the book handy in your tool box. It will help you better understand how your bike runs, lower repair costs and generally improve your satisfaction with the bike.

CHAPTER ONE

GENERAL INFORMATION

This book provides service and maintenance procedures for the Suzuki GS400, GS425 and GS450 motorcycles with a manual transmission and chain drive since 1977.

Repairing and maintaining your own motorcycle can be an enjoyable and rewarding experience. The following topics provide information on how to use this book as well as general service hints and techniques to make the work as easy and enjoyable as possible.

HOW TO USE THIS MANUAL

This manual has been specifically written and formatted for the amateur home mechanic. All procedures, tables, photos, etc., in this manual assume that the reader may be working on the bike or using this manual for the first time. This section is included to acquaint the home mechanic with what is in the manual and how to best take advantage of the information.

For the most frequently used general information and maintenance specifications refer to the *Quick Reference Data* pages. These colored pages in the front of the book represent a compilation of the most commonly "referred to" facts. The *Quick Reference Data* pages save you from searching each chapter of the manual every time this information is needed. Readily accessible information can help prevent serious and expensive mechanical errors.

To save time on all maintenance tasks, use the *Index*. The *Index* in the back of this manual has been carefully prepared and lists all major maintenance tasks by paragraph heading. Whether you want to remove the pistons or simply adjust the drive chain, a quick look in the *Index* will tell you exactly what page it is on.

For a better understanding of manual contents refer to the section on *Chapter Organization* in this chapter.

To save yourself time, energy and possible future aggravation, finish reading this entire chapter. If you acquaint yourself with all the special features of this manual it can become a valuable and indispensable tool. This manual can help you achieve a better maintained and more reliable machine.

CHAPTER ORGANIZATION

This chapter provides general information on how this manual is organized as well as special information and maintenance tips to aid all repair tasks. Read this entire chapter before performing any maintenance procedure.

Chapter Two, *Troubleshooting*, contains many suggestions and tips for finding and fixing troubles fast. Troubleshooting procedures discuss symptoms and logical methods to pinpoint the trouble.

Chapter Three, *Lubrication, Maintenance and Tune-up*, includes all normal periodic and preventive maintenance tasks designed to keep your machine in peak operating condition.

Subsequent chapters describe specific systems such as engine, clutch and fuel system. Each chapter provides complete disassembly, repair and reassembly procedures in easy to follow, step-by-step form. If a repair is impractical for home mechanics, it is so indicated. Usually, such repairs are more economically done by a Suzuki dealer or qualified specialist.

NOTES, CAUTIONS AND WARNINGS

NOTES, CAUTIONS, and WARNINGS appear throughout this manual and provide specific and important information to the reader. A NOTE usually provides extra or special information to make a step or procedure clearer. Disregarding a NOTE might cause inconvenience but will not cause damage or personal injury.

A CAUTION is provided in a procedure wherever mechanical damage of any type may occur. Failure to heed a CAUTION will most certainly result in some form of damage to the machine; however, personal injury is unlikely. WARNINGS are the most serious and are included in a procedure where personal injury may occur if the WARNING is not heeded. Mechanical damage may also occur.

PHOTOS, DRAWINGS AND TABLES

This manual contains literally hundreds of photos, drawings and tables that are used to support and clarify maintenance procedures. Each photo, drawing and table is referenced at least once within a specific procedure. When using a procedure, take full advantage of all the support data provided to make your job easier and help avoid costly errors.

MODEL IDENTIFICATION

Suzuki will often make modifications and improvements during a model year. Mid-year

changes are usually minor, however, if you are performing repair work you will want to install the latest, most improved parts possible. It is important to keep a record of your engine number and frame number when ordering parts. The applicability of all improved parts is always referenced by the engine number and/ or the frame number. The engine number is stamped on the top of the crankcase (**Figure 1**). The frame number is stamped on the steering head (**Figure 2**). When purchasing new parts, if possible, always compare them to the old parts. If the parts are not alike, have the parts or service manager explain the difference to you.

GENERAL MAINTENANCE HINTS

Most of the service procedures provided in this book can be performed by anyone reasonably handy with tools. It is suggested, however, that you carefully consider your own

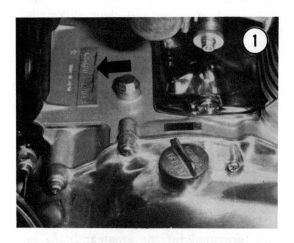

capabilities before attempting any repair task which involves major disassembly of the engine and transmission.

Crankshaft repairs, for example, require the use of a heavy-duty hydraulic press. This type of repair work must be performed by a competent machine shop or authorized dealer. Other procedures require precision measurements and, unless you have the skills and equipment to make them, it would be better to have a motorcycle shop do the work.

Repairs can be made faster and easier if the motorcycle is clean before you begin work. Good soap and pressurized water are usually the best to clean all but the most stubborn dirt or grease. High-pressure, coin-operated car washes do a good job of cleaning, however, the bike must be completely dried and lubricated after washing. High-pressure water and detergent can easily enter the wheels, swinging arm and other critical areas and cause corrosion if not treated immediately after cleaning. Clean all oily and greasy parts with cleaning solvent. An approved solvent is usually available in bulk form from many automobile service stations and parts stores. *Never use gasoline as a cleaning agent.* It presents an extreme fire hazard. Always work in a well-ventilated area when using cleaning solvent. Keep a fire extinguisher, rated for gasoline and oil fires, handy just in case. If you are not used to working with cleaning solvent wear rubber gloves, if possible, or treat your hands with a good skin lotion immediately after cleaning parts. Solvent will remove the skin oils from your hands and cause painful and irritating "solvent burns" if left untreated.

Special tools are required for some service procedures. All special tools necessary are referenced by a Suzuki part number and are available from an authorized dealer. If you are on good terms with the dealer's service department or know a professional motorcycle mechanic, you may be able to borrow what you need. Naturally, much of the labor charge made for repairs by a dealer is for removal and disassembly of other parts to reach the defective area. It is usually possible to perform much of the preliminary work yourself and

then take the affected part or assembly to the dealer for repair.

Once you decide to tackle a job yourself, read the entire section pertaining to the task. Study the procedures, illustrations, tables and other support data until you have a thorough idea of what is involved in the job. If special tools are required, make arrangements for them before beginning the work. It is very frustrating to get partway into a job and then discover you do not have the necessary parts or tools to complete it.

GENERAL MAINTENANCE AND REPAIR HINTS

Most of the service procedures covered in this manual are straightforward and can be performed by anyone reasonably handy with tools.

Simple wiring checks can be easily made at home; but knowledge of electronics is almost a necessity for performing tests with complicated electronic testing gear.

During disassembly of parts keep a few general cautions in mind. Force is rarely needed to get things apart. If parts are a tight fit, like a bearing in a case, there is usually a tool made to separate them. Never use a screwdriver to pry apart parts with machined surfaces such as crankcase halves and valve covers. You will mar the surfaces and end up with leaks.

Make diagrams wherever similar-appearing parts are found. For instance, case cover screws are often not the same length. You may think you can remember where everything came from—but mistakes are costly. There is also the possibility that you may be sidetracked and not return to work for days or even weeks—in which interval carefully laid out parts may have become disturbed.

Tag all similar internal parts for location and mark all mating parts for position. Record number and thickness of any shims as they are removed. Small parts such as bolts can be identified by placing them in plastic sandwich bags. Seal and label the bags with masking tape.

Wiring should be tagged with masking tape and marked as each wire is removed. Again, do not rely on memory alone.

Use a locking compound such as Loctite Lock N' Seal No. 2114 on all bolts and nuts, even if they are secured with lockwashers. This type of Loctite does not harden completely and allows easy removal of the bolt or nut. A screw lost from an engine cover or bearing retainer could easily cause serious and expensive damage before its loss is noticed.

When applying Loctite, use a small amount. If too much is used, it can squeeze out and stick to parts not meant to be stuck.

When replacing missing or broken bolts, particularly on the engine or frame components, always use Suzuki replacement bolts. They are specially hardened for each application. The wrong 15-cent bolt could easily cause many dollars worth of serious damage, not to mention rider injury.

When installing gaskets in the engine, always use Suzuki replacement gaskets *without* sealer, unless specifically designated. Suzuki gaskets are designed to swell when in contact with oil. Gasket sealer prevents the gaskets from swelling as intended, resulting in oil leaks. Suzuki gaskets are also cut from material of the precise thickness needed.

Disconnect battery ground cable before working near electrical connections and before disconnecting wires. Never run the engine with the battery disconnected; the alternator could be seriously damaged.

Protect finished surfaces from physical damage or corrosion. Keep gasoline and brake fluid off painted surfaces.

Avoid flames or sparks when working near a charging battery or flammable liquids such as brake fluid or gasoline.

No parts, except those assembled with a press fit, require unusual force during assembly. If a part is hard to remove or install, find out why before proceeding.

Cover all openings after removing parts to keep dirt, small tools, etc., from falling in.

When assembling two parts, start all fasteners, then tighten evenly.

Heavy grease can be used to hold small parts in place if they tend to fall out during assembly.

However, keep grease and oil away from electrical components or brake pads and discs.

Carburetors are best cleaned by disassembling them and soaking the parts in a commercial carburetor cleaner. Never soak gaskets and rubber parts in these cleaners. Never use wire to clean out jets and air passages; they are easily damaged. Use compressed air to blow out carburetor only if float has been removed first.

A baby bottle makes a good measuring device for adding oil to forks and transmissions. Get one that is graduated in ounces and cubic centimeters.

Take your time and do the job right. Do not forget that a newly rebuilt motorcycle engine must be broken in the same as a new one. Keep rpm within the limits given in your owner's manual when you get back on the road.

SAFETY FIRST

Professional motorcycle mechanics can work for years and never sustain a serious injury. If you observe a few rules of common sense and safety, you can enjoy many safe hours servicing your own machine. You could hurt yourself or damage the bike if you ignore these rules.

1. Never use gasoline as a cleaning solvent.
2. Never smoke or use a torch in the vicinity of flammable liquids such as cleaning solvent in open containers.
3. Never smoke or use a torch in an area where batteries are being charged. Highly explosive hydrogen gas is formed during the charging process.
4. If welding or brazing is required on the machine, remove the fuel tank to a safe distance, at least 50 feet away. Welding on gas tanks requires special safety procedures and must be performed by someone skilled in the process.
5. Use the proper sized wrenches to avoid damage to nuts and injury to yourself.
6. When loosening a tight or stuck nut, be guided by what would happen if the wrench slipped. Protect yourself accordingly.
7. Keep your work area clean and uncluttered.

8. Wear safety goggles during all operations involving drilling, grinding, or use of a cold chisel.

9. Never use worn tools.

10. Keep a fire extinguisher handy and be sure it is rated for gasoline and electrical fires.

EXPENDABLE SUPPLIES

Certain expendable supplies are required. These include grease, oil, wiping rags, cleaning solvent, and distilled water. Ask your dealer for the special locking compounds, silicone lubricants, and commercial chain lube products which make motorcycle maintenance

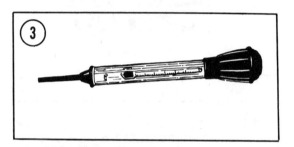

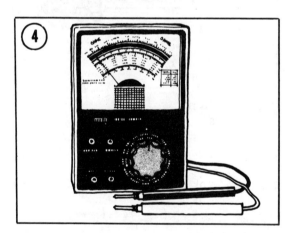

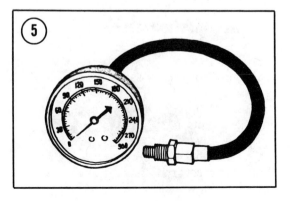

simpler and easier. Solvent is available at most service stations and distilled water for the battery is available at most supermarkets.

TOOLS

For proper servicing, you will need an assortment of ordinary handtools. As a minimum, these include:

a. Metric combination wrenches
b. Metric sockets
c. Plastic mallet
d. Small hammer
e. Snap ring pliers
f. Gas pliers
g. Phillips screwdrivers
h. Slot (common) screwdrivers
i. Feeler gauges
j. Spark plug gauges
k. Spark plug wrench
l. Dial indicator

Engine tune-up and troubleshooting procedures require a few more tools, described in the following section.

Hydrometer

This instrument measures state of charge of the battery, and tells much about battery condition. Such an instrument is available at any auto parts store and through most larger mail order outlets. See **Figure 3**.

Multimeter or VOM

This instrument (**Figure 4**) is invaluable for electrical system troubleshooting and service. A few of its functions may be duplicated by locally fabricated substitutes, but for the serious hobbyist, it is a must. Its uses are described in the applicable sections of this book.

Compression Gauge

An engine with low compression cannot be properly tuned and will not develop full power. A compression gauge measures engine compression. The one shown in **Figure 5** has a flexible stem which enables it to reach cylinders where there is little clearance between the cylinder head and frame. This type of gauge is available at auto accessory stores or by mail order from large catalog order firms.

Impact Driver

This tool might have been designed with the motorcyclist in mind. It makes removal of engine cover screws easy, and eliminates damaged screw slots. Good ones are available at larger hardware stores. See **Figure 6**.

Carburetor Gauge Set

A gauge set which can display manifold vacuum for both cylinders simultaneously will greatly simplify carburetor synchronization. **Figure 7** shows the Suzuki gauge set. Other aftermarket versions are available.

Strobe Timing Light

This instrument is necessary for tuning. It permits very accurate ignition timing by flashing a light at the precise instant the cylinder fires. Marks on the ignition advance governor are lined up with the side cover mark while the engine is running.

Suitable lights range from inexpensive neon bulb types ($2-3) to powerful xenon strobe lights ($20-40). See **Figure 8**. Neon timing lights are difficult to see and must be used in dimly lit areas. Xenon strobe timing lights can be used outside in bright sunlight. Both types work on this motorcycle; use according to the manufacturer's instructions.

Tappet Depressor and Tweezer

The Suzuki tappet depressor (**Figure 9**) is absolutely necessary for performing valve adjustments with the camshafts installed. It is used to hold valve tappets down so the adjustment shims can be removed. If you plan to do your own valve adjustments, order this tool (part No. 09916-64510) from your local dealer.

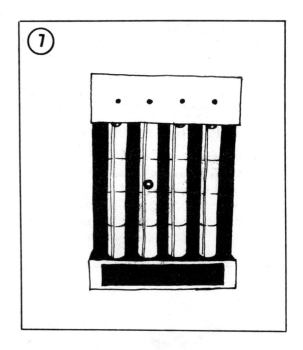

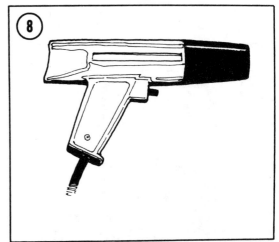

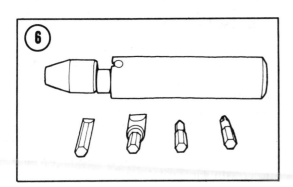

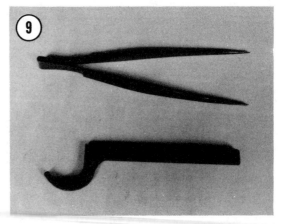

Valve Clearance Feeler Gauge

Valve clearances on GS models are critical and have very small tolerance (0.03-0.08 mm). This Suzuki special tool (part No. 09900-20803) is particularly useful for setting valve clearances because it contains gauges ranging from 0.02-1.00 mm with many small sizes not usually available in most feeler gauge

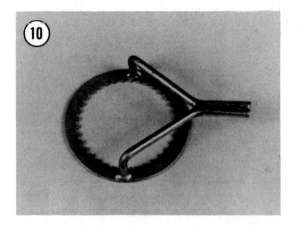

sets. This tool can be purchased from your local Suzuki dealer.

Clutch Hub Holding Tool

This handy tool (part No. 09920-51510) is used to hold the clutch hub so the hub nut can be removed (**Figure 10**). A substitute tool can easily be fabricated by welding steel rods to an old steel clutch plate; however, if you don't have access to a welder it may be cheaper to buy the tool than have one made. The tool is available from your local Suzuki dealer.

Compothane Mallet

This plastic covered "dead-blow" mallet is virtually indestructable and has become a favorite tool among most professional and amateur motorcycle mechanics. This mallet can be used on most metal surfaces without causing any damage to the surface. The mallet is available in a variety of shapes and weights and can be purchased from most professional tool distributors such as Snap-On and Mac.

CHAPTER TWO

TROUBLESHOOTING

Diagnosing mechanical problems is relatively simple if you use orderly procedures and keep a few basic principles in mind.

The troubleshooting procedures in this chapter analyze typical symptoms, and show logical methods of isolating causes. These are not the only methods. There may be several ways to solve a problem but only a systematic approach can guarantee success.

Never assume anything. Do not overlook the obvious. If you are riding along and the bike suddenly quits, check the easiest, most accessible problem spots first. Is there gasoline in the tank? Is the gas petcock in the ON or RESERVE position? Has a spark plug wire fallen off? Check ignition switch. Sometimes the weight of keys on a key ring may turn the ignition off suddenly.

If nothing obvious turns up in a cursory check, look a little further. Learning to recognize and describe symptoms will make repairs easier for you or a mechanic at the shop. Describe problems accurately and fully. Saying that "it won't run" isn't the same as saying "it quit on the highway at high speed and wouldn't start," or that "it sat in my garage for three months and then wouldn't start".

Gather as many symptoms together as possible to aid in diagnosis. Note whether the engine lost power gradually or all at once, what color smoke (if any) came from the exhaust, and so on. Remember that the more complicated a machine is, the easier it is to troubleshoot because symptoms point to specific problems.

After the symptoms are defined, areas which could cause the problems are tested and analyzed. Guessing at the cause of the problem may provide the solution, but it can easily lead to frustration, wasted time, and a series of expensive, unnecessary parts replacements.

You do not need fancy equipment or complicated test gear to determine whether repairs can be attempted at home. A few simple checks could save a large repair bill and time lost while the bike sits in a dealer's service department. On the other hand, be realistic and do not attempt repairs beyond your abilities. Service departments tend to charge heavily for putting together a disassembled engine that may have been abused. Some won't even take on such a job—so use common sense, don't get in over your head.

OPERATING REQUIREMENTS

An engine needs three basics to run properly: correct gas/air mixture, compression, and a spark at the right time. If one or more of these components are missing, the engine won't run.

The electrical system is the weakest link of the three. More problems result from electrical breakdowns than from any other source. Keep that in mind before you begin tampering with carburetor adjustments and the like.

If a bike has been sitting for any length of time and refuses to start, check the battery for a charged condition first, then look to the gasoline delivery system. This includes the tank, fuel pump, fuel petcock lines, and the carburetors. Rust may have formed in the tank, obstructing fuel flow. Gasoline deposits may have gummed up carburetor jets and air passages. Gasoline tends to lose its potency after standing for long periods. Condensation may contaminate it with water. Drain old gas and try starting with a fresh tankful.

TROUBLESHOOTING INSTRUMENTS

Chapter One lists many of the instruments needed and detailed instructions on their uses.

EMERGENCY TROUBLESHOOTING

When the bike is difficult to start or won't start at all, it does not help to grind away at the starter or kick the tires. Check for obvious problems even before getting out your tools. Go down the following list step-by-step. Do each one; you may be embarrassed to find your kill switch off, but that is better than wearing your battery down with the starter. If the bike still will not start, refer to the appropriate troubleshooting procedures which follow in this chapter.

1. Is there fuel in the tank? Remove the filler cap and rock the bike; listen for fuel sloshing around.

WARNING
Do not use an open flame to check in the tank. A serious explosion is certain to result.

2. Turn fuel petcock to RESERVE or PRIME to be sure that you get the last remaining gas.
3. Is the kill switch on?
4. Is the choke in the right position? It should be down for a cold engine and up for a warm engine.
5. Is the battery dead? Check it with a hydrometer.
6. Has the main fuse blown? Replace it with a good one.

STARTER

Starter system troubles are relatively easy to isolate. The following are common symptoms and cures. **Figure 1** shows a wiring diagram of the starting system. Use it to help isolate troubles.

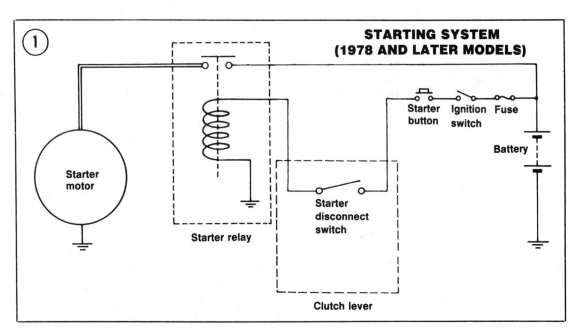

STARTING SYSTEM (1978 AND LATER MODELS)

Starter motor — Starter relay — Starter button — Ignition switch — Fuse — Battery — Starter disconnect switch — Clutch lever

1. *Engine cranks very slowly or not at all*—If the headlight is very dim or not lighting at all, most likely the battery or its connecting wires are at fault. Check battery using procedures described in Chapter Seven. Check wiring for breaks, shorts, and dirty connections.

If the battery and connecting wires check good, the trouble may be in the starter, solenoid, or wiring. To isolate the trouble, short the two large solenoid terminals together (not to ground); if the starter cranks normally, check the starter solenoid wiring. If the starter still fails to crank properly, remove the starter and test it.

2. *Starter engages but will not disengage when switch is released*—Usually caused by a faulty starter solenoid or switch.

CHARGING SYSTEM

Troubleshooting an alternator system is somewhat different from troubleshooting a generator system. For example, *never* short any terminals to ground on the alternator or voltage regulator.

The following symptoms are typical of alternator charging system troubles.

1. *Battery requires frequent charging*—The charging system is not functioning, or it is undercharging the battery. Test the alternator rectifier and voltage regulator as described in Chapter Seven.

2. *Battery requires frequent additions of water or lamps require frequent replacement*—The alternator is probably overcharging the battery. Have the voltage regulator checked or replaced.

3. *Noisy alternator*—Check for loose alternator rotor bolt.

IGNITION

Locating an ignition system miss or complete failure is a relatively simple and logical procedure. Check the obvious first. Is the ignition switch on? Is kill button in the RUN position?

1. Remove one or both spark plugs and reconnect the plug wires.

2. Lay the plug against the cylinder head so that its base makes a good connection with the head, and crank the engine over. A fat blue spark should be visible at the plug electrode. If there is no spark or a very weak spark, perform *Contact Breaker Point and Timing Adjustment* as outlined in Chapter Three.

3. After points have been cleaned and properly gapped, turn on the ignition switch and spring open the points repeatedly with a screwdriver. A small spark should be seen each time the points are opened and a fat blue spark should be visible at the spark plug electrode. A no-spark condition at the points indicates a possible fault in the battery circuit or bad connection or broken wire in the ignition primary circuit. Remove the fuel tank as outlined in Chapter Six; examine the breaker point wire connector (black and white wires) and check for shorted or broken wires.

4. If a small spark is visible at each breaker point set, but no spark or a very weak spark is visible at the spark plug, the malfunction is probably in an ignition coil or condenser. Special test equipment is required to properly test these components. Remove the coil/condenser units as outlined in Chapter Seven and have them tested by a dealer.

ENGINE

These procedures assume that the starter cranks the engine normally. If not, refer to *Starter* in this chapter.

Poor Performance

1. *Engine misses erratically at all speeds*—Intermittent trouble like this can be difficult to find and correct. The fault could be in the ignition system, exhaust system (restriction), or fuel system. Follow troubleshooting procedures for these systems to isolate the trouble.

2. *Engine misses at idle only*—Trouble could exist anywhere in the ignition system. Follow the *Ignition* troubleshooting procedure carefully. Trouble could exist in the carburetor's idle circuits. Check idle mixture adjustments (Chapter Three, *Carburetor Adjustment*) and check for restrictions in the idle circuits.

3. *Engine misses at high speed only*—Trouble could exist in the fuel system or ignition system. Check the fuel lines and valve as described under *Fuel System* in this chapter. Also check spark plugs and high-tension leads (see *Ignition* in this chapter).

4. *Poor performance at all speeds, lack of acceleration*—Trouble usually exists in ignition or fuel system. Check each with the appropriate procedure. Also check for dragging brakes, tight or bound wheel bearings, and correct tire pressure.

5. *Excessive fuel consumption*—This can be caused by a wide variety of seemingly unrelated factors. Check for clutch slippage, dragging brakes, and defective wheel bearings. Check tire pressure. Check ignition and fuel systems.

ENGINE NOISES

1. *Valve clatter*—This is a light to heavy tapping sound from the cam box. It is usually caused by excessive valve clearance. Adjust the clearance as described in Chapter Three. If the noise persists, disassemble the valve drive system as described in Chapter Four and check for worn or damaged cam lobes, broken springs, missing adjustment shims, etc.

2. *Knocking or pinging during acceleration*—May be caused by lower octane fuel that recommended or by poor fuel available from some "discount" service stations. It may also be caused by incorrect ignition timing or spark plugs or wrong heat range. See Chapter Three, *Spark Plug Replacement* and *Contact Breaker Point and Timing Adjustment*.

3. *Slapping or rattling noises at low speed or during acceleration*—May be caused by piston slap, i.e., excessive piston-to-cylinder wall clearance.

4. *Knocking or rapping during deceleration*—Usually caused by excessive rod bearing clearance.

5. *Persistent knocking and vibration*—Usually caused by excessive main bearing clearance.

6. *Rapid on-off squeal*—Compression leak around cylinder head gasket or spark plug.

EXCESSIVE VIBRATION

This can be difficult to locate without disassembling the engine. Usually this is caused by loose engine mounting hardware or worn engine and transmission bearings.

LUBRICATION TROUBLES

Excessive oil consumption—May be caused by worn rings and bores. Overhaul is necessary to correct this. See Chapter Four. It may also be caused by worn valve guides or defective valve guide seals. Also check for exterior leaks.

FUEL SYSTEM

Fuel system trouble must be isolated to the carburetor or fuel lines. These procedures assume that the ignition system has been checked and correctly adjusted.

1. *Engine will not start*—First determine that fuel is being delivered to the carburetors. Disconnect the fuel line at the carburetor. Insert the end of the line into a small container to catch the fuel. Turn the tap to PRIME. Fuel should run from the line. If not, remove tap from tank and clean and check. See Chapter Six.

2. *Rough idle or engine misses and stalls frequently*—Check carburetor adjustments. See Chapter Three.

3. *Stumbling when starting from idle*—Check idle speed adjustment. See Chapter Three.

4. *Engine misses at high speed or lacks power*—Possible fuel starvation. Check fuel delivery. Clean main jets and float needle valves.

5. *Black exhaust smoke*—Black exhaust smoke indicates a badly overrich mixture. Make sure the chokes disengage. Check idle mixture and idle speed. Check for leaky float needle valves and correct float level. Make sure jets are correct size. See Chapter Six.

CLUTCH

All clutch work except adjustment requires removal of the right engine cover. See Chapter Five.

1. *Slippage*—This is most noticeable when accelerating in a high gear from low speed. To check slippage, start the engine, select second gear, and release the clutch as if riding off in first gear. If the clutch is good, the engine will slow and stall. If the clutch slips, increased engine speed will be apparent.

Slippage results from insufficient clutch lever free play, worn plates, or weak springs.

2. *Drag or failure to release*—This usually causes difficult shifting and gear clash, particularly when downshifting. The cause may be excessive clutch lever free play, warped or bent plates, broken or loose lining, or lack of lubrication in clutch actuating mechanism.

3. *Chatter or grabbing*—Check for worn or warped plates. Check clutch lever free play.

TRANSMISSION

Transmission problems are usually indicated by one or more of the following symptoms:

    a. Difficulty shifting gears
    b. Gear clash when downshifting
    c. Slipping out of gear
    d. Excessive noise in neutral
    e. Excessive noise in gear

Transmission symptoms are sometimes hard to distinguish from clutch symptoms. Be sure that the clutch is not causing the trouble before working on the transmission.

BRAKES

1. *Brake lever or pedal goes all the way to its stop*—There are numerous causes for this including excessively worn shoes or pads, air in the hydraulic system, leaky brake lines, leaky calipers, or leaky or worn master cylinder. Check for leaks and thin brake pads. Bleed the brakes. If this does not cure the trouble, rebuild the calipers and/or master cylinder.

2. *Spongy lever*—Normally caused by air in the system; bleed the brakes.

3. *Dragging brakes*—Check for swollen rubber parts due to improper brake fluid or contamination, and obstructed master cylinder bypass port. Clean or replace defective parts. Also, check for brakes adjusted too tight.

4. *Hard lever or pedal*—Check brake pads for contamination. Also check for restricted brake lines and hoses.

5. *High speed fade*—Check for contaminated brake pads or shoes. Ensure that recommended brake fluid is installed. Drain entire system and refill if still in doubt.

6. *Pulsating lever or pedal*—Check for excessive brake disc runout. Undetected accident damage is also a frequent cause of this.

LIGHTING SYSTEM

Bulbs which continuously burn out may be caused by excessive vibration, loose connections that permit sudden current surges, poor battery connections, or installation of the wrong type bulb.

A majority of light and horn or other electrical accessory problems are caused by loose or corroded ground connections. Check those first, and then substitute known good units for easier troubleshooting.

FRONT SUSPENSION
AND STEERING

1. *Too stiff or too soft*—Make sure forks have not been leaking and oil is correct viscosity. If in doubt, drain and refill as described in Chapter Three.

2. *Leakage around seals*—There should be a light film of oil on fork tubes. However, large amounts of oil on tubes means the seals are leaking. Replace seals. See Chapter Eight.

3. *Fork action is rough*—Check for bent tube.

4. *Steering wobbles*—Check for correct steering head bearing tightness. See Chapter Eight.

CHAPTER THREE

3

PERIODIC MAINTENANCE AND LUBRICATION

A motorcycle, like any other precision machine, requires a certain amount of routine and preventive maintenance to ensure its safety, reliability, and performance.

The service lubrication intervals specified in **Table 1** are recommended for the average rider. Harder than average riding may require more frequent service to maintain peak reliability.

While time intervals are not provided, a correlation of 500 miles per month provides a good rule of thumb. For example, engine oil change is recommended every 1,500 miles. This approximates three months. If you ride less than 500 miles per month the oil should then be changed every three months regardless of miles.

If the motorcycle is used primarily in stop-and-go traffic it is a good idea to change the oil more often than is recommended. This is also true for excessive short haul use. Acids tend to build up rapidly under these conditions and if they are allowed to remain in the engine they will accelerate wear.

This chapter describes all periodic maintenance required to keep your bike running properly. Routine checks are easily performed at each fuel stop. Other periodic maintenance appears in order of frequency.

Engine tune-up is treated separately from other maintenance tasks because the various tune-up procedures interact with each other. All tune-up procedures should be performed in the specified order and at the same period of time.

Plan ahead for servicing and tune-ups. Make sure you have all supplies such as oil, spark plugs, etc., before starting the work. Nothing is more aggravating or time consuming than having to stop in the middle of a job pick up some forgotten item. This is particularly important when performing a valve adjustment. The engine must be dead cold, that is, it should not be run for at least 12 hours prior to adjustment.

ROUTINE CHECKS

The following simple checks should be carried out at each fuel stop.

Engine Oil Level

Place the motorcycle on the centerstand and allow several minutes for the oil to settle completely. On GS400 and GS425 models, check the oil level through the inspection window as shown in **Figure 1**. On GS450 models, unscrew and remove the filler cap/

dipstick (**Figure 2**). Maintain the oil level between the "F" and "L" marks (**Figure 1** or **Figure 3**). Top up the oil, if necessary, with the type recommended in **Table 2**.

General Inspection

1. Examine engine for signs of oil or fuel leakage.
2. Check tires for imbedded stones and pry them out.
3. Check the lights to make sure they work, especially the brake light. Motorists can't stop as quickly as you can and they need all the warning you can give them.

Battery and Connections

Remove the right side cover and check the electrolyte level in the battery. The electrolyte level must be between the upper and lower level marks on the battery case (**Figure 4**). Top up the level, if necessary, with distilled water.

To clean the battery connections and check the specific gravity of the electrolyte, refer to *Battery Service* in Chapter Seven.

Tire Pressure

Tire pressure should be checked and adjusted to accommodate the rider and any additional passenger or luggage weight. A simple, accurate gauge such as shown in **Figure 5** can be carried in the motorcycle tool kit. This type of gauge is generally preferred over the "dial" type gauge since the indication does not automatically return to zero when the gauge is removed. Maintain the tire pressures as specified in **Table 3**.

Tire Inspection

Check the tread for excessive wear, deep cuts and imbedded objects such as stones, nails, etc. If you find a nail in a tire, mark the location with a crayon before pulling it out. This helps to locate the hole in the tire when the tire is repaired. If a tire is punctured, most dealers recommend that the tube be replaced, not be repaired. Considering the amount of work involved to remove, repair and install the tube in the tire, it is not worth the trouble to duplicate the work should a patch fail. A patched tube should be considered an emergency repair.

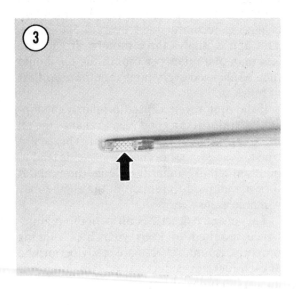

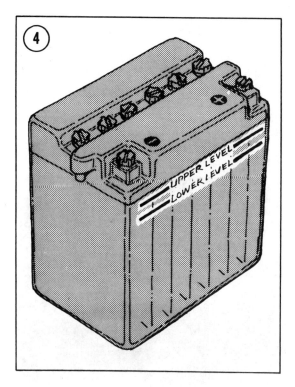

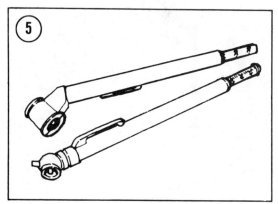

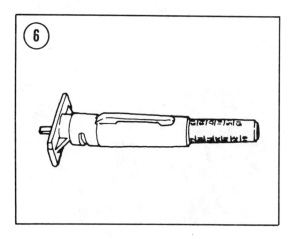

Check local traffic regulations concerning minimum tread depth. Measure the tread depth with a depth gauge (**Figure 6**). Suzuki recommends tire replacement when the tread depth is less than 1.6 mm (1/16 in.) on the front and 2.0 mm (3/32 in.) in the rear. Tread wear indicators appear across the tire when tread reaches minimum safe depth. Replace the worn tire at this point.

Wheel and Rim Inspection

On spoke wheels, inspect the rims for signs of damage and check for loose spokes. On models with aluminum alloy wheels, examine the wheels for cracks, bends or warpage. These wheels cannot be serviced, except for balancing. If the wheels are damaged they must be replaced.

Refer to Chapter Eight to "true" spoke wheels and balance all wheels.

PERIODIC MAINTENANCE

The following procedures are summarized in **Table 1**. A good way to ensure that all necessary items are covered during a periodic service is to make a check list and use it each time you service the motorcycle. Keep an up-to-date record of all items serviced and at what mileage; otherwise it is too easy to forget what was done and when.

1,000 KM (600 MILE) SERVICE

Drive Chain
Adjustment and Lubrication

The drive chain should be carefully inspected at least every 1,000 km (600 miles). Lubricate and adjust chain as often as necessary. The importance of proper drive chain service cannot be overemphasized. Accelerated drive chain wear growing out of neglect can prove very costly. At the least, a failed chain could severely damage the engine and transmission. At the worst, it could foul the rear sprocket and lock up the rear wheel.

WARNING
The drive chain supplied on all models is a continuous type without a master link. Do not break the chain and add a master link or chain failure may result.

1. Check the deflection (slack) in the drive chain as shown in **Figure 7**. The chain slack should be 15-20 mm (5/8-13/16 in.) for GS400 models and 20-30 mm (13/16-1 3/16 in.) for all other models.

2. If chain requires adjustment perform the following:

   a. Remove cotter pin securing axle nut and loosen nut (**Figure 8**).

   b. Loosen adjuster locknuts on each side (**Figure 9**).

   c. Turn adjuster bolts equally on both sides until chain deflection is as specified. Tighten adjuster bolt locknuts.

   d. Make sure index marks on adjusters are aligned equally on both sides (**Figure 10**).

   e. Torque rear axle nut to 8.5-11.5 mkg (62-83 ft.-lb.) and secure the nut with cotter pin.

3. Lubricate chain with a good grade of chain lubricant carefully following manufacturer's instructions.

4. Inspect sprockets for signs of wear and undercutting (**Figure 11**). Refer to Chapter Four for drive sprocket replacement and Chapter Nine for rear sprocket replacement.

2,500 KM (1,500 MILE) SERVICE

Engine Oil and Filter Change

Regular oil and filter changes will contribute more to engine longevity than any other single factor. It is recommended that the oil filter be changed at least every 5,000 km (3,000 miles); however, it is suggested that the filter be changed with each oil change if possible. Change both oil and filter more often in dusty

areas or if motorcycle is used primarily for short trips.

CAUTION
Never add STP or similar oil additives to the engine oil. These products will destroy the friction properties of the clutch, necessitating a complete flushing of the engine lubrication system and replacement of the clutch plates.

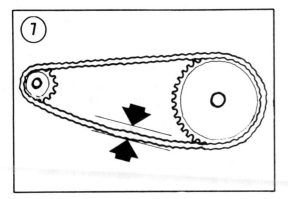

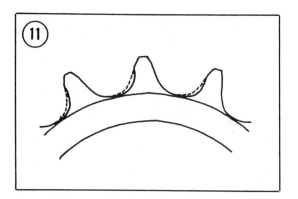

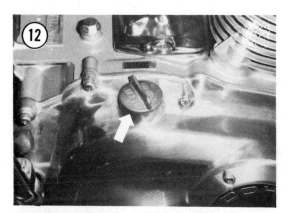

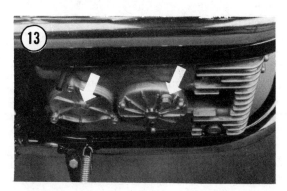

NOTE
Never dispose of motor oil in the trash or pour it, on the ground, or down a storm drain. Many service stations accept used motor oil. Many waste haulers provide curbside used motor oil collection. Do not combine other fluids with motor oil to be recycled. To find a recycling location contact the American Petroleum Institute (API) at www.recycleoil.org.

1. Warm up engine and place motorcycle on centerstand.
2. Remove the oil filler cap (**Figure 12**).
3. Place a drain pan under the engine and remove the drain plugs. See **Figure 13** for GS400 and GS425 models. See **Figure 14** for GS450 models.

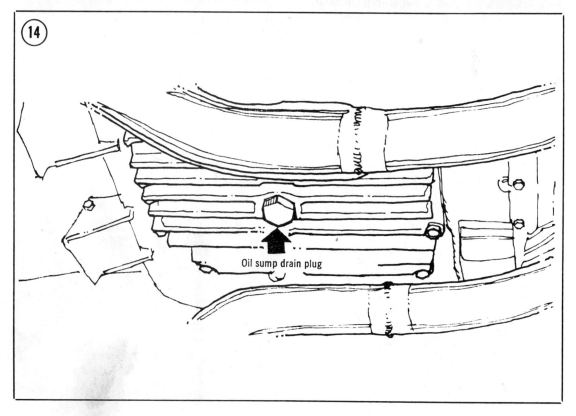

Oil sump drain plug

4. Unscrew the nuts securing the filter housing cover (**Figure 15**). Remove the cover from the bottom of the engine on GS400 and GS425 models (**Figure 16**). Remove the cover from the front of the engine on GS450 machines. Remove the oil filter and allow at least 10 minutes for all the old oil to drain.

5. Clean the oil drain plug, filter housing cover and filter housing with clean rags.

6. Inspect the gasket on the drain plug and the housing cover and replace them if they are not in good condition. Use a little grease to help hold the O-ring seal in position in the housing cover.

7. Install a new filter with the open end in toward the engine (**Figure 17**). Install the spring and housing cover and torque the nuts to 0.6-0.8 mkg (4.4-5.6 ft.-lb.).

8. Install the drain plugs and torque to 1 mkg (7 ft.-lb.).

9. Fill the crankcase through the filler opening with the recommended quantity and type of oil as specified in **Table 2** and **Table 4**.

10. Start the engine and run at an idle until the oil pressure warning light goes *off*. Warm up the engine a few minutes and shut it off. Allow the engine to sit for a few minutes and check the oil level through the window or with the dipstick. Add oil, if necessary, to maintain the level between the "L" and "F" marks.

11. Check carefully around the oil filter cover and drain plugs for any signs of leaks. Correct the leaks with new gaskets if necessary.

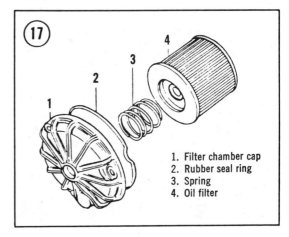

1. Filter chamber cap
2. Rubber seal ring
3. Spring
4. Oil filter

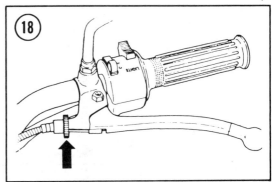

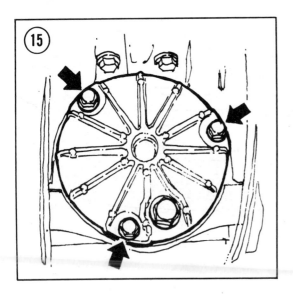

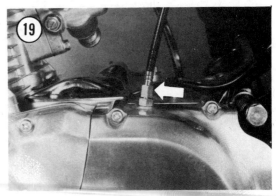

5,000 KM (3,000 MILE) SERVICE

Clutch Adjustment

1. Loosen large knurled locknut on clutch lever and turn adjuster in all the way (**Figure 18**).

2. Loosen locknut securing cable adjuster (**Figure 19**), and turn in on adjuster to provide maximum cable slack. Do not tighten locknut at this time.

3. Remove 2 screws securing clutch adjustment cover (**Figure 20**).

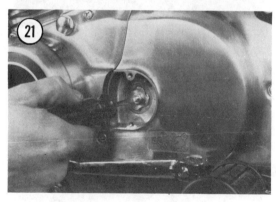

4. Loosen locknut on adjusting screw and back out screw 2 or 3 turns (**Figure 21**).

5. Slowly turn in on adjusting screw until resistance is felt as adjusting screw contacts the clutch pushrod. Back out adjusting screw 1/4-1/2 turn. Hold screw and secure adjustment with locknut. Install clutch adjustment cover.

6. Turn cable adjuster (**Figure 19**) until there is 4 mm (5/32 in.) of free play measured at the clutch lever (**Figure 22**). Tighten cable adjuster locknut.

Oil Pressure Check

A special gauge is required for checking oil pressure. Have the task performed by a dealer. Keep a record of pressure checks to determine if oil pressure is degenerating as the engine wear increases.

Rear Brake Adjustment

Rotate rear brake adjusting nut (**Figure 23**) until brake pedal free play is between 20-30 mm (3/4-1 3/16 in.). Check that brake arm movement does not exceed the brake lining wear limit (**Figure 24**). Refer to Chapter Ten for brake lining inspection and replacement.

Front Brake Adjustment

On models equipped with drum brakes, periodic brake adjustment is necessary. Models equipped with front disc brakes require no adjustment.

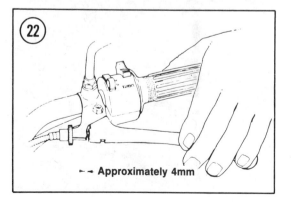

Approximately 4mm

Turn large knurled adjuster on brake lever in as far as it will go (**Figure 25**). Rotate the adjuster nut on front wheel (**Figure 26**) until there is approximately 5 mm (3/16 in.) free play in brake cable measured at the brake lever. Spin front wheel and make sure brake does not drag when *not* applied. Readjust if necessary.

Brake Fluid Level

Check brake fluid level in master cylinder reservoir on models equipped with front disc brake. Maintain fluid level between upper and lower marks on the reservoir (**Figure 27**).

> *WARNING*
> *If necessary to top off the master cylinder reservoir, only use brake fluid marked DOT 3 or DOT 4. All models use a glycol-based brake fluid. Mixing a glycol-based fluid with a petroleum-based or silicon-based fluid will cause brake component damage leading to brake failure.*

> *CAUTION*
> *Do not allow the brake fluid to spill on any painted surfaces or the paint may be damaged.*

Brake Pad Inspection

Brake pad wear depends on a number of factors including riding conditions and rider habits. If most of your riding is in mountainous areas, stop-and-go traffic, or if you know you are heavy on the brakes, check the pad life more frequently than recommended in **Table 1**.

Replace the front brake pads when they are worn down to the red line as shown in **Figure 28**. On GS400 and GS425 models, look between the caliper and disc to view the brake

pads. On GS450 models, the red line can be viewed through the window in the caliper (**Figure 29**). If dust has obscured the window, carefully pry off the plastic cover to view the pad wear red line. If the pads are worn past the limit, replace them as a set. Refer to Chapter Ten.

Brake Lines

Check the brake lines between the master cylinder and the caliper. If there is any leakage, tighten the connections or replace leaking lines

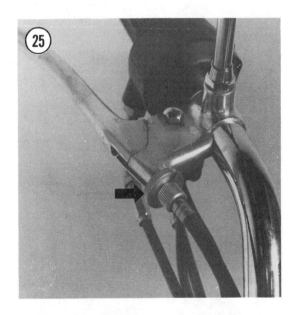

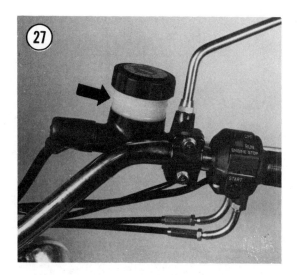

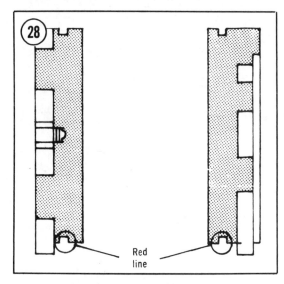

Red
line

and hoses and fill and bleed the system as described in Chapter Ten.

Brake Pedal

Lightly oil the rear brake pedal pivot shaft, working the oil in by moving the lever up and down.

Steering

Check the steering for play and adjust it if necessary as described in this chapter.

Wheel Hubs, Rims, and Spokes

Check wheel hubs and rims for bends and other signs of damage. Check both wheels for broken or bent spokes. Replace damaged ones immediately. See Chapters Eight and Nine. Tap each spoke lightly with a small hammer or wrench. All spokes should emit the same sound. A spoke that is too tight will have a higher pitch than the others; one that is too loose will have a lower pitch. If only one or two spokes are slightly out of adjustment, adjust them with a spoke wrench. If more are affected, the wheel should be removed and trued. See *Spoke Adjustment*, Chapter Eight.

Alloy Wheels

Check aluminum alloy wheels for cracks, bends, warpage or other signs of damage. These wheels cannot be serviced, except for balancing, and if found to be damaged they must be replaced. Refer to Chapter Eight for wheel balancing procedures.

Engine and Frame Fasteners

Constant vibration can loosen many fasteners on a motorcycle. Refer to **Table 5** and torque all engine and frame fasteners to the specified torque.

10,000 KM (6,000 MILE) SERVICE

Throttle Grip

Loosen, but do not remove, screws securing the throttle grip to the handlebar (**Figure 30**), and slide throttle grip off handlebar. Clean handlebar with solvent and wipe dry. Apply a light coat of grease to the handlebar and slide on throttle grip. Tighten screws securing throttle grip and check the action of the throttle. It should turn freely and snap back when released.

Front Fork Oil

The front fork is the most adjustable component of the motorcycle. A front suspension properly set up can improve the handling characteristics of the machine as well as make it more comfortable to ride.

The front suspension requires the correct amount of damping oil in each fork leg if it is to perform correctly. Damping characteristics depend on oil viscosity, therefore, the handling of the motorcycle can be altered by a change from one weight oil to another. Only personal experience will enable you to find the weight of oil that is best for you and your style of riding. As a rule, lighter weight oils are better suited for lighter riders and heavier weight oils are better suited for heavier riders or machines that are equipped with touring gear. Heavier oils should also be used if most of your riding is done with a passenger. Consult your local dealer concerning fork oils. He may be able to recommend the correct weight oil for your weight and the type of riding you will be doing. Refer to **Table 2** for the oil recommended by Suzuki.

If fork seal leakage is indicated by oil oozing out around the fork wiper boots, refer to Chapter Eight and replace the fork seals. It is impractical to add oil to a fork that has lost oil due to a leaky seal. The forks should be drained, flushed and refilled with the proper amount of oil after the leaky seal has been replaced.

The following procedure describes how to change fork oil with the fork installed. If desired, a more efficient flushing of the fork can be achieved by removing the fork tubes as outlined in Chapter Eight.

1. Remove the 4 bolts securing the handlebars (**Figure 31**). On models equipped with a foam cushion over the handlebars, remove the plugs covering the handlebar bolts, then remove the bolts (**Figure 32**). Place

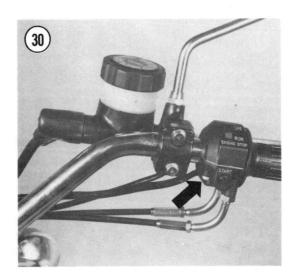

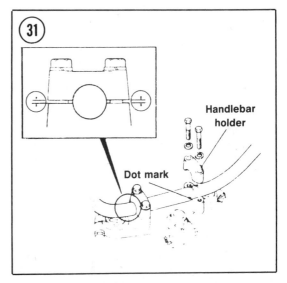

Handlebar holder

Dot mark

a few rags on the fuel tank and carefully lay the handlebars back on the fuel tank.

2. Loosen the upper fork pinch bolts (**Figure 33**).

3A. On 1977-1981 models, remove the fork tube caps (**Figure 34**).

3B. On 1982-on models perform the following:

   a. Remove the rubber cap from the top of the each fork tube.

   b. On models equipped with air valves, carefully bleed off the fork air pressure.

   c. Carefully press down against the spring stopper and remove the snap ring securing the stopper (A, **Figure 35**). Remove the spring stopper. Take care not to damage the O-ring.

4. Remove the fork springs from each fork tube. Have a few rags ready as the fork springs are quite oily.

5. Place a drain pan under each fork leg and remove the fork drain screw (**Figure 36**). Allow several minutes for the forks to drain completely. Compress the forks a few times to help force the oil out. Reinstall the drain screw.

6. Refer to **Table 2** and **Table 4** and add the specified amount and type of fork oil to each fork tube. Use a graduated baby bottle to ensure the oil amount is correct for each fork tube.

NOTE
Suzuki recommends that the fork oil level be measured, if possible, to ensure a more accurate filling.

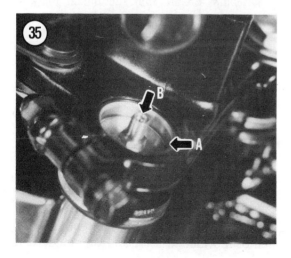

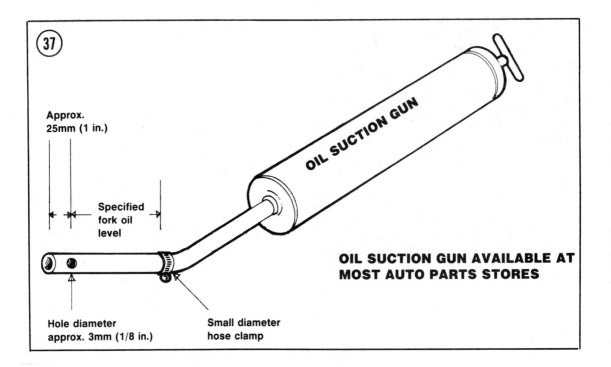

(37)

Approx.
25mm (1 in.)

Specified
fork oil
level

OIL SUCTION GUN

**OIL SUCTION GUN AVAILABLE AT
MOST AUTO PARTS STORES**

Hole diameter
approx. 3mm (1/8 in.)

Small diameter
hose clamp

7. Compress the forks completely.

8. Raise the rear of the motorcycle until the fork tubes are perfectly vertical. If it is inconvenient to raise the rear of the motorcycle, it will be necessary to remove both the fork tubes as described in Chapter Eight.

9. Use an accurate ruler or the Suzuki oil level gauge (part No. 09943-74110) to ensure the oil level is as specified in **Table 4**.

NOTE
*An oil level measuring device can be locally fabricated as shown in **Figure 37**. Fill the fork with a few cc's more than the required amount of oil. Position the hose clamp on the top edge of the fork tube and draw out the excess oil. Oil is sucked out until the level reaches the small diameter hole. A precise oil level can be achieved with this simple device.*

10. Allow the oil to settle completely and recheck the oil level measurement. Adjust the oil level if necessary.

11. Install the fork springs with the closer-wound coils facing down.

12A. On 1977-1981 models, ensure the O-ring on the fork cap is in good condition

and install the fork cap. Tighten the fork cap to 1.5-3.0 mkg (11-22 ft.-lb.). Torque the upper pinch bolt to 2.0-3.0 mkg (15-22 ft.-lb.).

12B. On 1982-on models, ensure the O-ring (**Figure 38**) is in good condition. Lightly oil the O-ring and install the spring stopper in the fork tube. Press down on the stopper until the snap ring groove is exposed and install the snap ring to secure the spring stopper. Ensure that the snap ring is fully engaged in the groove in the fork tube.

13. Refer to **Figure 31** and install the handlebars. Ensure that the punch mark is properly aligned and equal clearance is present on both sides of the handlebar holders. Torque the handlebar clamp bolts to 1.2-2.0 mkg (9-14 ft.-lb.).

14. On 1982-on models, install the rubber caps.

15. On models with air valves, refer to *Pressurizing Front Forks* in this chapter.

**Pressurizing Front Fork
(Models So Equipped)**

Proper suspension adjustment and "tuning" is necessary to provide optimum handling and comfort. Some 1982 and later models are

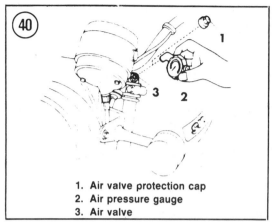

1. Air valve protection cap
2. Air pressure gauge
3. Air valve

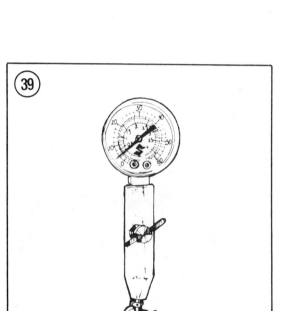

equipped with air valves in the fork tubes (B, **Figure 35**). Air valves allow air pressure to be pumped into the fork tubes to alter the handling characteristics of the motorcycle as well as help support the weight of any touring gear or accessories that may be installed.

Pressurizing the air fork is best performed with the Suzuki air gauge (part No. 09940-4410) as shown in **Figure 39**. This gauge allows air to be pumped into or bled from the fork tubes in a very precise manner. No pressure is lost from the fork tube when the gauge is removed.

If the Suzuki special gauge is not available, air pressure can be set reasonably accurately with the small air gauge supplied with the motorcycle (**Figure 40**). When using the small gauge make sure it is placed squarely on the air valve and removed quickly to prevent as little air loss as possible. Normal air loss when this type gauge is removed is 0.7-1.4 psi (0.05-0.10 kg/cm^2).

1. Place the motorcycle on the center stand and jack up the machine until the front wheel is clear of the ground.

2. Remove the rubber caps from the fork tubes and bleed off any remaining air pressure.

3. If using the Suzuki special air gauge (**Figure 38**), perform the following:
   a. Close the center valve on the air gauge.
   b. Back out the stem on the air valve.
   c. Carefully install the gauge on the air valve.
   d. Screw in the end valve stem. This opens the gauge chamber in the fork tube.

4. Connect a bicycle tire pump to the fork valve or the center valve on the special air gauge.

CAUTION
Never use a high-pressure air supply to pressurize the fork tubes or the fork seals will be damaged. Use only a hand-operated tire pump or special air pump.

5. Pump up pressure in the fork tube to approximately 1.0 kg/cm^2 (14 psi).

CAUTION
Do not exceed 2.5 kg/cm^2 (35 psi) or the fork seals may be damaged.

6. Slowly bleed air from the fork tubes until 0.5 kg/cm² (7.1 psi) is reached. Use the center valve on the special air gauge to bleed off the excess air pressure. Maximum allowable difference between fork tubes is 0.1 kg/cm² (1.4 psi).

7. Remove the special air gauge as follows:

   a. Close the center bleed valve.

   b. Back out the stem on the end valve.

   c. Carefully unscrew the gauge from the fork air valve.

8. Install the rubber fork tube caps.

Oil Pump Pickup Screen

Clean the oil pump pickup screen at least as frequently as specified in **Table 1**. Perform this task during an oil filter change.

1. Refer to *Engine Oil and Filter Change* as outlined in this chapter and drain the engine oil.

2. On models with an exhaust cross-over pipe under the engine, refer to Chapter Six and remove the exhaust system.

3. On GS400 and GS425 models, remove the bolts securing the pickup screen cover (**Figure 41**).

4. On GS450 models, remove the bolts securing the oil pan and carefully remove the pan.

5. Remove the screws securing the oil pickup screen (**Figure 42**) and remove the screen.

6. Thoroughly clean the screen and the screen cover or oil pan in solvent.

7. Apply blue Loctite (Lock N' Seal No. 2114) to the pickup screen screws and install the screen.

8. On GS400 and GS425 models, perform the following:

   a. Check the condition of the O-ring on the pickup screen cover. Replace the O-ring if it is not in good condition. Use a small amount of grease on the O-ring to help hold it in position.

   b. Install the screen cover. Torque the screen cover nuts to 0.6-0.8 mkg (4.3-5.8 ft.-lb.).

   c. Torque the drain plug to 1.0 mkg (7 ft.-lb.).

9. On GS450 models, use a new gasket on the oil pan and install the pan. Tighten the pan

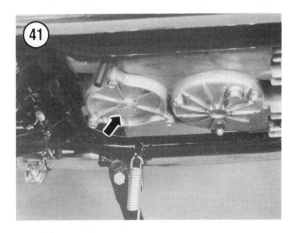

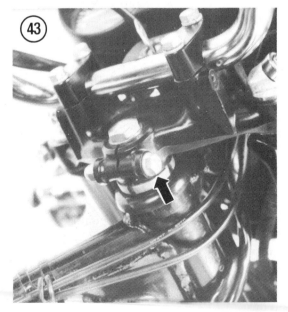

bolts gradually and evenly in a crisscross pattern. Torque the bolts to 1.0 mkg (7 ft.-lb.).
10. Refer to *Engine Oil and Filter Change* as outlined in this chapter and fill the engine with oil.

20,000 KM (12,000 MILE) SERVICE

Wheel Bearings

The wheel bearings should be checked, cleaned, and greased as described in Chapter Eight, *Front Wheel Disassembly/Assembly*, or as in Chapter Nine, *Rear Wheel Disassembly/Assembly*.

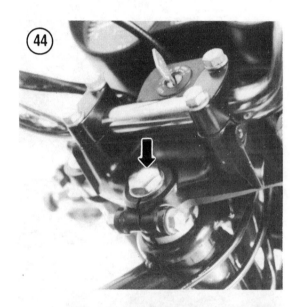

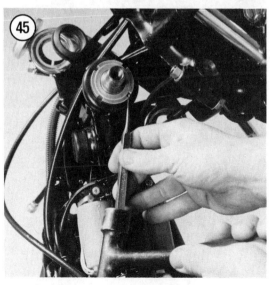

Speedometer Drive

The speedometer drive should be removed, cleaned, and greased when the front wheel bearings are serviced.

Steering Head
Lubrication and Adjustment

Lubricate the steering head bearings with grease as outlined under *Steering Head Disassembly* in Chapter Eight.

The steering head on all 1979 and earlier models is equipped with 36 loose ball bearings—18 bearing balls in each of the upper and lower bearing assemblies. The steering head on all 1980 and later models is fitted with 2 tapered roller bearings. The steering head on all models should be checked for looseness at least as frequently as specified in **Table 1**.

Jack up the motorcycle so that the front wheel is clear of the ground. Hold onto the front fork tubes and rock the fork assembly back and forth (front to rear). If any looseness can be felt, adjust the steering head as follows:
1. Place the motorcycle on the centerstand and place a block under the engine until the front wheel is clear of the ground.
2. Loosen the pinch bolt securing the steering stem head bolt or nut (**Figure 43**) and loosen the head bolt or nut (**Figure 44**).
3. Use the Suzuki spanner wrench (part No. 09940-10122) and adjust the steering stem locknut until all play is removed from the steering head, yet the front end turns freely from side to side, under its own weight. If the Suzuki spanner is not available the steering locknut can be gently tapped with a hammer and a punch or screwdriver as shown in **Figure 45**. Take care not to damage the locknut.
4. Torque the steering stem head bolt or nut and the steering stem pinch bolt as specified in **Table 5**.

Swinging Arm

Use a good grade of chassis grease in a grease gun to lubricate the swinging arm. On models not equipped with a grease fitting remove the pivot bolt. See Chapter Nine,

Swinging Arm Removal/Installation, and inject grease directly into swinging arm bearings.

EVERY 2 YEARS

Replace all fuel and brake hoses. Drain and fill brake system with fresh brake fluid. See Chapter Ten, *Changing Fluid*.

ENGINE TUNE-UP

An engine tune-up consists of several accurate and careful adjustments made in order to obtain maximum engine performance. Because different systems in an engine interact to affect overall performance, tune-ups must be carried out in the following order:

  a. Valve clearance adjustment
  b. Ignition adjustment and timing
  c. Carburetor adjustment

Perform an engine tune-up every 3,000 miles. During every other tune-up, spark plugs and breaker points should be replaced.

Refer to **Table 6** for tune-up specifications.

> *NOTE*
> *All models **manufactured** after January 1, 1978 are engineered to meet stringent E.P.A. (Environmental Protection Agency) regulations. All tune-up specifications must be strictly adhered to, whether the work is performed by the owner, dealer, or an independent repair shop. Modifications to ignition system, exhaust system, and carburetion are forbidden by law unless modifications (aftermarket exhaust systems, etc.) have received written approval from the E.P.A. Engine idle speed and carburetor synchronization adjustments are permissible. Carburetor air screw adjustments are preset and **must not** be altered. Failure to comply with E.P.A. regulations may result in heavy fines.*

Valve Clearance Adjustment

> *CAUTION*
> *Valve clearance adjustments must be performed when the engine is completely cold—not run for at least 12 hours. If engine is not cold, adjustments will not be accurate and engine damage may result.*

Proper valve clearance is essential for engine performance and longevity. If valve clearances are too small the valves may be burned or distorted. Excessive valve clearance will result in a noisy valve train and poor performance.

1. Remove the fuel tank as outlined in Chapter Six.
2. On GS400 and GS425 models remove screws securing end covers to cylinder head and remove the 4 covers.

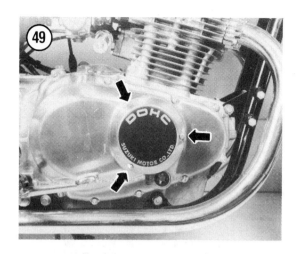

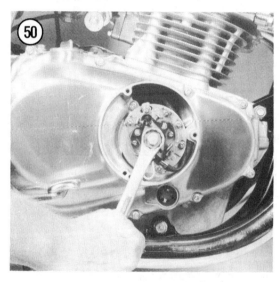

3. Loosen clamp and remove breather hose from breather cover.

4. Disconnect horn wires (**Figure 46**).

5. Remove bolt securing horn bracket to frame and remove horn.

6. On GS400 and GS425 models remove bolts securing breather cover (**Figure 47**) and remove cover.

7. Remove bolts securing cam cover to cylinder head and remove cover (**Figure 48**). Note the location of different length bolts.

8. Remove screws securing contact breaker point cover (**Figure 49**).

9. Remove spark plug leads by grasping the spark plug caps; never pull on the plug lead itself.

10. Blow away any dirt that may have accumulated around spark plugs and remove the plugs.

11. To rotate crankshaft use a wrench on the large hex portion of the advance governor (**Figure 50**).

CAUTION
Do not attempt to rotate crankshaft by using the small bolt that secures the advance governor or bolt may twist off.

Rotate crankshaft clockwise until one cam lobe is perpendicular to cylinder head surface (**Figure 51**).

12. Use a feeler gauge and check valve clearance (**Figure 52**). Clearance should be 0.03-0.08 mm (0.0012-0.0030 in.).

NOTE
It is recommended that Suzuki feeler gauge (part No. 09900-20803) be used to check valve clearances as it contains several small gauges not normally found in feeler gauge sets. Refer to Chapter One for tool description.

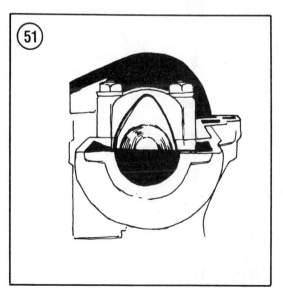

13. If valve clearance is within tolerance repeat Steps 11 and 12 for remaining valves. If valve clearance is not as specified, the adjustment shim on the top of the tappet must be replaced.

14. Rotate tappet by hand until notch in tappet is fully exposed (**Figure 53**).

15. Use Suzuki tappet depressor (part No. 09916-64510) and press down on tappet (**Figure 54**). Make sure depressor bears on edge of tappet and not on the shim (**Figure 55**).

16. Use a small screwdriver in tappet notch to pop shim loose from tappet, otherwise the surface tension caused by the oiled parts makes the shim difficult to remove. Use tweezers and lift out shim (**Figure 56**).

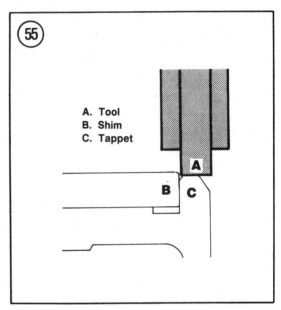

A. Tool
B. Shim
C. Tappet

3

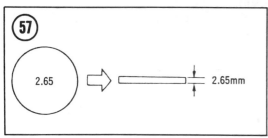

2.65 ⇨ 2.65mm

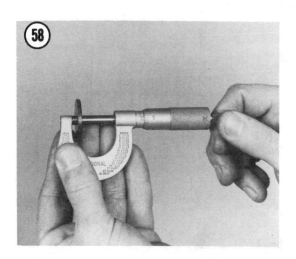

CAUTION
Never use a magnet to lift out adjustment shims. They are made of hardened steel and are easily magnetized. A magnetized part will attract and hold metal particles which will cause excessive wear. A magnetized adjustment shim could also lift out of a tappet while the engine is running and cause serious and expensive engine damage.

17. Write down the size the shim. Sizes are etched on each shim (**Figure 57**).

NOTE
*If etched size is not visible it will be necessary to measure shim thickness with a micrometer (**Figure 58**).*

18. Refer to **Table 7** and calculate required replacement shim as described in the following typical example:
 Actual valve clearance—0.10 mm
 Desired clearance (maximum)—0.08 mm
 Difference (too large)—0.02 mm
 Existing shim size—2.45 mm

The clearance in this case is at least 0.02 mm too large. It must be reduced by at least that amount, through the substitution of a thicker shim. **Table 7** indicates that the next larger shim, No. 8, is 2.50 mm. This shim will reduce the clearance by 0.05 mm. Clearance will then be 0.05 mm, well within the specified range.

19. Oil both sides of the replacement shim before installing on valve tappet. Install shim with etched number down against the tappet. Before purchasing all new shims, check to see if any shims removed from other valves may be reused. It is possible that one or several may work and save some expense.

20. After any shims have been replaced, rotate crankshaft several times to make sure shims are properly seated by the camshafts. Recheck valve clearances and readjust if necessary.

21. Check condition of cam cover gasket and replace if necessary. Install cam cover and torque bolts to 0.7-1.0 mkg (5.1-7.0 ft.-lb.) in the order shown in **Figure 59**.

22. Install breather cover, end covers, horn, and fuel tank. If complete tune-up is being performed, do not install breaker point cover or spark plugs.

Spark Plug Cleaning/Replacement

1. Grasp high-tension leads by the spark plug caps and pull them off; never pull on the lead itself.

2. Blow away dirt that may have accumulated in spark plug wells with compressed air.

> *WARNING*
> *Wear safety goggles or glasses when doing this to prevent particles from getting in your eyes.*

3. Remove spark plugs with a spark plug wrench.

> *NOTE*
> *If plugs are difficult to remove apply penetrating oil around the base of the plugs and allow it to soak in for 10-20 minutes.*

4. Inspect spark plugs carefully. Refer to **Figure 60**. Check for broken or cracked porcelain, excessively eroded electrodes, and excessive carbon or oil fouling. If deposits are light,

plugs may be cleaned in solvent with a wire brush or with a special spark plug sandblast cleaner.

5. Use a wire feeler gauge and gap plugs to 0.6-0.7 mm (0.024-0.028 in.) by bending the side electrode (**Figure 61**). Do not file electrodes to correct the gap.

6. Install spark plugs finger-tight and tighten an additional 1/8-1/4 turn. If a torque wrench is available, torque plugs to 1.9 mkg (14 ft.-lb.).

Ignition System
Tune-up Hints

The following list of general hints will help make a tune-up easier and more successful:

1. Always use good tools and tune-up equipment. The money saved from one or two home tune-ups will more than pay for good tools; from that point on you're money ahead. Refer to Chapter One for suitable types of tune-up/test equipment.

2. The purchase of a small set of ignition wrenches and one or two "screwholding" or magnetic screwdrivers will ease the work in replacing breaker points and help eliminate losing small screws.

3. Always purchase quality ignition components.

4. When using a feeler gauge to set breaker points, ensure that the blade is wiped clean before inserting between the points.

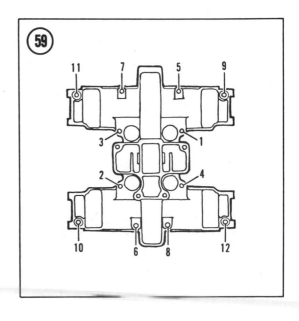

⑥⓪

SPARK PLUG CONDITION

NORMAL

- Identified by light tan or gray deposits on the firing tip.
- Can be cleaned.

GAP BRIDGED

- Identified by deposit buildup closing gap between electrodes.
- Caused by oil or carbon fouling. If deposits are not excessive, the plug can be cleaned.

OIL FOULED

- Identified by wet black deposits on the insulator shell bore and electrodes.
- Caused by excessive oil entering combustion chamber through worn rings and pistons, excessive clearance between valve guides and stems, or worn or loose bearings. Can be cleaned. If engine is not repaired, use a hotter plug.

CARBON FOULED

- Identified by black, dry fluffy carbon deposits on insulator tips, exposed shell surfaces and electrodes.
- Caused by too cold a plug, weak ignition, dirty air cleaner, too rich a fuel mixture, or excessive idling. Can be cleaned.

LEAD FOULED

- Identified by dark gray, black, yellow, or tan deposits or a fused glazed coating on the insulator tip.
- Caused by highly leaded gasoline. Can be cleaned.

WORN

- Identified by severely eroded or worn electrodes.
- Caused by normal wear. Should be replaced.

FUSED SPOT DEPOSIT

- Identified by melted or spotty deposits resembling bubbles or blisters.
- Caused by sudden acceleration. Can be cleaned.

OVERHEATING

- Identified by a white or light gray insulator with small black or gray brown spots and with bluish-burnt appearance of electrodes.
- Caused by engine overheating, wrong type of fuel, loose spark plugs, too hot a plug, or incorrect ignition timing. Replace the plug.

PREIGNITION

- Identified by melted electrodes and possibly blistered insulator. Metallic deposits on insulator indicate engine damage.
- Caused by wrong type of fuel, incorrect ignition timing or advance, too hot a plug, burned valves, or engine overheating. Replace the plug.

3

5. Ensure points are fully open when setting gap with a feeler gauge.

6. Be sure feeler gauge is not tilted or twisted when it is inserted between the contacts. Closely observe the points and withdraw the feeler gauge slowly and carefully. A slight resistance should be felt, however, the movable contact point must *not* "spring back" even slightly when the feeler gauge blade is removed.

7. If the breaker points are only slightly pitted, they can be "dressed down" lightly with a small ignition point file or Flex-Stone. *Do not* use sandpaper as it leaves a residue on the points.

8. After points have been installed, always ensure that they are properly aligned, or premature pitting and burning will result. See **Figure 62**. Bend only the *fixed* half of the points; not the movable arm.

9. When point gap has been set, clean contacts with lacquer thinner or special contact cleaner spray. Close the contacts on a clean piece of paper such as a business card and wipe contacts a few times to remove any trace of oil or grease. A small amount of oil or grease on the contact surfaces will cause the points to prematurely burn or arc.

10. When connecting a timing light or timing tester, always follow the manufacturer's instructions.

Contact Breaker Point and Timing Adjustment (GS400 and GS425 Models)

1. Remove breaker point cover (**Figure 63**).
2. Use a wrench on large hex portion of advance governor (**Figure 64**) and rotate crankshaft clockwise until breaker points for left cylinder are fully open.

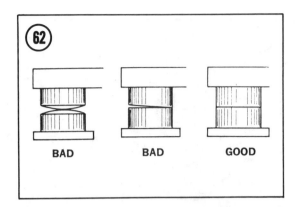

BAD   BAD   GOOD

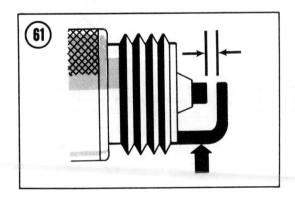

3. Loosen 2 screws securing breaker points to the breaker plate (**Figure 65**) and set point gap to 0.3-0.4 mm (0.012-0.016 in.). Tighten point screws.

4. Rotate engine clockwise until "F" mark for the left cylinder is aligned with mark on engine cover as viewed through window in breaker plate. See **Figure 66** (breaker plate removed for clarity). Make sure the "L" identifying the left cylinder is visible below the "F" mark.

5. Connect a timing tester or continuity device to electrical terminal (**Figure 67**) and a good ground on the engine.

6. Loosen 2 screws securing breaker plate (**Figure 68**) and rotate plate until points just begin to open (no continuity on tester). Tighten breaker plate screws. Rotate crankshaft a few turns to double check the adjustment. Readjust if necessary.

7. Rotate crankshaft clockwise until "F" mark for the right cylinder is aligned with mark on engine cover (**Figure 69**). Make sure the "R" identifying the right cylinder is visible below the "F" mark.

8. Connect continuity device to right cylinder point terminal (**Figure 70**) and ground.

9. Loosen screws securing half-plate (**Figure 71**) and adjust plate until points just begin to open (no continuity). Tighten screws, rotate engine, and double check the adjustment. Readjust if necessary.

NOTE
This completes breaker point adjustment and static engine timing. More precise engine timing can be achieved with a timing light. If a timing light is available proceed to the next step.

10. Connect the timing light to the left cylinder in accordance with the light manufacturer's instructions.

11. Start and warm up engine. Run engine below 1,500 rpm and direct timing light into window on breaker plate and observe timing marks. The "F" mark should be in perfect alignment (**Figure 66**). If timing is not correct, loosen breaker plate screws (**Figure 68**) and gradually move plate until marks are perfectly aligned. Tighten screws.

12. Increase engine speed above 3,600 rpm. Check that advance timing marks align (**Figure 72**). If the timing marks are not perfectly aligned, loosen breaker plate screws and move breaker plate until all marks are perfectly aligned. Tighten screws.

NOTE
If timing mark alignment is below 1,500 rpm and above 3,600 rpm is difficult to obtain, remove the breaker plate and make sure advance governor weights move freely without binding. If advance governor weights are free and a slight variation in timing marks still exists, set the timing using the 3,600 rpm marks. This ensures that timing is perfect during the engine's normal rpm range.

13. Repeat Steps 11 and 12 for the right cylinder. To adjust timing for right cylinder, loosen screws in the half-plate (**Figure 71**).

14. Install breaker point cover.

CAUTION
Do not carry clothing or rags under the seat or the air flow to the air cleaner will be restricted and adversely affect engine performance.

Ignition Timing
(1980 and Later Models)

All 1980 and later models are equipped with a breakerless electronic ignition system. No routine service or adjustment is necessary.

Air Filter

The air cleaner should be cleaned and reoiled with every tune-up or at least as often as specified in **Table 1**.

1. On GS400 and GS425 models, perform the following:

   a. Open the seat and remove the screws securing the filter cover (**Figure 73**).

   b. Remove the screw securing the filter assembly to the air box and remove the assembly (**Figure 74**).

   c. Remove the retaining band and separate the foam element from the metal frame. Proceed to Step 3.

2. On GS450 models, perform the following:

   a. Remove the seat. Slide back the metal retaining clips securing the air cleaner cover (**Figure 75**) and remove the cover.

   b. Fold the filter frame in the center and withdraw it from the air box as shown in **Figure 76**.

   c. Carefully remove the foam filter element (**Figure 77**).

3. Wash the foam filter element in solvent, then in hot, soapy water. Rinse the element in clean water and squeeze it between your palms to remove as much water as possible. The element can be pressed between several layers of paper towels to speed up the drying process. Allow the element to dry completely.

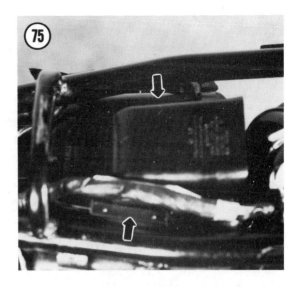

> *CAUTION*
> *Never wring or twist the foam element during the cleaning or reoiling process; the foam can easily be damaged.*

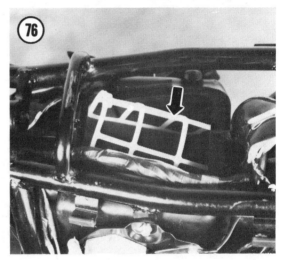

4. Carefully examine the element for any splits or tears in the foam (**Figure 78** or **Figure 79**). Replace the element if it is damaged in any way.

5. Apply engine oil or special air filter oil to the element and gently work the foam in your hands until the element is completely saturated with oil. Squeeze the element between your palms to remove all the excess oil.

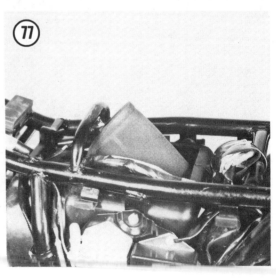

NOTE
A good grade of special air filter oil provides better protection against dirt and moisture than plain engine oil.

6. Thoroughly clean the inside of the air box and the filter sealing flange.

7. On GS400 and GS425 models, perform the following:

    a. Install the foam element in the metal frame and install the filter assembly into the air box.

    b. Ensure that the lip on the metal frame engages the clip in the air box as shown in **Figure 80**.

    c. Secure the filter assembly with the screw and install the filter cover.

8. On GS450 models, perform the following:

    a. Carefully install the foam element into the air box. Ensure that the edges of the element are correctly positioned around the inside of the air box.

b. Install the filter frame as shown in **Figure 81** to secure the foam element.

c. Install the filter cover. Slide the retaining clips forward to secure the cover.

Throttle Cable Adjustment

Throttle cable free play should be 1-1.5 mm (1/32-1/16 in.). If cable adjustment is necessary, loosen locknuts on cable adjusters (**Figure 82**) and turn adjusters in or out until specified free play is achieved. Tighten locknuts.

Carburetor Adjustments
(Models Manufactured Before
January 1, 1978)

> *NOTE*
> *Carburetors on models **manufactured** after January 1, 1978 are flow tested and preset at the factory for maximum performance within regulations set by the E.P.A. (Environmental Protection Agency). Under no circumstances*

should the carburetors be modified or the air screws adjusted. Heavy fines are imposed for such violations.

All other tune-up procedures must be carried out before the carburetors can be adjusted effectively.

3

1. Start and warm up engine. Turn throttle stop screw (**Figure 83**) until engine idles between 1,100 and 1,200 rpm.

2. Screw in air screw (**Figure 84**) on each carburetor until it bottoms out. Be careful not to overtighten and damage the screw. Back each screw out 1 1/4 turns. This is the basic setting.

3. Gradually adjust each air screw for maximum engine rpm. This should be between 3/4 and 1 1/4 turns open.

4. Reset idle speed to 1,100-1,200 rpm.

Carburetor Balancing (Synchronization)

Carburetor balancing, or synchronization, is essential for maximum performance. A special gauge, called a manometer, is required to do this job accurately. The one shown in **Figure 85** is marketed by Suzuki (part No. 00913-13120). There are other manometers on the market that work equally as well with virtually the same procedure.

1. Before beginning any work, the gauge must be calibrated; this must be done each time the gauge is used. Unscrew the 4 mm Allen bolt from the right cylinder (**Figure 86**). Screw in one balancer adapter. Connect the first hose of balancer to adapter.

2. Start engine and run it at a steady 1,750 rpm.

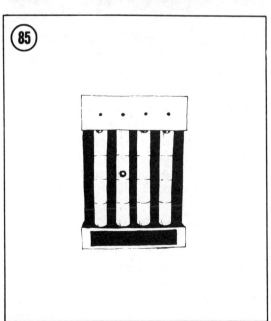

3. Turn air screw for the tube that is connected until steel ball lines up with center mark on tube (**Figure 85**).

4. Remove the calibrated hose from the right cylinder and connect one of the other hoses to the same cylinder adapter.

5. Turn air screw for the connected tube until steel ball lines up with center mark on tube. The 2 air tubes have now been calibrated to each other.

6. Remove 4 mm Allen bolt from left cylinder and install a balancer adapter. Remove the fuel tap's vacuum line from the carburetor and plug the fitting on the carburetor.

7. Connect hoses to both cylinders and run engine at a steady 1,750 rpm.

8. Adjust throttle balance screw (**Figure 87**) until both steel balls are aligned.

9. Remove hose adapters and install 4 mm Allen bolts. Make sure each bolt is fitted with a good washer.

10. Reset the idle speed, if necessary, to 1,100-1,300 rpm.

Compression Test

Every tune-up, check the cylinder compres-

sion. Record the results and compare them at the next check. A running record will show trends in deterioration so that corrective action can be taken before complete failure occurs.

Both a dry test and a wet test should be carried out to isolate trouble in cylinders or valves.

1. Warm the engine to normal operating temperature.

2. Remove spark plugs.

3. Connect compression tester to one cylinder following tester manufacturer's instructions.

4. Check to make sure the chokes are open. With assistance, hold the throttle fully open

and crank the engine until gauge needle ceases to rise. Record results and remove tester.

5. Repeat Steps 3 and 4 for the other cylinder.

When interpreting the results of a compression test refer to **Table 8** for compression specifications. If the compression of either cylinder is below the specified pressure, cylinder or valve repair must be performed. If the maximum pressure difference between cylinders exceeds the specified value, a complete engine overhaul is due.

To determine whether the compression problem is due to valves or piston rings, perform a second compression test with approximately 15cc (1/2 oz.) of motor oil in each cylinder. If the compression reading rises significantly, piston rings and/or cylinder bore are probably worn. If the wet compression test changes little from the dry test, the valves are probably burned.

STORAGE

Several months of inactivity can cause serious problems and general deterioration of your bike. This is especially important in areas with extremely cold winters. During the winter, you should prepare your bike carefully for "hibernation".

Selecting a Storage Area

Most cyclists store their bikes in their home garage. If you do not have a garage, there are other facilities for rent or lease in most areas. When selecting an area, consider the following points.

1. The storage area must be dry; there should be no dampness or excessive humidity. A heated area is not necessary, but the area should be insulated to minimize extreme temperature variations.

2. Avoid buildings with large window areas. If this is not possible, mask the window to keep direct sunlight off the bike.

3. Avoid buildings in industrial areas where factories are liable to emit corrosive fumes. Also avoid buildings near large bodies of salt water.

4. Select an area where there is a minimum risk of fire, theft, or vandalism. Check with your insurance agent to make sure that your insurance covers the bike where it is stored.

Preparing the Bike For Storage

Careful preparation will minimize deterioration and make it easier to restore the bike to service later. Use the following procedure.

1. Wash the bike completely. Make certain to remove any road salt which may have accumulated during the first weeks of winter. Wax all painted and polished surfaces, including any chromed areas.

2. Run the engine for 20-30 minutes to stabilize oil temperature. Drain oil, regardless of mileage since last oil change. Replace the oil filter and fill engine with a normal quantity of fresh oil.

3. Remove battery and coat cable terminals with petroleum jelly. If there is evidence of acid spillage in the battery box, neutralize with baking soda, wash clean, and repaint the damaged area. Store the battery in a warm area and recharge it every 2 weeks.

4. Drain all the gasoline from fuel tank, interconnecting hoses, and carburetors. Leave fuel petcock in the RESERVE position. As an alternative, a fuel preservative may be added to the fuel. This preservative is available from many motorcycle shops and marine equipment suppliers.

5. Remove spark plugs and add a small quantity of oil to each cylinder. Turn the engine a few revolutions by hand to distribute the oil and install the spark plugs.

6. Run a paper card, lightly saturated with silicone lubricant, between the points.

CAUTION
Do not use any other type of lubricant or the points will be burned when the bike is restored to service.

7. Check tire pressures. Move machine to storage area and store it on the centerstand.

After Storage

Before returning the motorcycle to service, thoroughly check all fasteners, suspension components and brake components. Check the oil level and top up if necessary. If possible, change the engine oil and filter. The oil may have become contaminated with condensation.

Make sure the battery is fully charged and the electrolyte level is correct before installing the battery. Fill the fuel tank with fresh gasoline.

Before starting the engine, remove the spark plugs and spin the engine over a few times to blow out the excess storage oil. Place a rag over the cylinder head to keep the oil off the engine. Install new spark plugs and connect the spark plug leads.

Table 1 MAINTENANCE AND LUBRICATION SCHEDULE

Every fuel stop or every month
- Check engine oil level
- Check tire condition and inflation
- Check battery electrolyte level
- Check wheels for damage or loose spokes

Initial 600 miles (1,000 km)
- Check all engine, exhaust system and frame fasteners and tighten if necessary
- Check and/or adjust valve clearance
- Check and/or adjust contact breaker points and ignition timing (1979 and earlier models)
- Change engine oil and oil filter
- Adjust engine idle speed
- Adjust clutch
- Check brake fluid level
- Check brake pad wear
- Clean, lubricate and adjust drive chain
- Check and/or adjust steering stem
- Adjust throttle cables
- Perform compression check

Every 2,000 miles (3,000 km)[1]
- Change engine oil (1979 and earlier models)

Every 4,000 miles (6,000 km)[2]
- Perform all maintenance items specified under initial 600 miles (1,000 km) plus the following:
- Change engine oil and filter (all GS450 models)
- Clean spark plugs and adjust gap
- Clean and reoil foam air cleaner element
- Inspect battery electrolyte level; check specific gravity of electrolyte with hydrometer
- Check oil pressure
- Change fork oil
- Lubricate throttle and clutch cables with oil or special cable lubricant
- Lubricate brake pedal shaft

Every 7,500 miles (12,000 km)[3]
- Perform all maintenance items specified under initial 600 miles
- (1,000 km) and 4,000 mile (6,000 km) service plus the following:
- Replace spark plugs
- Lubricate throttle grip with grease
- Lubricate speedometer and tachometer cables with grease
- Clean oil pickup screen

(continued)

Table 1 MAINTENANCE AND LUBRICATION SCHEDULE (cont.)

Every year
- Bleed and change brake fluid

Every 2 years, 15,000 miles (24,000 km)
- Replace fuel line
- Replace brake hoses
- Lubricate steering stem bearings and swing arm bearings

1. For all 1978 and earlier models, 1,500 miles (2,500 km).
2. For all 1978 and earlier models, 3,000 miles (5,000 km).
3. For all 1978 and earlier models, 6,000 miles (10,000 km).

Table 2 RECOMMENDED FUEL AND LUBRICANTS

Fuel	90 octane or higher
Engine oil	SAE 10W-40, rated SE or SD
Front fork oil	SAE 10W-30 motor mixed 50/50 with ATF (automatic transmission fluid)
Brake fluid	DOT 3, DOT 4, or SAE J1703

Table 3 RECOMMENDED TIRE PRESSURES

Tire	Psi	kg/cm²
Front tire (normal riding)		
Solo (GS400)	25	1.75
Solo (GS425N, EN, LN)	25	1.75
Solo (GS450ET, ST, LT, TX)	25	1.75
Solo (GS450EZ, ED)	24	1.75
Solo (GS450TZ, TXZ)	21	1.25
Solo (GS450TXD)	22	1.50
Solo (GS450LD, LF, LH)	28	2.00
Solo (GS450LF)	24	1.75
Dual (GS400)	25	1.75
Dual (GS425N, EN, LN)	25	1.75
Dual (GS450ET, ST, LT, TX)	25	1.75
Dual (GS450EZ, TZ, TXZ, ED)	24	1.75
Dual (GS450TXD, LG)	24	1.75
Dual (GS450LD, LF, LH)	28	2.00
Front tire (continuous high-speed riding) *		
Solo (GS400)	28	2.00
Solo (GS425N, EN, LN)	28	2.00
Solo (GS450ET, ST, LT, TX)	28	2.00
Solo (GS450EZ, ED)	28	2.00
Solo (GS450TZ, TXZ, TXD)	24	1.75
Solo (GS450LD)	28	2.00
Dual (all models)	28	2.00
Rear tire (normal riding)		
Solo (GS400)	28	2.00
Solo (GS425N, EN, LN)	28	2.00
Solo (GS450ET, ST, LT, TX)	28	2.00
Solo (GS450EZ, ED)	28	2.00
Solo (GS450TZ, TXZ, TXD)	24	1.75
Solo (GS450LD, LF, LH)	32	2.25
Solo (GS450LG)	28	2.00

(continued)

Table 3 RECOMMENDED TIRE PRESSURES (cont.)

Dual (GS400)	32	2.25
Dual (GS425N, EN, LN)	32	2.25
Dual (GS450ET, ST, LT, TX)	32	2.25
Dual (GS450EZ, ED)	32	2.25
Dual (GS450TZ, TXZ, TXD)	32	2.25
Dual (GS450LD, LF, LH)	36	2.50
Dual (GS450LG)	32	2.25
Rear tire (continuous high-speed riding)*		
Solo (GS400)	32	2.25
Solo (GS425N, EN, LN)	32	2.25
Solo (GS450ET, ST, LT, TX)	32	2.25
Solo (GS450EZ, ED)	32	2.25
Solo (GS450TZ, TXZ, TXD)	28	2.00
Solo (GS450LD)	32	2.25
Dual (all models)	36	2.25

* Suzuki does not provide inflation pressure information for continuous high-speed riding for 1985-on models.

Table 4 CAPACITIES

Fuel tank	Liters	U.S. gal.	Imp. gal.
GS400, GS425	14	3.7	3.1
GS450L	11	2.9	2.4
GS450E, S	15	4.0	3.3
GS450ET, ST, LT, TX	14	3.7	3.1
GS450LZ	11	2.9	2.4
GS450TZ, TXZ	12	3.2	2.6
GS450EZ	14.5	3.8	3.2
All 1983 models	16	4.2	3.5
All 1985-on models	13	3.4	2.9

Engine/transmission oil	cc	U.S. qt.	Imp. qt.
Without filter change			
GS400, GS425	2100	2.2	1.8
GS450	2600	2.7	2.3
With filter change			
GS400, GS425	2400	2.5	2.1
GS450	2900	3.1	2.6
At overhaul			
GS400, GS425	2700	2.8	2.4
GS450	3000	3.2	2.6

Fork oil	cc	U.S. oz.	Imp. oz.
GS400	145	4.9	5.1
GS425L	160	5.4	5.6
GS450N, C	145	4.9	5.1
GS450LZ	189	6.4	6.7
GS450EZ	178	6.0	6.3
GS450TZ	181	6.1	6.4
GS450TXZ	143	4.8	5.0
GS450ED			
Right leg	165	5.6	5.8
Left leg	187	6.3	6.6
GS450TXD	155	5.2	5.5
GS450LD, LF, LG, LH	277	9.4	9.8

(continued)

Table 4 CAPACITIES (cont.)

Fork oil level *	mm	in.
GS400	187	7.1
GS425L	173	6.8
GS425E	187	7.1
GS450LZ	117	4.6
GS450EZ	131	5.6
GS450TZ	125	4.9
GS450TXZ, TXD	208	8.2
GS450ED	190	7.5
GS450LD, LF, LG, LH	118.5	4.7

* Measure the oil level from the top of the fork leg with the fork leg held vertical, the spring removed and the fork leg completely compressed.

Table 5 TORQUE SPECIFICATIONS

Item	mkg	ft.-lb.
Front axle nut	3.6-5.2	26-38
Front axle holder nut	1.5-2.5	11-18
Front caliper mounting bolt	2.5-4.0	18-29
Front caliper axle bolt		
GS400, GS425 models	2.5-3.5	18-26
GS450 models	1.5-2.0	11-15
Upper fork pinch bolt	2.0-3.0	15-22
Lower fork pinch bolt	2.5-4.0	18-29
Steering stem pinch bolt	1.5-2.5	11-18
Steering stem head bolt or nut	3.6-5.2	26-38
Handlebar clamp bolt	1.2-2.0	f9-15
Fork cap bolts	1.5-3.0	11-22
Brake disc mounting bolt	1.5-2.5	11-18
Rear sprocket nut	2.5-4.0	18-29
Swinging arm pivot nut		
GS400, GS425 models	5.0-8.0	36-58
GS450 models	5.0-5.8	36-42
Shock absorber nut	2.0-3.0	15-22
Rear axle nut		
GS400; GS425	8.5-11.5	62-83
GS450	5.0-8.0	36-58
Torque link nut	2.0-3.0	15-22
Engine mounting bolts		
8 mm	2.0-3.0	15-22
10 mm	3.0-3.7	22-27
Foot rest mounting bolts		
8 mm	1.5-2.5	11-18
10 mm	2.7-4.3	20-31

Table 6 TUNE-UP SPECIFICATIONS

Recommended spark plug	
1977-1985	NGK B8ES or ND W24ES
1986-on	NGK B8ES or ND W24ES-U
Spark plug gap	0.6-0.8 mm (0.024-0.031 in.)

(continued)

Table 6 TUNE-UP SPECIFICATIONS (cont.)

Breaker point ignition (GS400, GS425)	
Point gap	0.3-0.4 mm (0.012-0.016 in.)
Dwell angle	
GS400	180°
GS425	190°
Valve clearance (cold)	0.03-0.08 mm ((0.0012-0.0031 in.)
Ignition timing*	
GS400, GS425	10° BTDC below 1,500 rpm
	40° BTDC above 3,600 rpm
GS450	10° BTDC below 1,650 rpm
	40° BTDC above 3,500 rpm
Idle speed	1,100-1,300 rpm
Carburetor air screw	
All models manufactured	
after January 1978	Pre-set @ factory (non-adjustable)
All earlier models	1 1/4 turns open

* Timing on GS450 models is pre-set. No routine timing adjustment is necessary.

Table 7 TAPPET SHIM SIZES

No.	Thickness (mm)	Part No.	No.	Thickness (mm)	Part No.
1	2.15	12892-45000	11	2.65	12892-45010
2	2.20	12892-45001	12	2.70	12892-45011
3	2.25	12892-45002	13	2.75	12892-45012
4	2.30	12892-45003	14	2.80	12892-45013
5	2.35	12892-45004	15	2.85	12892-45014
6	2.40	12892-45005	16	2.90	12892-45015
7	2.45	12892-45006	17	2.95	12892-45016
8	2.50	12892-45007	18	3.00	12892-45017
9	2.55	12892-45008	19	3.05	12892-45018
10	2.60	12892-45009	20	3.10	12892-45019

Table 8 COMPRESSION SPECIFICATIONS

	Standard	Service limit
Compression pressure		
GS400, GS425	130-184	100 psi
	(9-13 kg/cm²)	(7.0 kg/cm²)
GS450	130-170 psi	100 psi
	(9-12 kg/cm²)	(7.0 kg/cm²)
Maximum difference between cylinders		
GS400, GS425	—	14 psi (1 kg/cm²)
GS450	—	28 psi (2 kg/cm²)

CHAPTER FOUR

ENGINE

All "GS400 series" engines are air-cooled, 2-cylinder, 4-cycle models equipped with dual overhead camshafts (DOHC). A gear-driven balancer shaft is installed forward of the crankshaft to smooth out engine vibrations.

The crankshafts and balancer shafts in GS400 and GS425 models are supported in ball and roller bearings. The connecting rods also pivot on the crankshaft in roller bearings.

All GS450 models are equipped with a one-piece forged crankshaft. The crankshaft main bearings, connecting rod bearings and balancer shaft bearings are automotive style "plain" insert bearings.

Both camshafts are chain-driven from the crankshaft. The cam chain tension is controlled automatically by a spring-loaded slipper tensioner which bears against the rear vertical run of the chain.

The engine and transmission are lubricated from a common wet-sump oil supply. Oil is pumped throughout the engine by an oil pump driven by the clutch. The oil pump on GS400 and GS425 models is a high-volume, low-pressure type. The pump on GS450 models is a high-pressure type necessary to provided lubrication to "plain" insert type bearings. A wet-plate clutch is installed inside the right engine cover.

This chapter provides complete service and overhaul procedures for the "GS400 series" engine. Refer to Chapter Five for transmission and clutch repair procedures.

All engine upper end repair, including camshafts, cylinder head and cylinder block, can be performed with the engine installed in the motorcycle. Engine removal is necessary to perform repair on the crankshaft, transmission and certain components of the gearshift and kickstarter mechanisms.

Refer to **Table 1** for all engine torque specifications. **Tables 1-11** are located at the end of the chapter.

CAMSHAFTS

Removal

1. Remove the fuel tank as outlined in Chapter Six.
2. On GS400 and GS425 models remove screws securing end covers to cylinder head (**Figure 1**) and remove 4 covers.

3. Loosen clamp and remove breather hose from breather cover (**Figure 2**).

4. Disconnect horn wires (**Figure 3**).

5. Remove bolt securing horn bracket to frame and remove horn.

6. On GS400 and GS425 models remove bolts securing breather cover (**Figure 4**) and remove cover.

7. Remove bolts securing cam cover to cylinder head and remove cover (**Figure 5**). Note location of different length bolts.

8. Loosen locknut on cam chain tensioner and turn slotted lockscrew clockwise to lock tensioner pushrod (**Figure 6**).

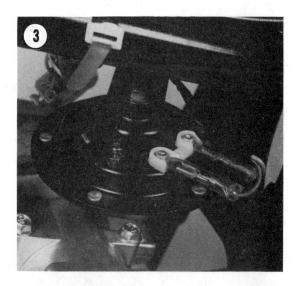

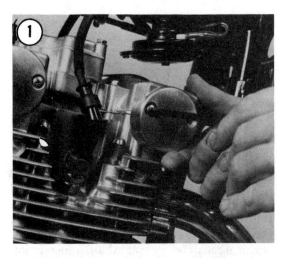

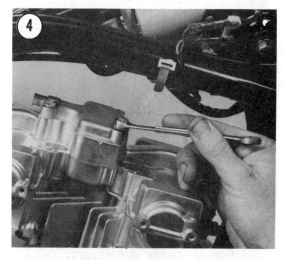

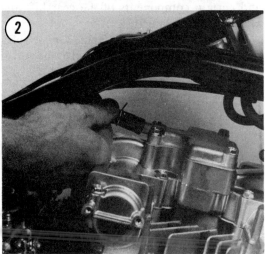

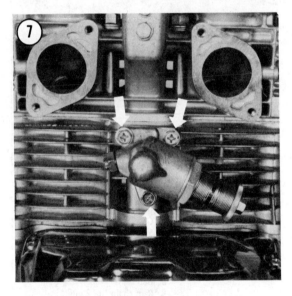

9. Remove bolts (**Figure 7**) and remove cam chain tensioner. See **Figure 8**.

10. On GS400 and GS425 models gradually loosen, then remove, 4 bolts securing cam chain idler (**Figure 9**). Lift off idler assembly taking care that the cushions and spacers do not fall into the cam chain opening.

NOTE
If idler cushion and spacer are accidentally dropped down the cam chain opening, they can be removed by a strong magnetic tool retriever.

11. Gradually and evenly, loosen bolts securing cam bearing caps (**Figure 10**), and remove caps.

NOTE
*Cam bearing caps are marked "A," "B," "C," and "D" with corresponding marks on the cylinder head (**Figure 11**).*

12. Lift up on cam chain and lift out intake (rear) camshaft (**Figure 12**).

13. Tie a piece of wire or cord to cam chain (**Figure 13**) to prevent chain from falling into engine. If the engine is still installed in the motorcycle, attach the wire or cord to the frame to hold the chain.

14. Disengage chain and remove exhaust cam (**Figure 14**).

15. Perform *Inspection* procedure below.

Inspection

NOTE
*The following procedure describes how to use Plastigage to measure camshaft bearing journal wear. Plastigage can be purchased from most auto supply stores and is available in several sizes. Make sure you purchase Plastigage small enough to measure the camshaft bearing clearance as specified in **Table 2**.*

1. Carefully examine both camshafts for evidence of excessive or abnormal wear on the lobes or bearing journals.

2. Inspect each cam sprocket for signs of wear. Excessive wear is unlikely except in engines with high mileage or misaligned sprockets. If sprockets are worn, they must be replaced in pairs and a new cam chain must be installed.

NOTE
*The cam chain is a one piece unit. To replace the chain it is necessary to remove the crankshaft. Refer to **Lower End Disassembly**.*

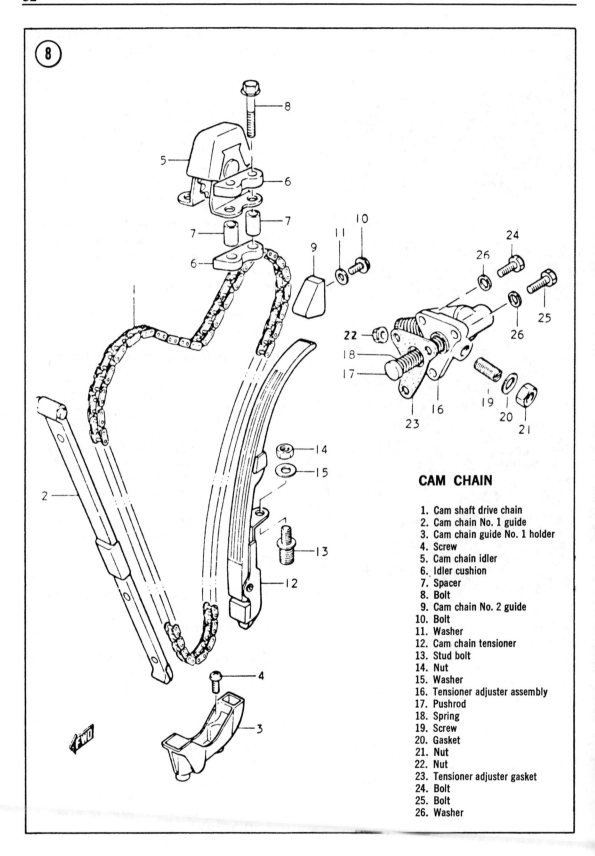

CAM CHAIN

1. Cam shaft drive chain
2. Cam chain No. 1 guide
3. Cam chain guide No. 1 holder
4. Screw
5. Cam chain idler
6. Idler cushion
7. Spacer
8. Bolt
9. Cam chain No. 2 guide
10. Bolt
11. Washer
12. Cam chain tensioner
13. Stud bolt
14. Nut
15. Washer
16. Tensioner adjuster assembly
17. Pushrod
18. Spring
19. Screw
20. Gasket
21. Nut
22. Nut
23. Tensioner adjuster gasket
24. Bolt
25. Bolt
26. Washer

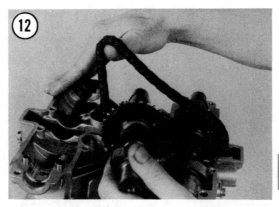

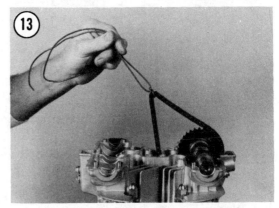

3. If sprockets are replaced, ensure that they are positioned on the camshafts correctly. Refer to **Figure 15** for the correct positioning of the marks in relation to the notches on the ends of the camshafts. Apply a couple of drops of blue Loctite (Lock N' Seal No. 2114) to the sprocket bolts and torque them to 0.9-1.2 mkg (6.5-8.5 ft.-lb.). On GS450 engines, make sure the sprockets are aligned with the camshaft locating pins as shown in **Figure 16**. Fold over the metal tabs to secure the bolts.

NOTE
Suzuki replacement part camshafts and sprockets for GS400 and GS425 models use a locating pin, hex head bolts and folding locking washers as installed on GS450 models. When installing new stock replacement part camshafts and sprockets on GS400 and GS425 models, use the procedure steps outlined for GS450 models.

4. Use a micrometer and measure the height of each camshaft lobe as shown in **Figure 17**. Refer to **Table 2** for wear specifications.

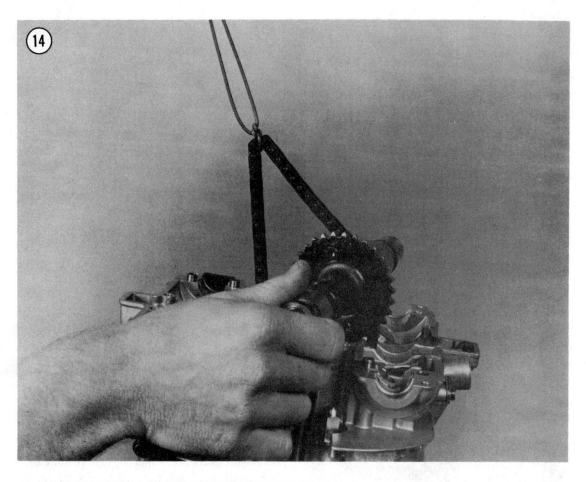

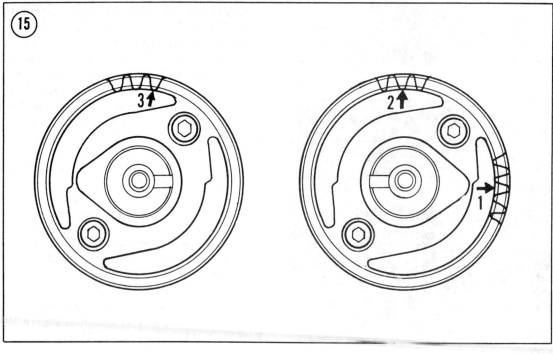

5. Measure bearing journal wear with Plastigage as follows:

a. Wipe off all oil from the bearing journal and camshaft bearing surfaces and place the camshaft on the cylinder head.

b. Place a small strip of Plastigage on each bearing surface as shown in **Figure 18**.

c. Install the bearing caps and tighten the bolts gradually and evenly in a crisscross pattern. Torque the bolts to 0.8-1.2 mkg (6.0-8.5 ft.-lb.).

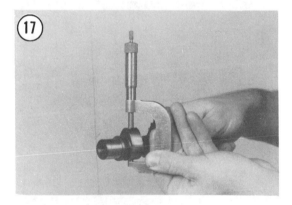

NOTE
It is not necessary to install the cam chain over the camshafts to check the bearing clearance with Plastigage. Do not allow the camshaft to turn while tightening the bearing cap bolts. If the camshaft is allowed to turn, the Plastigage will be damaged and the whole procedure must be repeated.

6. Remove the bearing caps as outlined under *Camshaft Removal*. Measure the thickness of the Plastigage with the wrapper as shown in **Figure 19**. The Plastigage may adhere to the camshaft or the bearing cap; either location will provide a correct indication. Refer to **Table 2** for the specified bearing journal clearance. If the clearance exceeds the service limit, determine the defective component as follows:

a. Measure the diameter of the camshaft bearing journals with a micrometer. If the camshaft journal diameter measurements are not within tolerances specified in **Table 2**, the camshafts must be replaced.

b. Install the camshaft bearing caps on the cylinder head without the camshafts. Tighten the bolts gradually and evenly in a crisscross pattern then torque to 0.8-1.2 mkg (6.0-8.5 ft.-lb.). Use an inside micrometer and measure the inside diameter of each bearing journal on the cylinder head. If the inside diameter exceeds the tolerances specified in **Table 2** the cylinder head must be replaced.

7. Place each camshaft in V-blocks and use a dial indicator to measure the camshaft runout (**Figure 20**). Replace either camshaft if runout exceeds 0.10 mm (0.004 in.).

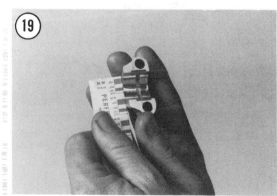

Installation and Timing

1. Using large hex shoulder of advance governor (**Figure 21**) rotate engine until timing mark (T) for right (R) cylinder aligns with mark on engine cover (**Figure 22**). This positions right piston at TDC (top dead center).

NOTE
The "T" timing mark is viewed through the window in the ignition plate. Due to the small window size and the recessed location of the timing marks, it is recommended that the ignition plate be removed to allow a better view for a more precise alignment of the marks. Remove the screws securing the ignition plate and carefully remove the plate. See **Figure 23** *for GS400 and GS425 models and* **Figure 24** *for GS450 models.*

2. Lubricate the camshaft lobes and bearing journals with molybdenum disulfide lubricant such as Bel-Ray Moly Lube. Spread the lubricant evenly without leaving any dry spots. Lubricate the bearing journals in the cylinder head with engine oil.

3. Lift up the cam chain and install the exhaust camshaft in the cylinder head (**Figure 25**). The exhaust cam is marked "EX". The notch in the end of the camshaft is positioned on the *right* side of the engine. Rotate the end of the tachometer drive gear as the camshaft is installed to ensure that the gear correctly engages the camshaft.

CAUTION
The tachometer drive gear must correctly engage the camshaft as the camshaft is installed or the gear will be damaged.

4. Check that the TDC timing mark "T" is correctly positioned as shown in **Figure 22**. Pull up on cam chain to remove all slack and install chain over cam sprocket so No. 1 arrow (**Figure 26**) points directly toward or slightly below (1-2 mm) gasket surface on cylinder head. Ensure that TDC mark is still correctly

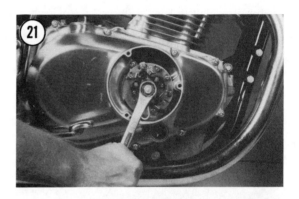

positioned and no slack exists in the front of the chain.

5. Install camshaft bearing caps. Make sure cast letters on caps correspond to cast letters on cylinder head as shown in **Figure 27**. Tighten bolts securing bearing caps gradually and evenly.

CAUTION
Bearing cap bolts are specially hardened and are identified by a "9" cast on bolt head. Use of any other type of bolt could cause serious engine damage.

NOTE
It is necessary to hold cam chain in position on sprocket while tightening bearing caps. Valve spring tension against cam lobe will cause cam to rotate slightly as bearing caps are tightened. If chain is not held in place, it will jump off alignment by 1 or 2 teeth and the procedure will have to be done over from the beginning.

When bearing cap bolts are tight, recheck timing mark alignment and readjust if necessary. If alignment is correct, engine can be rotated slightly to relieve valve spring load on cam lobe and lessen chance of chain slipping.

6. Lubricate and install the intake camshaft (marked "IN", **Figure 28**) carefully through cam chain and position cam into bearing journals. Make sure right and left ends are in correct locations.

7. Position the cam chain on the intake cam sprocket so that exactly 20 chain pins (GS400, GS425 models) or 18 chain pins (GS450 models) are between arrow No. 2 on the exhaust cam and arrow No. 3 on the intake cam as shown in **Figure 29** or **Figure 30**.

8. Install the bearing caps. Make sure the cast letters on the caps correspond to the cast letters in the cylinder head (**Figure 27**) and that the "triangles" enclosing the marks point forward. Tighten the bearing cap bolts gradually and evenly in a crisscross pattern. Torque the bolts to 0.8-1.2 mkg (6.0-8.5 ft.-lb.).

9. On GS400 and GS425 models, install the cam chain idler assembly. Gradually and evenly tighten the bolts securing the idler. Torque the bolts to 0.6-1.0 mkg (4.4-7.0 ft.-lb.).

10. Loosen the locknut and lockscrew on the cam chain tensioner assembly. Push in on the spring-loaded plunger while rotating the large knurled nut counterclockwise (**Figure 31**). When the plunger is pushed in as far as possible, secure it with the lockscrew.

11. Make sure the gasket is in place and install the chain tensioner assembly (**Figure 32**). Torque the bolts to 0.6-0.8 mkg (4.5-6.0 ft.-lb.).

12. Back out the lockscrew approximately 1/4 turn to release the spring-loaded plunger. Secure the lockscrew with the locknut (**Figure 33**).

NOTE
Do not back out the lockscrew more than 1/2 turn or the plunger may become disengaged from the tensioner body. If this should occur it will be necessary to remove the tensioner assembly to install the plunger into the tensioner body.

13. Use a 19 mm wrench on the end of the crankshaft and rotate the crankshaft several turns to make sure the camshafts and chain operate smoothly and freely. Recheck the camshaft timing in relation to the TDC marks.

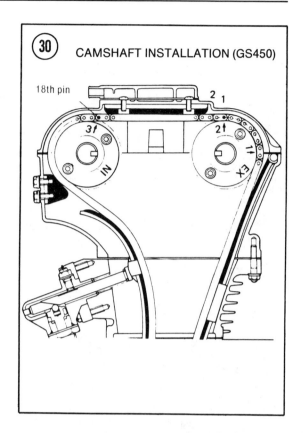

(30) CAMSHAFT INSTALLATION (GS450)

(31)

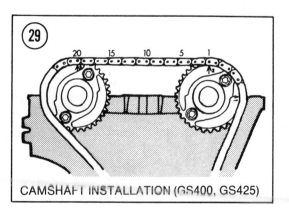

(29)

CAMSHAFT INSTALLATION (GS400, GS425)

4

NOTE
Rotate the large knurled nut on the cam chain tensioner counterclockwise while slowly rotating the crankshaft counter-clockwise. This rotation will cause the cam chain to push back against the tensioner plunger. Release the knurled nut and slowly rotate the crankshaft clockwise (normal rotation). The knurled nut should rotate clockwise as the plunger takes up the slack in the cam chain. If the knurled nut does not re-spond as described, the plunger lock-screw may be too tight or the plunger may be sticking. If necessary, refer to **Cam Chain Tensioner** *as outlined in this chapter to disassemble the tensioner assembly.*

14. Install the ignition plate if it was removed.

15. Perform *Valve Clearance Adjustment* as outlined in Chapter Three.

16. Use approximately 50 cc (2 oz.) of engine oil and pour the oil over each camshaft bearing and the tachometer drive gear.

17. Install the cam cover gasket. Use a new gasket if possible. Make sure that all 4 half-moon shaped rubber end plugs (**Figure 34**) are in place.

18. On GS450 models, ensure that the screws securing the end caps are tight (**Figure 35**).

19. Carefully position the cam cover on the cylinder head so the gasket is not disturbed.

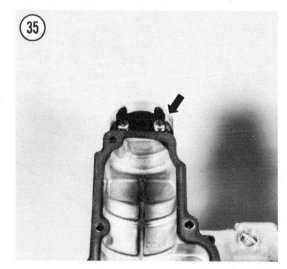

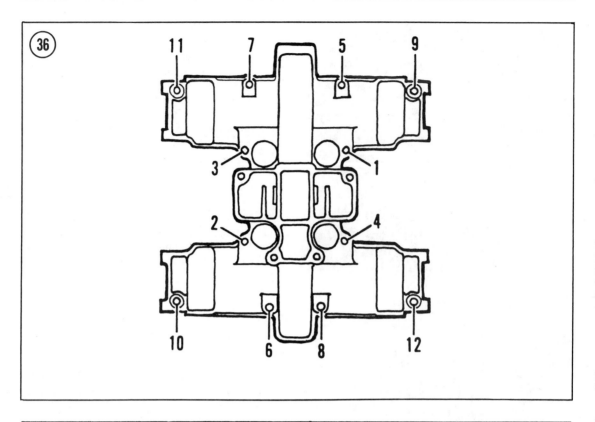

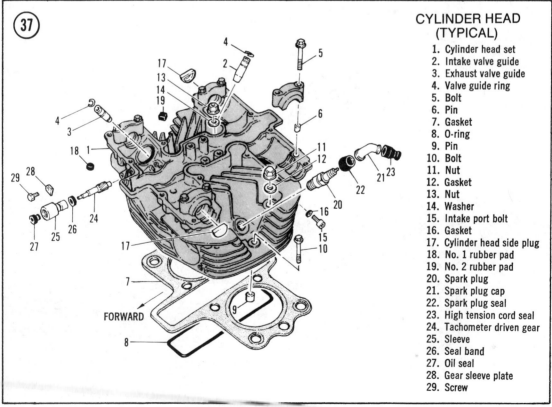

CYLINDER HEAD
(TYPICAL)

1. Cylinder head set
2. Intake valve guide
3. Exhaust valve guide
4. Valve guide ring
5. Bolt
6. Pin
7. Gasket
8. O-ring
9. Pin
10. Bolt
11. Nut
12. Gasket
13. Nut
14. Washer
15. Intake port bolt
16. Gasket
17. Cylinder head side plug
18. No. 1 rubber pad
19. No. 2 rubber pad
20. Spark plug
21. Spark plug cap
22. Spark plug seal
23. High tension cord seal
24. Tachometer driven gear
25. Sleeve
26. Seal band
27. Oil seal
28. Gear sleeve plate
29. Screw

20. Install the cam cover bolts. Tighten all the bolts gradually and evenly in the order shown in **Figure 36**. Torque the bolts to 0.9-1.0 mkg (6.5-7.0 ft.-lb.).

21. Install the breather cover gasket and install the breather cover. Install the cover bolts and torque to 0.9-1.0 mkg (6.5-7.0 ft.-lb.). Connect the breather hose to the breather cover and air box.

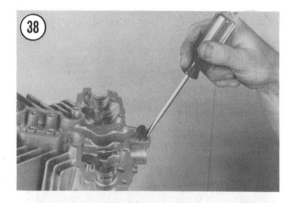

22. On GS400 and GS425 models, install the 4 camshaft end covers.
23. Install the horns and connect the horn wires.
24. Install the fuel tank as outlined in Chapter Six.
25. Connect the tachometer drive cable.
26. Connect the spark plug leads. Make sure the caps fit securely over the spark plugs.

CYLINDER HEAD

The cylinder head can be removed while the engine is installed in the motorcycle frame. Refer to **Figure 37** for a typical cylinder head assembly.

Removal

1. Perform *Camshaft Removal* as outlined in this chapter.
2. Perform *Exhaust System Removal* as outlined in Chapter Six.
3. Gently pry up on the end of the forward chain guide until the end is free from the head (**Figure 38**). Pull the chain guide straight up and out of the engine. If the engine is still installed in the frame, it will be necessary to pull the chain guide up between the upper frame tubes in order to clear the engine with the lower end of the guide (**Figure 39**).
4. On GS400 and GS425 engines, remove the two 6 mm bolts from each end of the cylinder head (**Figure 40**).
5. On GS450 engines, remove the 6 mm bolt from the front of the engine between the center exhaust ports (**Figure 41**).

6. Refer to **Figure 42** and gradually and evenly remove the head nuts in descending order. Numbers denoting sequence are cast in the head close to each head nut (**Figure 43**).

> *NOTE*
> *Use a magnetic tool retriever to lift the head nuts and washers out of the center recesses (**Figure 44**).*

7. Tap around the base of the cylinder head with a plastic or rubber mallet to break the head loose from the cylinder and carefully lift off the head (**Figure 45**).

> *CAUTION*
> *The cooling fins on the cylinder head are fragile. Tap the cylinder head carefully to avoid damaging the fins. Never use a metal hammer.*

8. Remove and discard the old head gasket. On GS400 and GS425 engines, remove and discard the rectangular O-ring (**Figure 46**).

9. Perform *Inspection*.

Inspection

> *NOTE*
> *Remove the tappets and adjusting shims from each valve to prevent them from falling out during cylinder head inspection.*

1. Use a small screwdriver in the tappet notch to pop the shim loose from the tappet and remove the shims as shown in **Figure 47**. Remove the tappets (**Figure 48**).

> *CAUTION*
> *Never use a magnet to lift out valve tappets or adjustment shims. They are made of hardened steel and are easily magnetized. A magnetized part will attract and hold metal particles which will cause excessive wear. A magnetized adjustment shim could also lift out of a tappet while the engine is running and cause serious and expensive damage. All component parts of each valve assembly must be kept together in the proper order as they are removed. Do not mix any parts with like components from other*

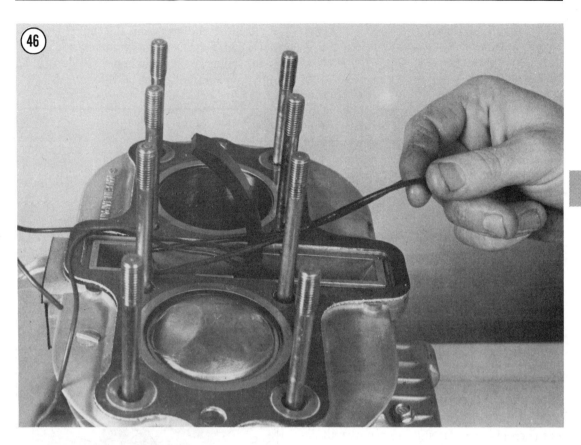

valve assemblies. Wear patterns have developed on these moving parts and damage or rapid and excessive wear may result if the parts are intermixed. An egg carton makes an excellent storage unit to keep the valve components in order.

2. Carefully clean all traces of gasket and sealant residue from the combustion chamber side and camshaft side of the cylinder head.

3. Without removing the valves, remove all carbon deposits from the combustion chambers with a wire brush and solvent. Stubborn deposits can be removed with a blunt scraper made of hardwood or a piece of aluminum that has been rounded and smoothed on one end as shown in **Figure 49**. Never use a hard metal scraper. Small burrs resulting from gouges in the combustion chamber will create hot spots which can cause preignition and heat erosion of the head and piston. After all carbon has been removed from the combustion chamber and exhaust ports, clean the entire head in solvent.

NOTE
*If valve inspection and/or repair is desired, refer to **Valves** as outlined in this chapter.*

4. Carefully examine the combustion chambers and ports for cracks or damage. Some types of cracks and/or damage can be repaired with heliarc welding. Refer such work to an authorized dealer or welding shop experienced with cylinder head repair.

5. Use a straightedge and check the gasket surface of the head in several places as shown in **Figure 50**. Such an inspection might be best performed by a dealer or machine shop. Replace the head if the gasket surface is warped beyond the service limit of 0.1 mm (0.004 in.).

Installation

1. Ensure that the gasket surface on the cylinder is clean and free of old gasket residue.
2. Clean all the carbon from the pistons. Wipe out each cylinder carefully to remove all debris.
3. Install a new head gasket over the studs on the cylinder (**Figure 51**). On GS400 and GS425 engines, install a new rectangular O-ring on the cylinder block.
4. Pull the cam chain up through the opening in the head and carefully lower the head down over the cylinder studs (**Figure 52**). Make sure the alignment dowels are engaged, then press the head down against the gasket.
5. On GS400 and GS425 engines, install the 4 dome nuts with copper washers on the exposed studs and the 4 plain nuts and steel washers on the recessed studs. Use a screwdriver to help route the washers over the studs.

NOTE
Stuff rags into the cam chain tunnel before attempting to install the washers over the head studs. A copper washer accidentally dropped into the chain tunnel obviously cannot be removed with a magnetic tool retriever. Dropping a washer into the engine could easily cause a lot of extra work and aggravation.

6. Remove the rags from the cam chain tunnel. Tighten the head nuts gradually and evenly in the sequence shown in **Figure 53**. Torque the nuts to 3.5-4.0 mkg (26-29 ft.-lb.).

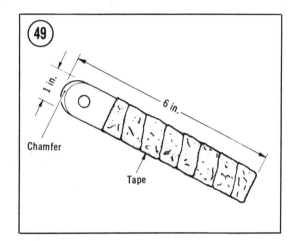

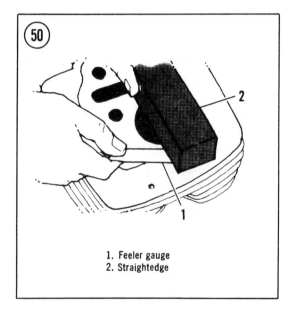

1. Feeler gauge
2. Straightedge

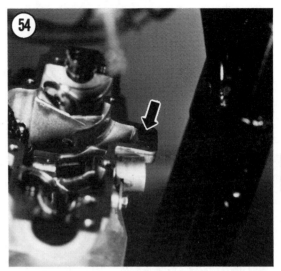

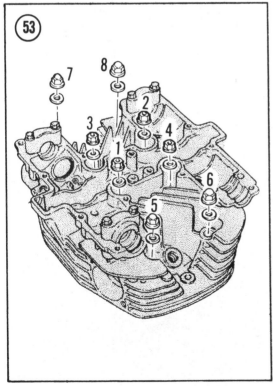

7. On GS400 and GS425 engines, install the two 6 mm bolts in each end of the head (**Figure 40**). On GS450 engines, install the one 6 mm bolt between the center exhaust ports (**Figure 41**).

8. Install the forward chain guide. The lower end of the guide must "slip into place" and feel secure in the bottom of the engine. If the bottom of the guide is correctly installed, it will be necessary to slightly spring back the upper portion of the chain guide in order to install it in the upper cylinder head groove. Make sure that the upper end of the guide fits securely in the groove as shown in **Figure 54**.

9. Install the tappets and shims if removed during inspection.

10. Perform *Camshaft, Installation and Timing* as outlined in this chapter.

11. Refer to Chapter Six and install the exhaust system.

12. Refer to Chapter Three and perform *Valve Adjustment*.

VALVES

Valve servicing requires the use of a valve spring compressor tool to remove the valves from the head. Suitable valve spring compressors can be rented from most rental shops, however, it may be less expensive to have a dealer or other motorcycle repair shop remove the valves from the head.

Removal

Refer to **Figure 55** for this procedure.

1. Perform *Cylinder Head, Removal* and *Inspection* as outlined in this chapter.

2. Install one end of the valve spring compressor against one valve head. Place the other end of the tool squarely over the valve retainer (**Figure 56**).

> *CAUTION*
> *All component parts of each valve assembly must be kept together in the proper order as they are removed. Do not mix any parts with like components from other valve assemblies. Wear patterns have developed on these moving parts and damage or rapid and excessive wear may result if the parts are intermixed. An egg carton makes an excellent storage unit to keep the valve components in order.*

3. Tighten the valve spring compressor until the split valve keeper separates. Lift out both split keepers with needlenose pliers as shown in **Figure 57**.

4. Gradually loosen the compressor tool and remove it from the cylinder head. Lift off the upper valve retainer (**Figure 58**).

5. Remove the inner and outer valve springs (**Figure 59**). Keep the springs together as they are a matched pair.

6. Tip up the head and remove the valve (**Figure 60**).

7. Use needlenose pliers and remove the valve guide oil seal (**Figure 61**). Discard the old seal as it will be destroyed when it is removed.

> *NOTE*
> *Valve guide oil seals should be routinely replaced whenever the valves are removed. Failure to replace the seals may result in excessive oil consumption.*

8. Lift out the lower valve seat (**Figure 62**).
9. Repeat the procedure for the other valves.
10. Perform *Inspection*.

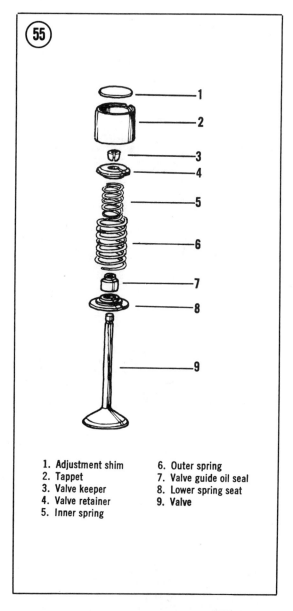

1. Adjustment shim
2. Tappet
3. Valve keeper
4. Valve retainer
5. Inner spring
6. Outer spring
7. Valve guide oil seal
8. Lower spring seat
9. Valve

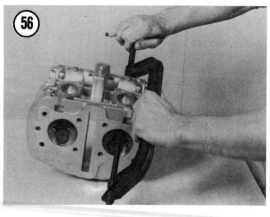

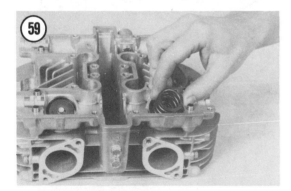

Inspection

NOTE
Some of the following inspection steps require the use of special measuring devices that most home mechanics do not own. If full valve inspection is desired, have the specialized measurements performed by an authorized dealer.

1. Clean the valves with a wire brush and solvent.

2. Inspect the contact surface of each valve for burning or pitting. Each valve should have a precise seating "ring" as shown in **Figure 63**. Replace any valve that is burned, pitted, warped or cracked. The valves are made from a specially hardened material and should not be ground or refaced.

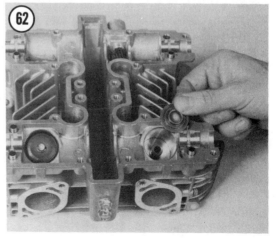

3. Measure the valve stem with a micrometer as shown in **Figure 64**. Replace the valve if worn beyond the limits specified in **Table 3**.

4. Remove all carbon and varnish from the valve guides with a stiff spiral wire brush.

5. Insert each valve in its guide. Hold the valve just slightly off its seat and rock it sideways in opposite directions. If it rocks more than slightly, the guide is worn and must be replaced. If a dial indicator is available, a more accurate measurement can be made as shown in **Figure 65**. Replace any guides that exceed the valve-to-guide clearance specified in **Table 3**. If guides must be replaced, refer the task to an authorized dealer or machine shop.

6. Use a dial indicator and V-blocks as shown in **Figure 66** and measure the valve stem deflection or runout. Replace valves if the stem deflection exceeds the limits specified in **Table 3**.

7. Use a dial indicator and one V-block as shown in **Figure 67** and measure the runout or deflection of the valve head. Replace valves if the head deflection exceeds the limits specified in **Table 3**.

8. Measure valve spring heights as shown in **Figure 68**. All springs should be as specified in **Table 3** with no bends or distortions. Replace defective springs in pairs.

9. If the valve seats in the cylinder head have ever been reconditioned, the ends of the valve stems can be refaced if necessary, however, the end of the valve must not be less than 4.0 mm (0.16 in.) as shown in **Figure 69**.

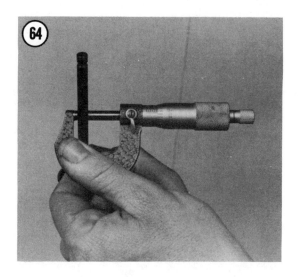

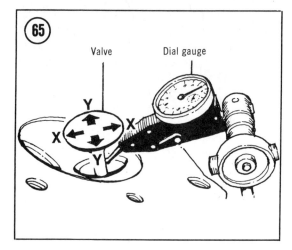

Valve   Dial gauge

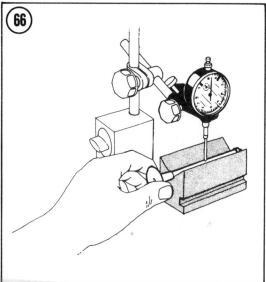

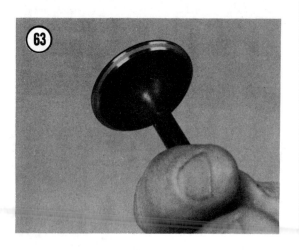

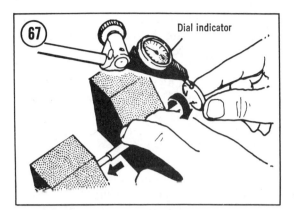

Dial indicator

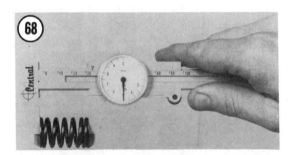

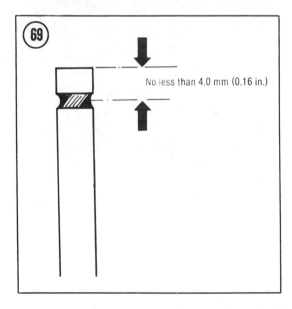

No less than 4.0 mm (0.16 in.)

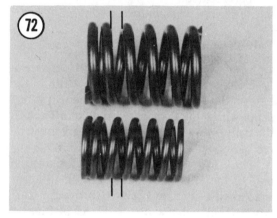

Installation

1. Install the lower spring seat over the valve guide (**Figure 62**).

2. Lubricate the lip on the new valve guide seal with engine oil and install the seal over the valve guide. If using the special seal installation tool, position the seal into the tool. If the special tool is not available, use a 10 mm socket as shown in **Figure 70** and gently tap the seal into place. Ensure that the seal is seated squarely over the valve guide and is locked into place (**Figure 71**).

3. Install the inner and outer valve springs. Note that the coils are closer together on the bottom end (toward cylinder head) of the springs (**Figure 72**). Ensure that the springs are installed correctly.

4. Lubricate the valve stems with Bel-Ray Moly Lube or equivalent and install the valves in the head.

5. Place the upper spring retainer over the valve springs. Install the spring compressor tool and tighten the compressor until the end of the valve is exposed enough to install the split keepers.

6. Apply a small amount of grease to each keeper half and stick the keeper to a small screwdriver to aid installation (**Figure 73**). Install the split keepers on the valve stem and back off the spring compressor until the split keepers secure the valve mechanism.

7. Remove the valve spring compressor. Use a soft drift or a soft-faced hammer and tap the end of each valve to make sure the keepers are properly seated.

8. Perform *Cylinder Head, Installation.*

Valve Seat and Seal Inspection

1. Remove the valve as previously described.

2. Use a caliper and measure the width of the seat on the valve (**Figure 74**). If the seat width is not within the tolerance specified in **Table 3**, the valve seat in the cylinder head must be reconditioned.

3. The most accurate method for checking the seal of the valve is to use Prussian Blue or machinist's dye, available from auto part stores or machine shops. If Prussian Blue or dye is available, perform the following:

   a. Thoroughly clean the valve and valve seat with solvent or detergent.

   b. Spread a thin layer of Prussian Blue or machinist's dye evenly on the valve face.

   c. Moisten the end of a "suction cup" valve tool (**Figure 75**) and attach it to the valve. Insert the valve into the guide.

   d. Tap the valve up and down in the head. Do not rotate the valve or a false indication will result.

   e. Remove the valve and examine the impression left by the Prussian Blue or dye. If the impression left in the dye (on the valve or in the head) is not even and continuous and the valve seat width (**Figure 63**) is not within specified tolerance (**Table 3**) the seat in the cylinder head must be reconditioned. Refer to *Valve Seat Reconditioning.*

4. Inspect the valve seats in the cylinder head. The seats should be smooth and even with a smooth polished seating "ring" as shown in **Figure 76**. If the seats are burned or damaged they must be reconditioned. Refer to *Valve Seat Reconditioning.*

5. Perform *Valves, Installation.*

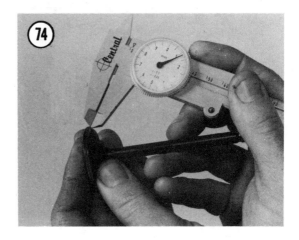

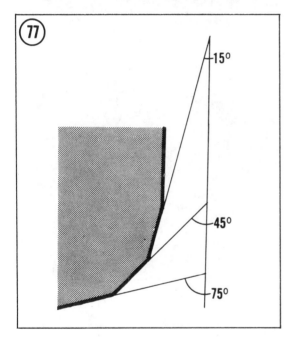

Valve Guide Replacement

When guides are worn so that there is excessive stem-to-guide clearance or valve tipping, they must be replaced. Replace all, even if only one is worn. This job should only be done by a dealer as special tools are required.

Valve Seat Reconditioning

This job is best left to your dealer or local machine shop. They have the special equipment and knowledge for this exacting job. You can still save considerable money by removing the cylinder head and taking just the head to the shop. The following procedure is provided in the event that you are not near a dealer and the local machine shop is not familiar with the seat reconditioning specifications.

1. With a 15° valve seat cutter, remove just enough metal to make bottom of seat concentric. See **Figure 77**.
2. With a 75° valve seat cutter, remove just enough metal from top of seat to make it concentric.
3. With a 45° valve seat cutter, cut a seat that is 1.0-1.2 mm (0.039-0.047 in.) wide.

CYLINDER BLOCK AND PISTONS

Cylinder block and piston repair work can be performed with the engine installed in the motorcycle.

Removal

1. Perform *Cylinder Head, Removal* as outlined in this chapter.
2. Tap around the base of the cylinder with a rubber mallet or plastic hammer to break the cylinder loose from the crankcase.
3. Gently lift up and remove the cylinder block from the engine (**Figure 78**). Note that the arrows on all the pistons point forward (**Figure 79**).
4. Remove and discard the cylinder base gasket. On GS400 and GS425 engines, remove the triangular O-rings (**Figure 80**).
5. Stuff clean rags into the crankcase openings around each connecting rod to prevent dirt and piston pin snap rings from falling into the engine.

6. Use a small screwdriver or awl and carefully pry out the snap ring through the notch in the piston (**Figure 81**). Partially cover the opening in the piston with your thumb to prevent the snap ring from flying out. Discard the old snap ring.

7. Use a wooden dowel or socket extension to push out the piston pin and remove the piston (**Figure 82**).

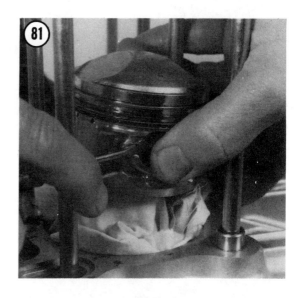

> *CAUTION*
> *On some engines (particularly those with high mileage) the piston pin may be difficult to remove. Do not attempt to drive out the pin or connecting rod damage may result. If the piston pin cannot be pushed or gently tapped out, use a piston pin extractor tool as shown in **Figure 83**. Refer to **Figure 84** for an example of a locally fabricated type. If such a tool is not available, have a dealer remove the piston pin. It is a quick and inexpensive job with the right tools and will prevent expensive engine damage.*

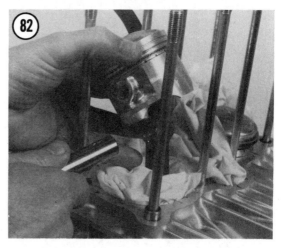

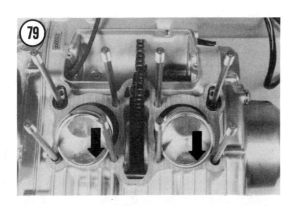

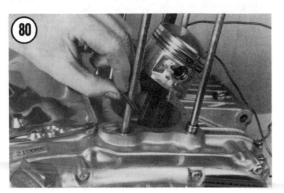

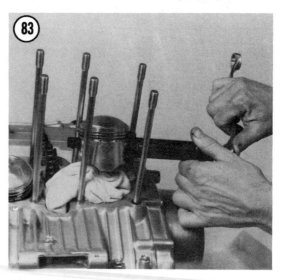

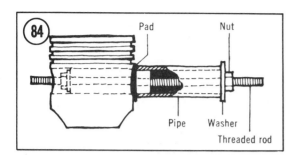

Pad   Nut

Pipe   Washer

Threaded rod

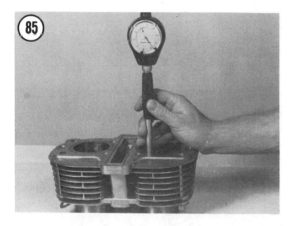

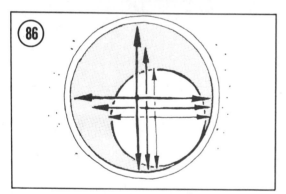

8. Mark the inside of the piston with a felt pen or scribe to identify its location. Repeat the removal procedure for the other pistons.

NOTE
If the engine is to be completely disassembled, it may be desirable to leave one piston installed. An installed piston can be used with a piston holding fixture to prevent the crankshaft from turning. This may be required if the magneto rotor or ignition advance governor must be removed. Refer to **Lower End Disassembly***.*

9. Perform *Cylinder Block Inspection* and *Piston and Ring Inspection*.

Cylinder Block Inspection

The following procedure requires the use of highly specialized and expensive measuring equipment. If such equipment is not available, have a dealer or machine shop perform the following measurements.

1. Use an inside micrometer or cylinder bore gauge and measure the cylinder bore (**Figure 85**). Measure the bore at 3 locations as shown in **Figure 86** and in 2 positions, 90° apart. Compare the measurements with the specifications in **Table 4**, **Table 5** or **Table 6** and rebore the cylinder if necessary.

2. Examine the condition of the cylinder bore (**Figure 87**). The cylinder should be rebored if the surface is scored or abraded. Pistons are available in oversize increases of 0.5 mm and 1.0 mm. Purchase the oversize pistons before having the cylinder bored. The pistons must first be measured and the cylinder bored to match them in order to maintain the specified piston-to-cylinder clearance. All pistons should be replaced as a set.

3. Use a feeler gauge and straightedge as shown in **Figure 88** and check the head gasket surface of the cylinder block for distortion. Check the cylinder at several places. If the distortion in any spot exceeds 0.1 mm (0.004 in.) the cylinder block must be replaced.

Piston and Ring Inspection

1. Measure the pistons at the point shown in **Figure 89**. If any piston is not within the tolerance specified in **Table 4**, **Table 5** or **Table 6**, replace both pistons as a set.

2. Use a bore gauge or a snap gauge and micrometer and measure the piston pin bore in each piston (**Figure 90**). Use a micrometer and measure each piston pin in the center and at both ends. Subtract the piston pin dimension from the inside piston pin bore dimension to obtain the piston pin/pin bore clearance. If the bore clearance dimension exceeds the service limit of 0.12 mm (0.0047 in.), replace the piston and pin as a set.

3. Clean the top of the pistons with a soft metal scraper to remove carbon (**Figure 91**). Use a piece of old piston ring to clean the ring grooves (**Figure 92**). Thoroughly clean the pistons in solvent or detergent and hot water.

4. Use a feeler gauge and check the side clearance of the rings in the piston grooves (**Figure 93**). If the clearance is greater than that specified in **Table 7**, measure the ring thickness, then the groove width, to determine which part is worn. All parts worn beyond their respective service limits must be replaced. Refer to **Table 7** for ring thickness and groove width specifications.

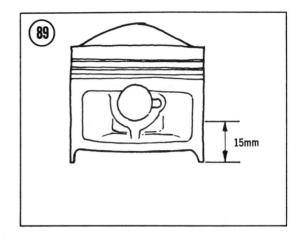

15mm

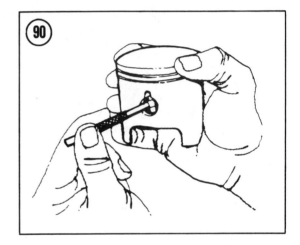

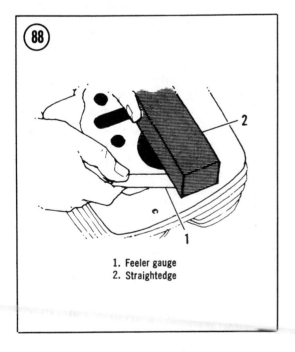

1. Feeler gauge
2. Straightedge

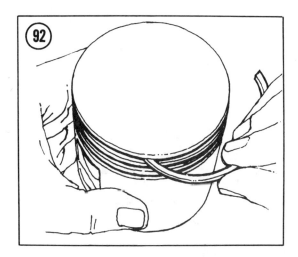

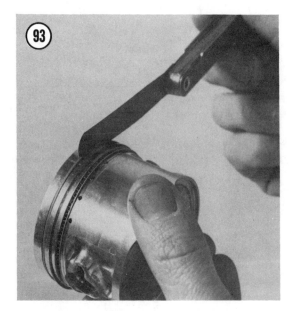

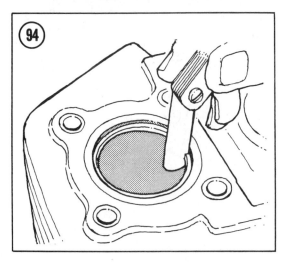

5. Place the 2 top piston rings, one at a time, into the cylinder bore and measure the ring end gap (**Figure 94**). Use the piston to push the ring squarely into the cylinder bore approximately 25 mm (1 in.). This measurement is required for new rings as well as old ones. Compare the actual ring gap to **Table 7** and replace the old rings if their gap is greater than the specified service limit. For new rings it is more likely that the gap will be less than minimum. If such is the case, clamp a fine file in a vise and carefully file the ring ends as shown in **Figure 95**.

6. Measure the free-state ring gap as shown in **Figure 96**. If the free-state ring gap is less than specified, the ring does not have sufficient spring tension to seat well. Such rings should be replaced. Note that the free-state ring gap is slightly different for "N" (Nippon) and "R" (Riken) type piston rings.

7. Existing rings that are oversize can be identified in the following manner:

   a. The top 2 rings are stamped with code numbers next to the letter on the ring end. A 0.5 mm oversized ring is stamped with the number "50" while a 1.0 mm oversize ring is stamped with the number "100."

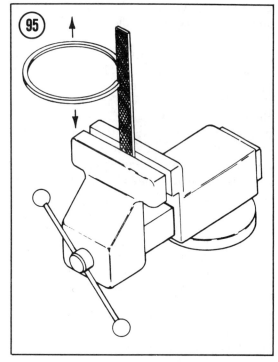

   b. An oversize oil ring spacer is identified by color codes. A 0.5 mm oversize spacer is painted red while a 1.0 mm oversize spacer is painted yellow.

   c. Oversize oil ring side rails must be measured with a caliper to determine their size. Oversize oil ring side rails are 0.5 mm and 1.0 mm larger than the standard bore size.

8. Carefully examine each piston around the area of the skirt, pin and ring grooves for signs of cracks, stress or metal fatigue. Replace all the pistons as a set if any signs of abnormal wear are present on any piston.

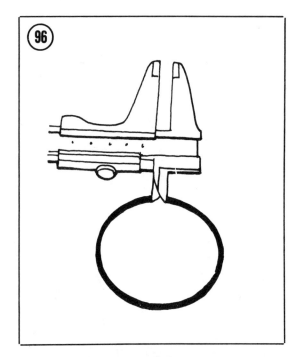

Installation

1. Carefully spread the piston rings with your thumbs as shown in **Figure 97** and install the rings in the appropriate grooves (**Figure 98**). The 2 top rings are stamped with either a letter "R" or "N" as shown in **Figure 99**. The identifying letters on the ring ends always face toward the top of the piston.

2. Two types of oil ring spacers are used (**Figure 100**). The "R" type spacer must always be installed with "R" type upper rings and the "N" type spacer with "N" type upper rings. The side rails on the oil rings are not marked and can be used with either type of oil ring spacer.

3. Install the oil ring spacer first. The 2 side rails can then be installed. There is no top or bottom designation for the side rails. Ensure that the side rails fit around the spacer as shown in **Figure 101**. Some clearance may be present between the ends of the oil ring spacer (**Figure 102**) or the ends may butt together. Do not allow the ends of the oil spacer to overlap.

4. Install one new snap ring into the pistion pin groove.

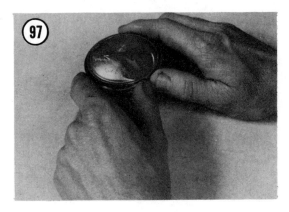

CAUTION
If possible, always use new snap rings to secure the piston pin. An old snap ring could work out and cause serious and expensive engine damage.

5. Lubricate the piston, piston pin and connecting rod with assembly oil or engine oil and install the piston on the connecting rod (**Figure**

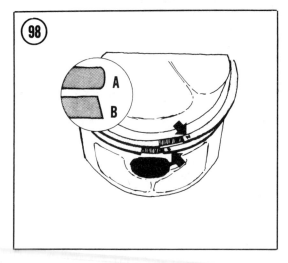

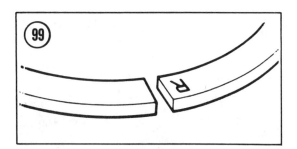

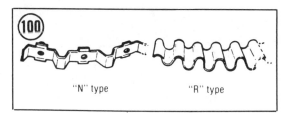

"N" type   "R" type

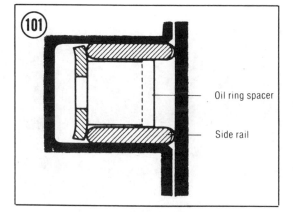

Oil ring spacer

Side rail

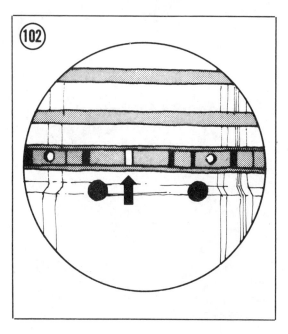

103). Make sure that the arrow on the piston points forward toward the front of the engine (**Figure 104**).

CAUTION
Never use STP or similar friction reducing products as assembly lubricant. Even a small amount will combine with the engine oil and destroy the friction properties of the clutch. If this should occur, the entire engine's lubrication system must be flushed and new clutch plates installed. If it is necessary to tap the piston pin into the connecting rod, do so with a soft-faced hammer. Make sure you support the piston to prevent the lateral shock from being transmitted to the lower connecting rod bearing.

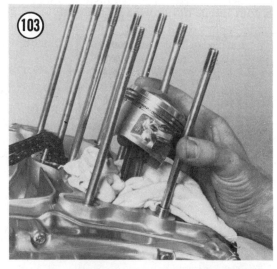

6. Partially hold a new snap ring in position with your thumb and install the snap ring into the piston groove (**Figure 105**). Make sure the snap ring locks into the groove. Rotate the snap ring so that a solid portion of the snap ring is opposite the notch in the piston (**Figure 106**).

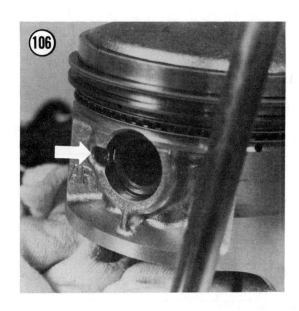

7. Make sure that the engine base and the bottom of the cylinder block are clean and free of old gasket residue. Install a new base gasket on the crankcase. On GS400 and GS425 engines ensure that the new triangular O-rings are properly positioned in the grooves (**Figure 107**).

8. Remove the old O-rings from the base of each cylinder liner and replace with new ones (**Figure 108**).

9. Stagger the rings on each piston so that the end gaps are approximately 120° from each other (**Figure 109**).

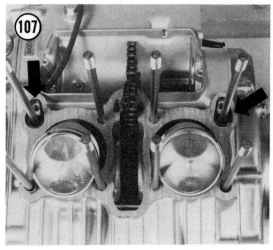

10. Install a piston holding fixture under one of the pistons to hold the pistons in position while installing the cylinder block. Carefully rotate the crankshaft until the piston is firmly against the holding fixture.

NOTE
A simple homemade holding fixture can be made of wood. Refer to **Figure 110** *for approximate dimensions.*

11. Oil each piston and cylinder bore with assembly oil or engine oil. Feed the cam chain

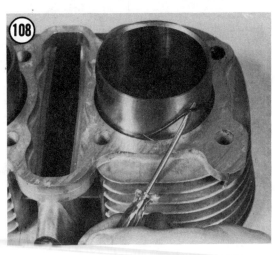

up through the chain tunnel and start the cylinder block down over the studs. Compress the rings with your fingers or a ring compressor and carefully slide the cylinder block over the pistons until the cylinder block contacts the other piston.

NOTE
A large hose clamp (Figure 111) can be used for an effective and inexpensive ring compressor.

12. Install the piston holding fixture under the other piston. Using your fingers or a ring compressor, carefully compress the rings on the piston while pushing down on the cylinder block until all 3 rings on each piston are fully installed into the cylinder bores.

13. Remove the ring compressor and piston holding fixture. Push the cylinder down completely against the base gasket.

14. Perform *Cylinder Head, Installation.*

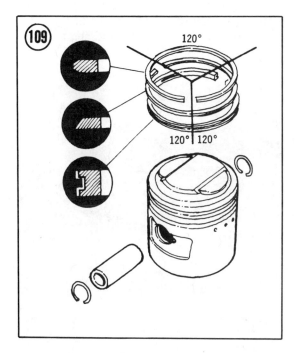

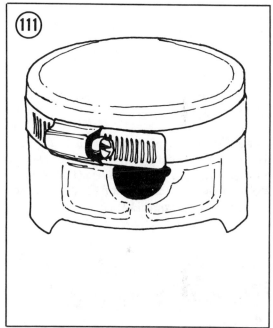

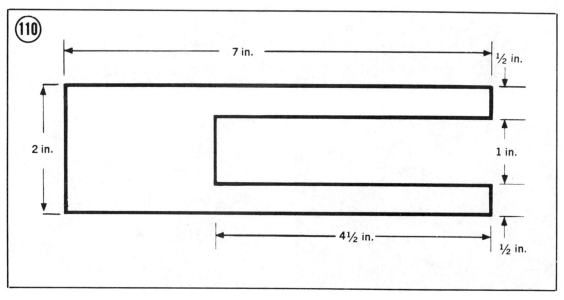

ENGINE LOWER END

Engine must be removed from motorcycle to perform repair on crankshaft and transmission. If you are performing repair work without assistance, it may be easier to first remove cylinder head and cylinder block. Head and block removal will greatly reduce bulk and weight of engine, making engine removal much more manageable for one person. Refer to *Cylinder Head Removal* and *Cylinder Block Removal*.

If only transmission repair is to be performed, it is not necessary to remove cylinder head and block.

Engine Removal/Installation

1. Place motorcycle on centerstand and remove any accessories such as fairings or safety bars.
2. Remove drain plug and drain engine oil. Remove bolts securing oil filter cover and oil pickup cover and remove covers (**Figure 112**).
3. Remove bolts securing left footrest and remove footrest (**Figure 113**).
4. Remove gearshift pinch bolt and remove gearshift lever (**Figure 114**). Bolt must be removed completely, not just loosened.
5. Use hammer driven impact tool and loosen 5 screws securing sprocket cover (**Figure 115**). Remove screws and swing cover up out of way with clutch cable still attached (**Figure 116**).
6. Use a chisel and fold back tab lockwasher securing engine sprocket nut (**Figure 117**).
7. Temporarily install gearshift lever and shift transmission into gear. Hold rear brake on and remove engine sprocket nut (**Figure 118**). Note that recess in nut (**Figure 119**) is installed toward sprocket. Slide sprocket off shaft (**Figure 120**) and disengage from drive chain.

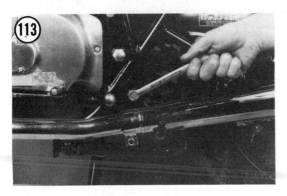

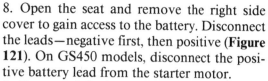

8. Open the seat and remove the right side cover to gain access to the battery. Disconnect the leads—negative first, then positive (**Figure 121**). On GS450 models, disconnect the positive battery lead from the starter motor.

9. Remove left side cover and open rubber boot to gain access to alternator wires (**Figure 122**). Disconnect yellow, white/green, and white/blue alternator wires.

10. Pull back rubber boot and remove starter lead from starter solenoid (**Figure 123**).

4

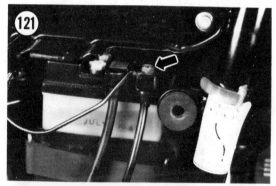

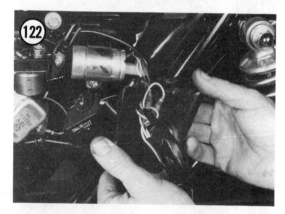

11. Remove bolt securing rear of fuel tank to frame (**Figure 124**).

12. Turn fuel valve to ON. Disconnect 2 rubber hoses from fuel valve.

13. Lift up on rear of tank and slide back to disengage from rubber mounting pads (**Figure 125**). Make sure rubber washers on mounting bolt are not lost (**Figure 126**).

14. Disconnect the ignition wires. See **Figure 127** for the breaker point wires on GS400 and GS425 models. See **Figure 128** for the signal generator wires on GS450 models.

15. Disconnect wire connector for gearshift indicator and blue neutral indicator wire (**Figure 129**). Unfasten clamps securing wires to frame.

16. Unscrew tachometer drive cable from cylinder head (**Figure 130**).

17. Remove bolts from exhaust pipe flange (**Figure 131**) and slide flange down exhaust pipe.

18. Remove bolts securing muffler to frame (**Figure 132** and **Figure 133**).

19. Loosen the clamp bolts securing each side of the crossover pipe, on models so equipped.

20. Slide the exhaust pipe out of the cylinder head and remove the pipe and muffler as a unit (**Figure 134**).

21. Loosen the locknuts securing the throttle cable adjusters (**Figure 135**). Turn the cable adjuster to provide cable slack and disconnect the cable ends from the carburetor throttle shaft.

22. Loosen the clamp screws securing each carburetor to the air box and intake flange (**Figure 136**).

23. On GS400 and GS425 models, perform the following:

    a. Remove the bolts securing each carburetor mounting flange (**Figure 137**).

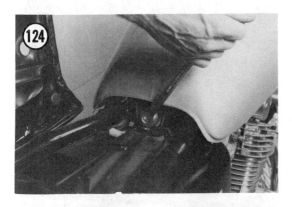

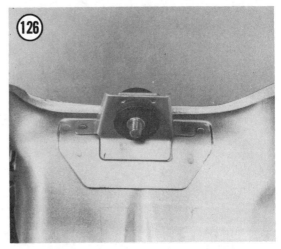

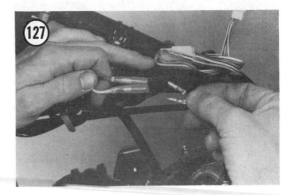

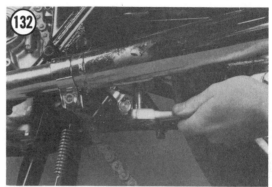

4

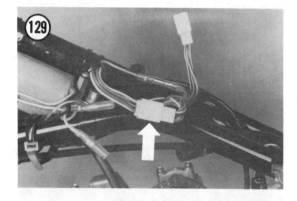

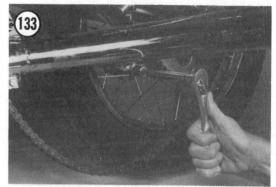

b. Use a hammer and a small piece of wood (such as a dowel) and gently tap the large spacer from between the cylinder head and the carburetor flange (**Figure 138**).

c. Hold the carburetors back against the air box and remove the mounting flanges from the carburetors as shown in **Figure 139**.

d. Slide the carburetors forward out of the air box and remove the carburetors.

24. On GS450 models, perform the following:

a. Remove the strap securing the battery and remove the battery (**Figure 140**).

b. Remove the screws securing the air box to the frame. See **Figure 141** for the left side and **Figure 142** for the right side.

c. Shift the air box back as far as possible and disengage the carburetors from the air box.

d. Pull the carburetors back out of the intake flanges and remove the carburetors.

25. Refer to **Figure 143** and remove the nuts and bolts securing the engine to the frame. On GS400 and GS425 models, note the following:

a. The lower engine mounting bolts are secured by nut plates (**Figure 144**).

b. The battery ground strap is installed under the top, rear engine mounting bolt (**Figure 145**).

26. Carefully lift the engine out of the frame from the right side.

27. Engine installation is the reverse of these steps. Keep the following items in mind during installation:

   a. On GS400 and GS425 models, ensure that the battery vent tube is routed through the frame clamp as shown in **Figure 146**.

   b. Install the long engine mounting bolts from the right side.

   c. Torque the 8 mm engine mounting bolts to 2.0-3.0 mkg (15-22 ft.-lb.). Torque the 10 mm engine mounting bolts to 3.0-3.7 mkg (22-27 ft.-lb.).

   d. Route the oil drain line from the air box between the engine and the swing arm (**Figure 147**).

   e. Install the drive chain on the sprocket then install the sprocket. Install the locking washer and sprocket nut with the recess in toward the engine.

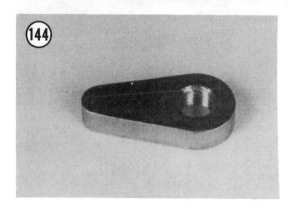

f. Temporarily install the shift lever and shift the transmission into gear. Hold on the rear brake and torque the sprocket nut to the specification given in **Table 1**. Fold over the locking washer to secure the nut.

g. Install the right and left footrests and torque the bolts as specified in **Table 1**.

h. Slide the exhaust pipes into the cylinder ports and install the rear footrest/muffler mounting bolts to secure the rear of the exhaust system. Leave the bolts loose at this time so the exhaust system can be shifted around as it is secured. Hold the exhaust pipes in the cylinder ports and secure the pipes with the flanges. Tighten the bolts finger-tight at this time.

i. Tighten the bolts securing the rear footrests and mufflers to the frame. Torque the bolts to 2.7-4.3 mkg (20-31 ft.-lb.).

j. Make sure all the exhaust pipe flanges are correctly positioned and the exhaust pipes are correctly aligned. Torque the flange bolts to 1.5-2.0 mkg (11-15 ft.-lb.). Torque the clamp bolts securing the crossover pipe to 0.9-1.4 mkg (7-10 ft.-lb.).

k. Lightly lubricate the fuel tank mounting pads with rubber lubricant or WD-40 and install the fuel tank. Connect the fuel line and engine vacuum line to the fuel valve before securing the rear of the fuel tank to the frame.

l. Clamp the carburetor vent tubes to the frame as shown in **Figure 148**.

28. Refer to Chapter Three and perform the following procedures:
   a. Install the oil filter and add engine oil
   b. Perform *Engine Tune-up*
   c. Perform *Clutch Adjustment*
   d. Perform *Drive Chain Adjustment*

Lower End Disassembly

It is necessary to split the crankcase to gain access to the crankshaft, connecting rods, transmission and inner gearshift components.

The following procedures represent a complete step-by-step process that should be followed if an engine is to be completely reconditioned. However, if you are replacing a known failed part, the disassembly need only be carried out until the failed part is accessible.

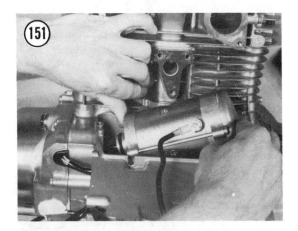

Further disassembly is unnecessary as long as you know that the remaining components are in good condition and that they were not affected by the failed part.

1. Perform *Engine Removal*.

2. On GS400 and GS425 models, if the crankshaft is to be removed it is necessary to remove the cylinder head and cylinder block. Perform *Cylinder Head Removal* and *Cylinder Block Removal* as outlined in this chapter.

NOTE
On GS450 engines, the connecting rods can be separated from the crankshaft. If desired, the crankshaft can be removed without removing the cylinder head or cylinder block.

3. Remove the screws securing the starter motor cover and remove the cover (**Figure 149**).

4. On GS450 models, remove the upper crankcase bolt (**Figure 150**).

5. Remove the bolts securing the starter and slide out the starter motor (**Figure 151**).

6. Remove the screws and the retaining clip securing the gearshift indicator switch (**Figure 152**) and remove the switch. Note how the wiring is routed. Do not lose the spring-loaded plunger in the end of the shifting cam (**Figure 153**). Remove the O-ring.

7. Use a hammer-driven impact tool and loosen the screws on the left engine cover as shown in **Figure 154**. Remove the screws,

cover and gasket. Note the location of the different length screws. Keep a few rags handy as some oil usually runs out when the cover is removed.

> *CAUTION*
> *Do not attempt to pry the cover loose with a screwdriver or similar sharp tool. The sealing surfaces on the cover and the crankcase will be damaged. The cover is held tight against the engine by the magnetic attraction of the alternator rotor. A strong pull is required to overcome the magnetic field.*

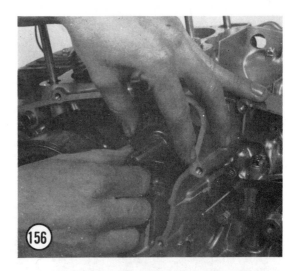

8. On GS400 and GS425 engines, remove the outside thrust washer from the starter idler gear (**Figure 155**). If the washer is not on the shaft, it is stuck to the inside of the engine cover.

9. Hold the idler gear in place and withdraw the gear shaft as shown in **Figure 156**. Remove the idler gear (**Figure 157**).

10. On GS400 and GS425 engines, remove the inner thrust washer (**Figure 158**).

> *NOTE*
> *It is not necessary to remove starter clutch assembly to remove crankshaft. If starter clutch removal is desired, perform Steps 11 and 12. If removal is not required, proceed to Step 13.*

11. To remove starter clutch assembly it is necessary to use a slide hammer. If such a tool

is not available, take engine to your local dealer and have him perform the task. If slide hammer is available perform the following:

a. Place 2 small blocks of wood under one piston to hold crankshaft from turning.

b. Remove bolt securing starter clutch assembly (**Figure 159**).

c. Install slide hammer on starter clutch assembly and pull clutch assembly from tapered end of crankshaft (**Figure 160**).

NOTE
*Clutch assembly contains 3 rollers and 3 spring loaded plungers (**Figure 161**). Take care that no parts are lost as some rollers often fall out when clutch is removed. Roller installation is described under **Lower End Assembly**.*

12. Remove large starter gear. On GS400 and GS425 models slide off 2 bearings and brass thrust washer (**Figure 162**). Note that chamfer on washer (**Figure 163**) faces toward engine.

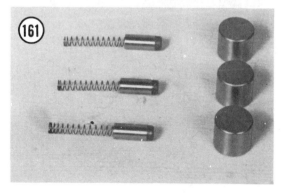

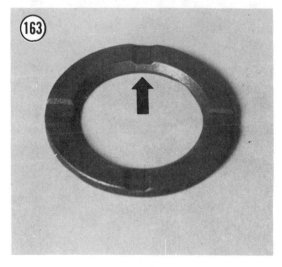

13. Bend back tabs securing seal retainer bolts. Remove bolts (**Figure 164**) and retainer on models so equipped.

14. Refer to Chapter Five and remove clutch and gearshift components.

15. Remove 4 screws securing bearing retainer and remove retainer (**Figure 165**).

16. On GS400 and GS425 models, gradually and evenly loosen, then remove bolts securing top half of crankcase (**Figure 166**). Note that 2 nuts are located in starter motor recess.

> *NOTE*
> *Before removing crankcase bolts, cut a cardboard template. Punch holes in template for each bolt location. Place bolts in template holes as they are removed. This procedure will greatly speed up assembly time by eliminating the search for the correct bolt.*

17. On GS400 and GS425 models remove crankcase nut from left side of engine (**Figure 167**).

18. Turn engine over to gain access to bottom crankcase bolts.

> *NOTE*
> *Have plenty of rags ready. Approximately one pint of oil is trapped in engine and will run out when engine is turned over.*

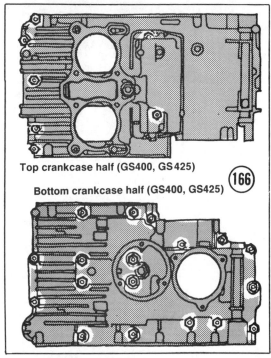

Top crankcase half (GS400, GS425)

Bottom crankcase half (GS400, GS425)

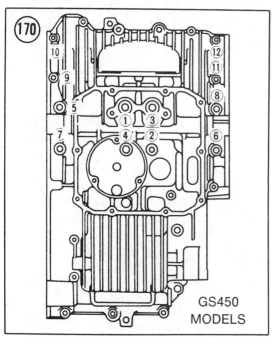

GS450
MODELS

19. On GS450 engines, perform the following:
   a. Gradually and evenly loosen then remove the bolts securing the oil sump and remove the oil sump. It may be necessary to tap around the edge of the sealing surface with a plastic or rubber mallet to help break the sump loose from the crankcase.
   b. Remove the screws securing the oil pickup screen (**Figure 168**) and remove the screen.

CAUTION
*The oil pickup screen must be removed. One crankcase bolt is located beneath the screen (**Figure 169**).*

20. Remove the 6 mm bolts and 8 mm bolts securing the bottom crankcase half. Refer to **Figure 166** for GS400 and GS425 engines and **Figure 170** for GS450 engines. Remove the bolts in descending order. The numbers are cast in the crankcase.

NOTE
Before removing the crankcase bolts cut a cardboard template, as previously described, to keep the bolts in the proper order.

21. On GS400 and GS425 engines, remove the bolts located in the oil filter cavity.
22. On GS450 engines, remove the 8 mm Allen bolts accessible through the oil filter cavity (**Figure 171**).

23. Make sure you remove the bolt located by the drive shaft (**Figure 172**). This bolt is often covered with dirt and grease.

24. Gently tap around the bottom crankcase half with a rubber or plastic mallet to break it loose, then lift off the crankcase half (**Figure 173**).

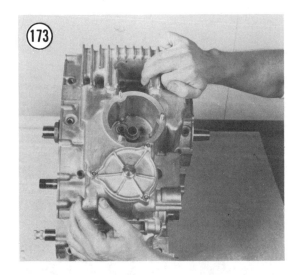

> *CAUTION*
> *Never attempt to pry the crankcase halves apart with a screwdriver or similar tool (except at designated pry points). Serious damage will result to the crankcase sealing surfaces. The crankcase halves are a matched set and are very expensive. Damage to one crankcase half necessitates replacing the entire set.*

> *NOTE*
> *On GS450 engines, a pry point is located at the rear of the crankcase (**Figure 174**). A large screwdriver can be used at this pry point to help separate the crankcases.*

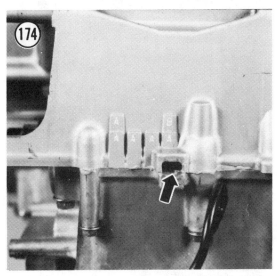

25. Lift out and remove the balancer shaft assembly, if desired (**Figure 175**).

26. At this point of disassembly, major service can be performed on the crankshaft, balancer shaft, transmission and gearshift components. On GS450 engines, crankshaft, connecting rod and balancer shaft insert bearings can be re-

moved and replaced and all major inspections can be performed. If transmission and/or gearshift repairs are desired, refer to Chapter Five.

27. On GS400 and GS425 engines, remove the screws securing the oil pump pickup assembly (**Figure 176**) and remove the assembly.

28. On GS450 engines, perform the following steps, if further disassembly is desired:

    a. Remove the nuts securing each connecting rod to the crankshaft (**Figure 177**). Carefully lift off each bearing cap and remove each rod assembly.

> *NOTE*
> *Use a felt tip pen or scribe and carefully mark the location of each connecting rod and rod cap as well as the position of the bearing inserts if they are to be reused. Do not mark on the bearing surface, mark on the exterior of the connecting rod and bearing cap. Do not be confused by the numbers etched on the connecting rods (**Figure 178**). These numbers are used only for bearing sizing and do not represent connecting rod locations in the engine.*

> *CAUTION*
> *All parts must be installed in the exact position and location from which they were removed as wear patterns have developed on all parts. If the parts are intermixed with other like connecting rod components, rapid and excessive wear may result. Do not attempt to remove the bolts from the connecting rods. The bolts are factory-fit and aligned with each bearing cap. If the bolts are disturbed, the bearing cap alignment will be disturbed.*

    b. If crankshaft removal is desired, carefully lift out the crankshaft assembly.

    c. Lift out the oil pressure relief valve (**Figure 179**). Take care not to damage the O-ring.

    d. To determine the condition of the connecting rods and the crankshaft, refer to the appropriate inspection procedure. If new bearing inserts are to be installed on the connecting rods as well as on the crankshaft and balancer shaft, refer to the appropriate bearing selection procedures.

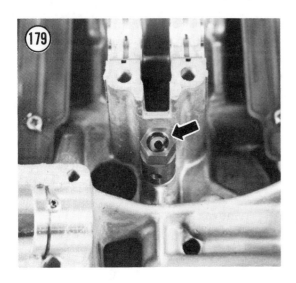

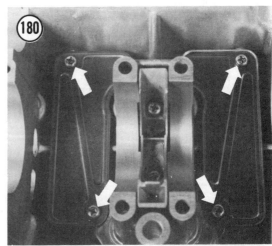

29. Remove the screws securing the oil separator plates in the bottom crankcase half (**Figure 180**).

30. Use solvent and thoroughly clean all parts and fasteners. Ensure that all the sludge deposits are cleaned from the bottom half of the crankcase.

Crankshaft Inspection (GS400 and GS425)

Except for preliminary checks, crankshaft service should be entrusted to a dealer. The crankshaft is pressed together and requires a press to separate it and assemble it as well as considerable expertise to correctly align it.

1. Carefully examine condition of crankshaft bearings. Bearings must spin freely without excessive play or roughness. If in doubt as to bearing condition, have them examined and/or replaced by a dealer.

2. Measure big end side clearance on connecting rod with a feeler gauge (**Figure 181**). The clearance should be 0.1-0.65 mm (0.0039-0.0256 in.), with a service limit of 1.0 mm (0.04 in.). If side clearance is out of tolerance, refer crankshaft assembly to a dealer for repair.

3. Examine condition of bearings on crankshaft balancer assembly (**Figure 182**). Bearings should spin freely without excessive play or roughness. If condition of bearings is in doubt, have bearings examined and/or replaced by a dealer.

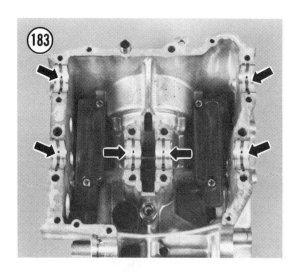

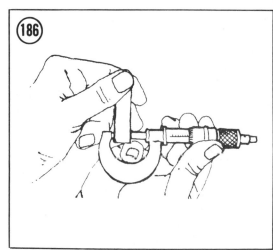

4

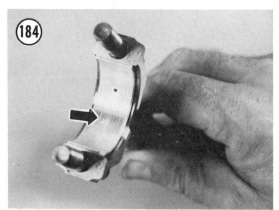

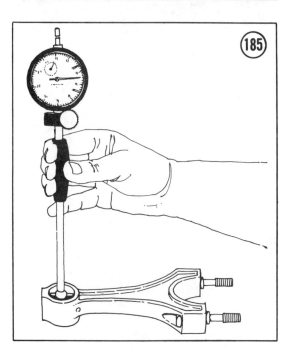

Crankshaft, Balancer Shaft and Connecting Rod Inspection (GS450 Engines)

NOTE
*Some steps in the following procedure require the use of highly specialized and expensive measuring equipment. If such equipment is not available, have a dealer or machine shop perform the measurements. Refer to **Table 8** and **Table 9** for crankshaft and connecting rod specifications.*

1. Carefully examine the crankshaft, balancer shaft and connecting rod bearing inserts. See **Figure 183** and **Figure 184**. The bearings should be replaced if there are any signs of bluish tint (burned), flaking, abrasion or scoring. If the bearing inserts are good they may be reused, provided the bearing clearance is within tolerance. Refer to the appropriate bearing clearance inspection procedure following. If any insert is questionable, replace the entire set.

2. Use a bore gauge or inside micrometer and measure the piston pin bore in each connecting rod (**Figure 185**). Use a micrometer and measure the diameter of each piston pin (**Figure 186**). If the clearance exceeds 0.080 mm (0.0031 in.) replace the out-of-tolerance connecting rod and piston pin as a set.

3. Use a feeler gauge and measure the side clearance between each connecting rod and the

crankshaft (**Figure 187**). If the clearance exceeds 0.3 mm (0.012 in.), the connecting rod or crankshaft must be replaced. Perform the following to determine which component is worn excessively:

 a. Use a micrometer and measure the width of the big end of the connecting rod (**Figure 188**). If the big end width is not as specified in **Table 8**, replace the connecting rod.

 b. Use an inside micrometer and measure the inside width of the crank pin journal (**Figure 189**). If the journal width is not as specified in **Table 8**, replace the crankshaft.

4. Place the crankshaft on 2 V-blocks, one on each end, and position a dial indicator against one of the center main bearing journals. Rotate the crankshaft to determine the amount of runout or deflection. If the runout exceeds 0.05 mm (0.002 in.), the crankshaft must be replaced.

5. Use a feeler gauge and measure the thickness of both crankshaft thrust bearings (**Figure 190**). If either bearing width is less than the 2.85 mm (0.112 in.) service limit, replace both thrust bearings as a set.

6. Use a micrometer and *accurately* measure the diameter of each main bearing journal and crank pin journal on the crankshaft (**Figure 191**). Measure each balancer shaft bearing journal (**Figure 192**). All bearing journals must be within the specifications in **Table 8** and **Table 9** or the balancer shaft and/or the

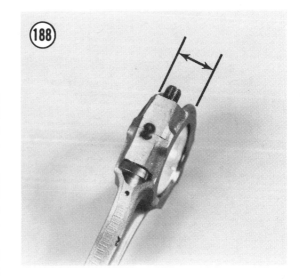

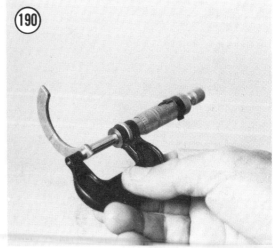

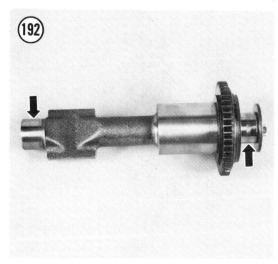

crankshaft must be replaced. Write down all measurements. The measurements can be used to determine the required bearing inserts, if new inserts are to be installed.

**Connecting Rod Bearing
Clearance Inspection (GS450 Engines)**

To accurately measure the bearing clearance it is necessary to use Plastigage. A strip of Plastigage is installed between the bearing surface and the crankshaft and is compressed when the bearing cap is tightened to the proper torque. The thickness of the compressed Plastigage is then measured with the Plastigage wrapper. This method, when properly performed, results in an accurate measurement of the bearing clearance.

1. Remove the nuts securing the connecting rod bearing cap and carefully remove the bearing cap from the connecting rod (**Figure 193**).

> *CAUTION*
> *Use a felt tip pen or scribe and carefully mark the location of each connecting rod and rod cap as well as the position of the bearing inserts if they are to be reused. Do not mark on the bearing surface, mark on the exterior of the connecting rod and bearing cap. All parts must be installed in the exact position and location from which they were removed as wear patterns have developed on all parts. If the parts are intermixed with other like connecting rod components, rapid and excessive wear may result. Do not attempt to remove the bolts from the connecting rods. The bolts are factory-fit and aligned with each bearing cap. If the bolts are disturbed, the bearing cap alignment will be disturbed.*

2. Clean the connecting rod bearing surface as well as the crank pin journal with solvent or contact cleaner.

3. Place a strip of green Plastigage on the top or bottom (TDC or BDC) of the crank pin journal. Make sure the strip does not cover the oil hole in the journal. Use a strip as long as the journal so the clearance can be checked at both ends of the bearing.

NOTE
Plastigage is available in different colors, corresponding to the range of measurement possible. Green Plastigage provides the proper range of measurement necessary to determine the connecting rod bearing clearance.

4. Carefully install the connecting rod and bearing cap on the crank pin journal. Make sure the connecting rod is installed with the oil hole (**Figure 194**) toward the *rear* of the engine.

NOTE
Do not allow the crankshaft to turn or the Plastigage strip will be ruined. The connecting rod must then be removed and a new strip of Plastigage installed.

5. Tighten the bearing cap nuts in 2 steps to make sure they are properly torqued. Tighten each bearing cap nut a little at a time to 1.2-1.8 mkg (8.5-13.0 ft.-lb.) then torque each nut to the final value of 3.0-3.4 mkg (21.5-25.0 ft.-lb.).
6. Carefully remove the nuts securing the bearing cap and remove the cap and connecting rod.
7. Use the Plastigage wrapper and measure the clearance at both ends of the Plastigage strip as shown in **Figure 195**. If the clearance indicated by the Plastigage exceeds the service limit of 0.080 mm (0.0031 in.), the bearing inserts must be replaced. If the indicated clearance varies more than 0.025 mm (0.001 in.) on each end of the Plastigage strip, the crank pin journal is tapered excessively. The crankshaft must be reground or replaced.

NOTE
The Plastigage may adhere to the bearing cap, connecting rod or crank pin journal. Any of these locations will provide an accurate indication of bearing clearance.

8. If the bearing inserts must be replaced, proceed to *Connecting Rod Bearing Insert Selection and Installation.* If the bearing clearance is within tolerance and the bearing inserts appear serviceable, install the connecting rods and bearing caps as outlined in *Lower End Assembly (GS450 Engines).*

Crankshaft Main Bearing and Balancer Shaft Bearing Clearance Inspection (GS450 Engines)

To accurately measure the bearing clearance it is necessary to use Plastigage. A strip of Plastigage is installed between the bearing insert and the bearing journals of the crankshaft and balancer shaft. The Plastigage is compressed when both crankcase halves are bolted together and the bolts are tightened to the proper torque. The thickness of the compressed Plastigage is then measured with the Plastigage wrapper. This method, when properly performed, results in an accurate measurement of the bearing clearance.

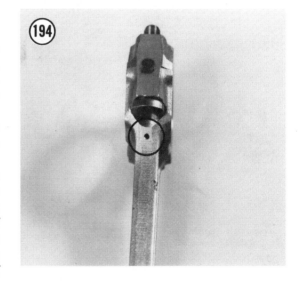

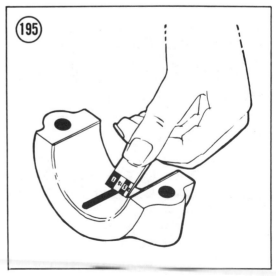

1. Remove the crankshaft and balancer shaft as described under *Disassembly*. Do not remove the bearing inserts at this time.

2. Use solvent or contact cleaner and clean the main bearing journals on the crankshaft and balancer shaft as well as the main and balancer shaft bearing inserts in both crankcase halves.

3. Clean all the sealant residue from the sealing surfaces of both crankcase halves.

CAUTION
Make sure all sealant residue is removed from the crankcase sealing surfaces. Leftover sealant residue may "bunch up" in places and not allow the crankcase halves to bolt together completely. The Plastigage may then not be completely compressed between the bearing surfaces, resulting in an incorrect bearing clearance indication.

4. Place the upper crankcase half on a workbench and carefully install the crankshaft and balancer shaft in the upper crankcase half.

CAUTION
Make sure the crankshaft is installed correctly or inaccurate bearing clearance indications will result. When the engine is viewed from the inside with the crankshaft at the top, the alternator end of the crankshaft must be on the right end (Figure 196).

5. Place a strip of green Plastigage on each crankshaft main bearing and balancer shaft journal. Make sure the strip does not cover the oil hole in the journal. Use a strip as long as each journal so the clearance can be checked at both ends of the bearing.

NOTE
Plastigage is available in different colors, corresponding to the range of measurement possible. Green Plastigage provides the proper range of measurement necessary to determine the main bearing clearance.

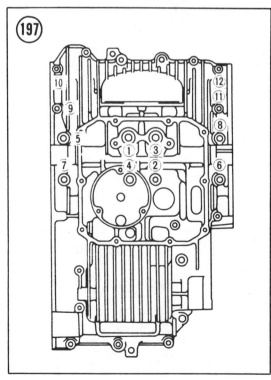

6. Carefully install the lower crankcase half over the upper half. Install all the crankcase bolts finger-tight.

NOTE
Do not allow the crankshaft to turn or the Plastigage strips will be ruined. The lower crankcase must then be removed and new strips of Plastigage installed on all the main bearing journals.

7. Tighten the crankcase bolts in 2 steps to make sure they are properly torqued. Tighten all the bolts in the order designated in **Figure 197**. Tighten bolts 1-8 (in designated order) to

1.3 mkg (9.5 ft.-lb.) and bolts 9-12 (in designated order) to 0.6 mkg (4.5 ft.-lb.). Torque each 6 mm bolt to the final value of 0.9-1.3 mkg (6.5-9.5 ft.-lb.) and each 8 mm bolt to 2.0-2.4 mkg (14.5-17.5 ft.-lb.).

8. Remove the bolts securing the crankcase halves and carefully lift off the lower crankcase half.

9. Use the Plastigage wrapper and read the clearance at both ends of the Plastigage strip as shown in **Figure 198**. If the clearance indicated by the Plastigage exceeds the service limit of 0.080 mm (0.0031 in.), the bearing inserts must be replaced. If the indicated clearance varies more than 0.025 mm (0.001 in.) on each end of the Plastigage strip, the main bearing journal or balancer shaft journal is tapered excessively. The crankshaft or balancer shaft journals must be reground or the shafts replaced.

NOTE
The Plastigage may adhere to the bearing insert or the bearing journal. Either location will provide an accurate indication of bearing clearance.

10. If the bearing inserts must be replaced, proceed to *Crankshaft Main Bearing and Balancer Shaft Bearing Insert Selection and Installation*. If the bearing clearance is within tolerance and the bearing inserts appear serviceable, install the crankshaft as outlined in *Lower End Assembly (GS450 Engines)*.

Connecting Rod Bearing Insert Selection and Installation (1980-1981 GS450 Engines)

Refer to **Table 10** for this procedure.

1. Perform *Crankshaft and Connecting Rod Inspection* to determine if crank pin journals and connecting rods are serviceable.

2. Perform *Connecting Rod Bearing Clearance Inspection* to determine if the bearing clearance is within tolerances specified in **Table 8**. If bearing clearance is not as specified, the bearing inserts must be replaced as a set.

3. Each connecting rod is etched with a code number "1" or "2" as shown in **Figure 199**.

4. Each crank pin journal on the crankshaft is stamped with a code number "1," "2" or "3" as shown in **Figure 200**.

NOTE
*Do not confuse the crank pin code numbers "1," "2" and "3" with the letters "A," "B" or "C" on the crankshaft. The **letter** codes are used to select crankshaft main bearing inserts.*

5. Each bearing insert is color-coded on the edge of the bearing (**Figure 201**).

6. Bearing selection is determined by the connecting rod code and crank pin code as shown in **Table 10**. If the crank pin dimensions are within the tolerances stated for each number code, the bearings can be simply selected by color-code. For example, the crank pin shown in **Figure 200** is stamped

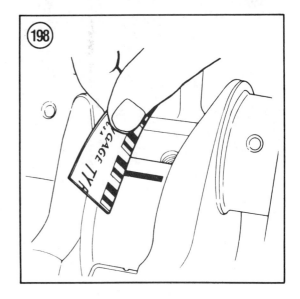

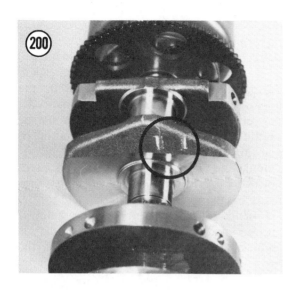

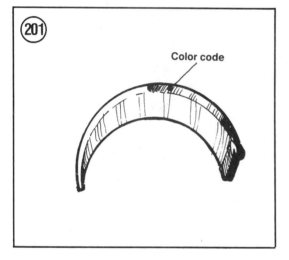

Color code

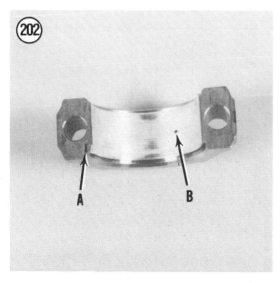

A   B

"1". It was determined with a micrometer, during inspection, that this crank pin measured 33.997 mm (1.3385 in.). This is within the tolerances stated in **Table 10** for a number "1" crank pin. The connecting rod used on this crank pin is etched "2" as shown in **Figure 199**. The required bearing insert for a "2" connecting rod and a "1" crank pin journal is color-coded black as specified in **Table 10**.

7. If any crank pin measurements taken during inspection do not fall within the tolerance range for the stamped numbered code, the serviceability of the crankshaft must be carefully examined. If the crank pin journal in question is not tapered, out-of-round, or scored the crankshaft may still be used, however, the bearing selection will have to be made based on the measured diameter of the crank pin and not by the stamped number code. Suzuki recommends the crankshaft be replaced whenever a crank pin journal dimension is beyond the specified range of the stamped code number.

8. To install new connecting rod bearing inserts, perform the following:

   a. Use a small screwdriver or awl and carefully pry out each old insert by the "tab."

CAUTION
Do not touch the bearing surface of new inserts. The bearing surfaces are easily contaminated and damaged by dirt, grit and skin acids.

   b. Make sure the inner surfaces of each connecting rod and bearing cap are perfectly clean. Engage the "tab" on the insert with the notch in the connecting rod or bearing cap and carefully press the other end of the insert into place. Make sure the "tabs" are correctly positioned in the notches as shown in A, **Figure 202**.

CAUTION
The oil hole in the bearing insert (B, Figure 202) must be aligned with the oil hole in the connecting rod (Figure 203).

NOTE
*Both connecting rod bearing inserts in
a set are equipped with oil holes,
therefore, the inserts are
interchangeable; they can be installed
in either the connecting rod or the
bearing cap. The bearing cap is not
fitted with an oil hole.*

c. Make sure each insert is flush with the
edge of the connecting rod or bearing
cap.

9. Install the connecting rods as outlined in
Lower End Assembly (GS450 Engines).

Connecting Rod Bearing Insert Selection and Installation (1982-on GS450 Engines)

1. Perform Steps 1 through 6 of *Connecting
Rod Bearing Insert Selection and Installation
(1980-1981 GS450 Engines)* in this chapter.

2. On all GS-450 models manufactured after
June 1982, disregard the location of the
number codes for each crank pin journal as
described in Step 4 of the 1980-1981
prodedure. On the 1982 and later models, the
location of the number code that identifies the
size of each connecting rod crank pin journal
is changed. The new location for the number
code for both crank pins is on the right-hand
web of the left cylinder crankshaft throw
(**Figure 204**). In some engines, after a period
of operation, the code number may no longer
be visible. If such is the case, each crank pin
journal must be accurately measured with a
micrometer as outlined in *Crankshaft,
Balancer Shaft and Connecting Rod
Inspection (GS450 Engines)* in this chapter.

3. If any crank pin measurements taken
during inspection do not fall within the
tolerance range for the stamped number code,
the serviceability of the crankshaft must be
carefully examined. If the crank pin journal in
question is not tapered, out-of-round or
scored, the crankshaft may still be used;
however, the bearing selection will have to
made based on the measured diameter of the
crank pin journal and not by the stamped
number code. If the crank pin journal is
damaged, it may be possible to avoid the
expense of purchasing a new crankshaft by

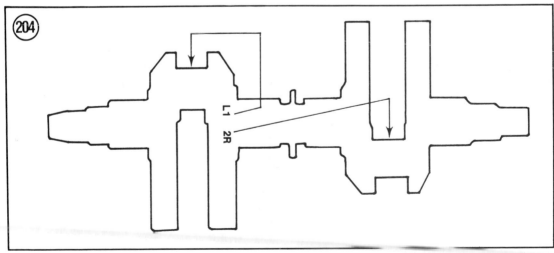

having the damaged journal reground undersize by a machine shop. Undersize connecting rod bearing inserts are available in 0.25 mm and 0.50 mm sizes as specified in **Table 11**.

4. Perform Steps 8 and 9 of *Connecting Rod Bearing Insert Selection and Installation (1980-1981 GS450 Engines)* in this chapter.

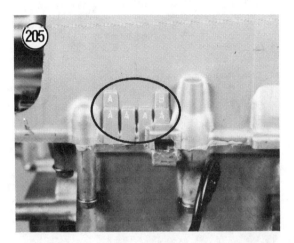

Crankshaft Main Bearing and Balancer Shaft Bearing Insert Selection and Installation (1980-1981 GS450 Engines)

Refer to **Table 12** for this procedure.

1. Perform *Crankshaft and Connecting Rod Inspection* to determine if the crankshaft main bearing journals and balancer shaft journals are serviceable.

2. Perform *Crankshaft Main Bearing and Balancer Shaft Clearance Inspection* to determine if the bearing clearances are within tolerances specified in **Table 9**. If bearing clearances are not as specified, the bearing inserts must be replaced as a set.

3. Each crankcase main bearing and balancer shaft bearing is identified by a letter code "A" or "B" stamped on panels at the rear of the upper crankcase half as shown in **Figure 205**. These stamped letter codes correspond to each crankcase bearing in the order shown in **Figure 206**.

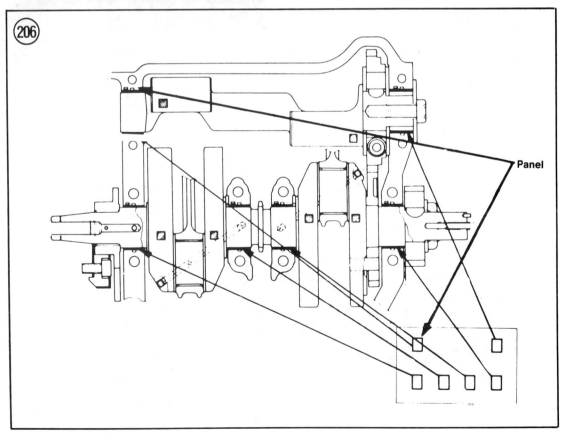

Panel

4. Each main bearing journal on the crankshaft and each bearing journal on the balancer shaft are identified by a code letter "A," "B" or "C." Crankshaft code letters are stamped on the crankshaft counterweight as shown in **Figure 207**. The letter code for each journal is always stamped on the counterweight closest to the journal.

> *NOTE*
> *Do not confuse the main bearing code letters "A," "B" and "C" with the numbers "1", "2" or "3" on the crankshaft counterweights. The **number** codes are only used to select connecting rod bearing inserts.*

5. On earlier engines, both code letters for the balancer shaft journals are etched on the balancer counterweight as shown in **Figure 208**.

> *NOTE*
> *On later engines, the code letter for the right-hand end (gear end) of the balancer shaft journal is etched directly on the journal. If the etched code letter is no longer visible, the bearing journal*

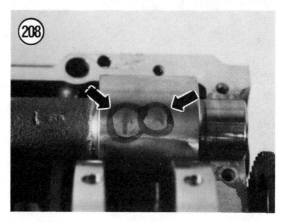

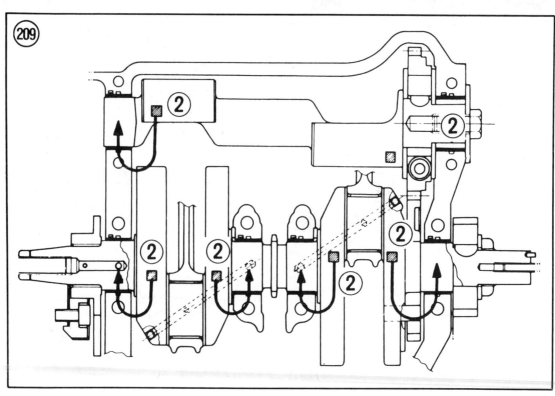

*diameter must be measured with a micrometer. See **Figure 209** for the code letter location on the later engines.*

6. Each bearing insert is colored-coded on the edge of the bearing (**Figure 210**).

7. Bearing selection is determined by the crankcase code and the crankshaft and balancer shaft counterweight code as shown in **Table 12**. If the crankshaft main bearing or balancer shaft bearing dimensions are within the tolerances stated for each letter code, the bearings can be simply selected by color-code. For example, the main bearing journal is stamped "B" as shown in **Figure 207**. It was determined with a micrometer, during inspection, that this journal measured 32.989 mm (1.2594 in.). This is within the tolerances

stated in **Table 12** for a letter "B" main bearing journal. The crankcase code for this main bearing is stamped "A" as shown in **Figure 205**. The required bearing insert for a "A" crankcase bearing and a "B" crankshaft main bearing journal is color-coded black as specified in **Table 12**.

8. If any main bearing journal or balancer shaft journal measurements taken during inspection do not fall within the tolerance range for the stamped letter codes, the serviceability of the crankshaft or the balancer shaft must be carefully examined. If the bearing journals in question are not tapered, out-of-round or scored the crankshaft or the balancer shaft may still be used, however, the bearing selection will have to be made based on the measured diameter of the bearing journal and not by the stamped letter code. Suzuki recommends the crankshaft or balancer shaft be replaced whenever a bearing journal dimension is beyond the specified range of the stamped code letter.

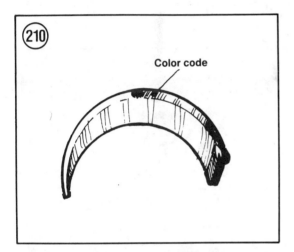

Color code

NOTE
The right-hand end (gear end) bearing journal of the balancer shaft can be purchased separately. The bearing journal (called a spacer by Suzuki) is randomly issued by the parts department in "A" or "B" sizes. Ensure that the proper bearings inserts are ordered to correspond to the new bearing journal size.

9. To install new bearing inserts, perform the following:

    a. Use a small screwdriver or awl and carefully remove each old insert by prying up on the locating "tab" (**Figure 211**).

CAUTION
Do not touch the bearing surface of the new inserts. The bearing surfaces are easily contaminated and damaged by dirt, grit and skin acids.

    b. Make sure the inner bearing surfaces of both crankcase halves are perfectly clean. Engage the "tab" on the insert

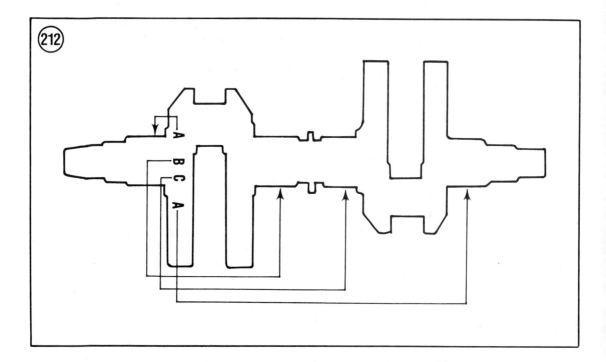

with the notch in the crankcase and carefully press the other end of the insert into place.

NOTE
Both bearing inserts in a set are equipped with oil holes, therefore, the inserts are interchangeable; they can be installed in either crankcase half.

c. Make sure each insert is flush with the edge of the crankcase.

10. Install the crankshaft and balancer shaft as outlined in *Lower End Assembly (GS450 Engines)*.

Crankshaft Main Bearing and Balancer Shaft Bearing Insert Selection and Installation (1982-on GS450 Engines)

1. Perform Steps 1 through 6 of *Crankshaft Main Bearing and Balancer Shaft Bearing Insert Selection and Installation (1980-1981 GS450 Engines)* in this chapter.
2. On all GS450 models manufactured after June 1982, disregard the location of the letter codes for each main bearing journal as described in Step 4 of the 1981-1982 procedure. On the 1982 and later models, the

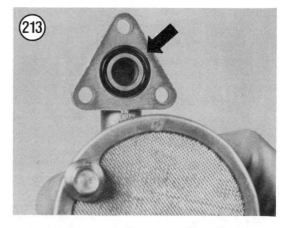

location of the letter code that identifies the size of each main bearing journal is changed. The new location for the letter code for all journals is on the left-hand web of the left cylinder crankshaft throw (**Figure 212**). In some engines, after a period of operation, the code letter may no longer be visible. If such is the case, each main bearing journal must be accurately measured with a micrometer as outlined in *Crankshaft, Balancer Shaft and Connecting Rod Inspection (GS450 Engines)* in this chapter.
3. If any main bearing journal measurements taken during inspection do not fall within the

Lower End Assembly
(GS400 and GS425)

CAUTION
Never use STP or similar products as assembly lubricant. Even a small amount will combine with engine oil and destroy the friction properties of the clutch, necessitating a complete flushing of the engine's lubrication system and installation of new clutch plates. Use thread locking compound such as Loctite Lock N' Seal No. 2114 on all fasteners during engine assembly. A small bolt or screw working loose inside the engine could have disastrous and expensive consequences.

1. Make sure all engine parts are clean and all fasteners are in good condition. Replace all bolts, nuts, and screws with damaged heads or stripped threads.
2. Install oil separator plates in bottom crankcase half.
3. Install new O-ring in oil pump assembly (**Figure 213**). Install pickup assembly in bottom crankcase half.
4. Carefully install crankshaft assembly in crankcase.

NOTE
On engines undergoing a complete rebuild, it is recommended that cam chain be replaced prior to crankshaft installation.

Make sure groove on crankshaft bearing engages C-ring in crankcase half. Outer bearing races on other 3 crankshaft bearings have a small indentation that must engage a dowel installed in the crankcase half. Slowly rotate bearing races until you can feel the indentation engage the dowels. Small punch marks on bearing races should be nearly perpendicular to case sealing surface when bearing races are in proper position (**Figure 214**). Rotate races on outside bearing until locating pin engages notch in crankcase (**Figure 215**).

tolerance range for the stamped letter code, the serviceability of the crankshaft must be carefully examined. If the main bearing journal in question is not tapered, out-of-round or scored, the crankshaft may still be used; however, the bearing selection will have to made based on the measured diameter of the main bearing journal and not by the stamped letter code. If the main bearing journal is damaged, it may be possible to avoid the expense of purchasing a new crankshaft by having the damaged journal reground undersize by a machine shop. Undersize main bearing inserts are available in 0.25 mm and 0.50 mm sizes as specified in **Table 13**.
4. Perform Steps 9 and 10 of *Main Bearing and Balancer Shaft Bearing Insert Selection and Installation(1980 1981 GS450 Engines)* in this chapter.

5. Install C-ring bearing retainer for crankshaft balancer end bearing (**Figure 216**).

6. Engage gear on crankshaft balancer with gear on crankshaft, so punch marks are aligned (**Figure 217**). Slowly rotate crankshaft and lower balancer until it is positioned in crankcase.

7. Rotate outer bearing races on balancer assembly until locating pins engage notches in crankcase (**Figure 218**). Make sure punch marks are perfectly aligned on balancer and crankshaft gears (**Figure 219**).

8. If transmission or gearshift components were removed from crankcase for repair, install them at this time. Refer to Chapter Five for applicable installation procedures.

9. Carefully apply a non-hardening sealant compound to sealing surface of bottom crankcase half. Use Suzuki Bond No. 4 or Permatex Forma Gasket Non-hardening Sealant 2B. Do not use silicone sealant. Use just enough sealant to cover all sealing surfaces (**Figure 220**). Do not apply a thick layer or allow sealant to run inside crankcase. Wipe off any sealant that may have gotten on bearing surfaces. Use lacquer thinner to clean off any excess sealant.

10. Install a new O-ring in the crankcase (**Figure 221**).

11. Check that all bearing locating pins are properly engaged in crankcase notches. Check that sealing surface of upper crankcase half is

clean and all old sealant has been removed. Carefully install lower crankcase half over upper half. Gently tap crankcase together with a rubber mallet or block of wood.

CAUTION
Crankcase halves should fit together without force. If crankcase halves do not fit together completely, do not attempt to pull them together with the bolts. Remove bottom half and investigate the cause of interference. Upper and lower crankcases are a matched set and are very expensive. Do not risk damage by trying to force cases together.

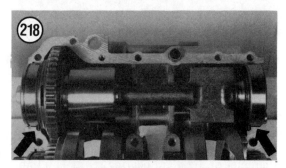

12. Install bolts in bottom crankcase and tighten 8 mm bolts gradually and evenly in the order shown in **Figure 222**. Gradually tighten all 6 mm bolts. Torque 8 mm bolts to 2 mkg (14.5 ft.-lb.). Torque 6 mm bolts to 1.0 mkg (7.2 ft.-lb.).

13. Turn engine over and install all upper crankcase bolts. Tighten bolts gradually and

evenly to 1.0 mkg (7.2 ft.-lb.). Do not forget to tighten nut on left side of engine (**Figure 223**).

CAUTION
Hold slack out of cam chain and rotate over several times. Engine should rotate freely and easily with no binding or stiff spots. If something does not feel right, investigate and correct the problem now. An engine that feels rough when rotated by hand will not "wear in," and will likely cause expensive damage if run.

14. Install bearing retainer and secure with 3 screws (**Figure 224**).

15. Install clutch and gearshift components as outlined in Chapter Five.

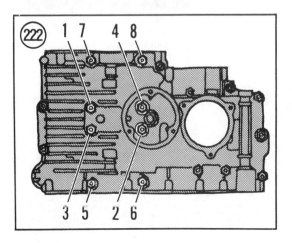

16. Install seal retainer and secure bolts by bending the locking tabs over bolt heads (**Figure 225**).

17. Install brass thrust washer and 2 bearings. Ensure that chamfer on thrust washer faces toward engine. Slide on large starter gear.

18. Wipe tapered end of crankshaft clean with solvent or lacquer thinner and install starter clutch/alternator rotor. Tighten the rotor retaining bolt to 6.0-7.0 mkg (43.4-50.6 ft.-lb.). If rollers fell out of clutch assembly during removal, refer to **Figure 226** and perform the following:

  a. Place assembly on a clean surface and install spring and plunger (push piece). Hold plunger in position with a small drill bit inserted through hole in assembly body (**Figure 227**).

  b. Slide roller in assembly and gently withdraw drill bit so spring tension holds roller into place (**Figure 228**). Repeat for other rollers.

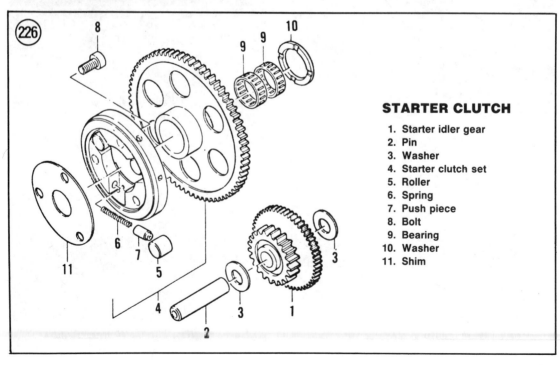

STARTER CLUTCH

1. Starter idler gear
2. Pin
3. Washer
4. Starter clutch set
5. Roller
6. Spring
7. Push piece
8. Bolt
9. Bearing
10. Washer
11. Shim

19. Install starter idler gear as follows:
   a. Lightly grease inner washer to hold it in place on engine.
   b. Hold the idler gear in place and align shaft hole.
   c. Insert idler gear shaft through gear into engine. Install washer on outside of gear.

20. Use a new gasket and install left engine cover. Ensure that rubber grommet around alternator wires is correctly located in engine cover. Route wires around engine as shown in **Figure 229**.
21. Install large O-ring and spring loaded plunger in gearshift cam. Install gearshift indicator switch. Secure switch and route wires as shown in **Figure 230**.
22. Carefully install starter motor (**Figure 231**) and secure with 2 bolts. Route wires from breaker point assembly and starter through notch in engine as shown in **Figure 232**.
23. Make sure gasket is correctly positioned and install cover over starter motor.
24. Install cylinder block and head if removed, and install engine.

Lower End Assembly (GS450 Engines)

working loose inside the engine could have disastrous and expensive consequences.

1. Make sure all engine parts are clean and all fasteners are in good condition. Replace all bolts, nuts and screws with damaged heads or threads.

2. Carefully remove all traces of old sealant residue from the sealing surfaces on both crankcase halves. Use a wooden scraper or similar device to clean off the old sealant. Never use a metal scraper or the sealing surfaces can be damaged. Wipe the surfaces clean with solvent or lacquer thinner.

3. Install the oil baffle plates in the bottom crankcase half (**Figure 233**).

4. Install the oil pressure release valve, if removed (**Figure 234**).

5. Apply a thin film of molybdenum disulfide lubricant such as Bel-Ray Moly Lube on the bearing inserts in both crankcase halves as well as on the bearing journals of the crankshaft and balancer shaft.

6. Install the cam chain over the crankshaft sprocket.

NOTE
On engines undergoing a complete rebuild, it is recommended that a new cam chain be installed.

7. Install the crankshaft thrust bearings on each side of the center main bearing inserts as shown in **Figure 235**. The notch in the bearing (**Figure 236**) must be positioned toward the outside of the engine.

8. Route the cam chain into the chain tunnel and carefully place the crankshaft into the upper crankcase half.

9. Engage the gear on the balancer shaft with the gear on the crankshaft so that the punch marks are aligned. Slowly rotate the crankshaft and lower the balancer shaft into the crankcase. Ensure that the punch marks on each gear are correctly aligned as shown in **Figure 237**.

10. If the connecting rods were removed from the crankshaft, perform the following:

    a. Apply engine assemby oil or Bel-Ray Moly Lube to both halves of each connecting rod bearing insert (**Figure 238**).

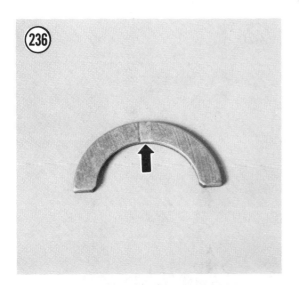

b. Carefully install each connecting rod over the correct crank pin journal with the oil hole (**Figure 239**) toward the *rear* of the engine. Install the bearing cap over the connecting rod bolts with the etched numbers on the connecting rods together as shown in **Figure 240**.

CAUTION
*Make sure all connecting rod components are installed exactly as removed. Intermixing connecting rod components may cause serious and excessive engine wear. If the connecting rods are not installed with the oil holes (**Figure 239**) toward the rear of the engine, expensive engine damage will result.*

4

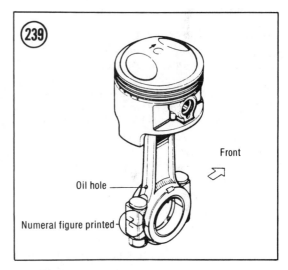

Oil hole

Front

Numeral figure printed

c. Install all connecting rod nuts finger-tight. Tighten each nut a little at a time to a torque value of 1.2-1.8 mkg (8.5-13.0 ft.-lb.). Gradually and evenly tighten the nuts to a final torque value of 3.0-4.0 mkg (21.5-25.0 ft.-lb.) as shown in **Figure 241**.

11. Install the oil control jet in the transmission bearing journal (**Figure 242**) if removed.

12. If transmission or internal gearshift components were removed for repair, install the C-rings and seal retainers (**Figure 243**) at this time. Install the transmission and gearshift components. Refer to Chapter Five for applicable installation procedures. Make sure the locating pins on the transmission bearings are properly fitted into the crankcase notches (**Figure 244**).

> *NOTE*
> *Two different type drive shaft and clutch pushrod seals are installed on 1980 GS450 engines; lipped and non-lipped types. The non-lipped seals are retained by an external seal retainer (**Figure 245**). The lipped seals are retained by grooves machined in both crankcase halves. If the drive shaft and pushrod seals are replaced, be sure that the correct seals are purchased. All crankcases have machined grooves to accept lipped seals, however, non-lipped seals can only be installed on engines equipped with an external seal retainer.*

13. Slide the rear cam chain tensioner into place. Make sure the ends of the tensioner completely engage the notches in the crankcase.

14. Install the 2 rubber cushions over the ends of the chain tensioner (**Figure 246**). The small tips of the cushions must point *up* toward the inside of the engine.

15. Carefully apply a thin layer of Suzuki Bond No. 4 (or equivalent) to the sealing surfaces on the lower crankcase half.

CAUTION
*Apply crankcase sealant with care. All surfaces must be covered or oil leaks may occur. **Do not** allow any sealant to contact any of the bearing surfaces. Use only a thin layer of sealant or the excess may squeeze into the crankshaft or transmission bearing areas.*

16. Make sure that all transmission and gearshift internal parts are correctly installed as outlined in Chapter Five. Ensure that the bearing locating pins are properly engaged in the crankcase notches.

17. Make sure that the sealing surface of the upper crankcase half is clean and all the old sealant has been removed.

CAUTION
*Hold the slack out of the cam chain and rotate the crankshaft several times. The crankshaft, balancer shaft and transmission shafts should rotate freely and easily with no binding or stiff spots. If something does not feel right, **stop** and correct the problem now. Do not attempt to run an engine that does not feel right when rotated by hand or serious and expensive damage may result.*

18. Carefully install the lower crankcase half over the upper half. Gently tap the crankcase halves together with a rubber mallet or block of wood. The dowel pins should align and both sealing surfaces should fit together. If the lower crankcase half does not fit down fully, stop and investigate the interference.

CAUTION
The crankcase halves should fit together without force. If they do not fit together fully, do not attempt to pull them together with the crankcase bolts or the crankcases will be damaged. Remove the bottom half and investigate the cause of the interference. The upper and lower crankcases are a matched set and are very expensive. Do not risk damage by trying to force the cases together.

19. Install all the crankcase bolts finger-tight. Tighten the crankcase bolts in 2 steps to make sure they are properly torqued. Tighten all the bolts in the order designated in **Figure 247**. Tighten bolts 1-8 a little at a time (in the designated order) to 1.3 mkg (9.5 ft.-lb.). Tighten bolts 9-13 (in the designated order) to 0.6 mkg (4.5 ft.-lb.). Torque each 6 mm bolt to the final value of 0.9-1.3 mkg (6.5-9.5 ft.-lb.) and each 8 mm bolt to 2.0-2.4 mkg (14.5-17.5 ft.-lb.). Do not forget to install the Allen bolts located in the oil filter housing (**Figure 248**).

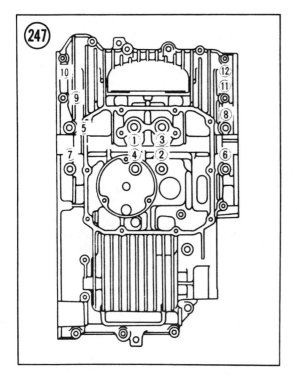

20. Apply blue Loctite (Lock N' Seal No. 2114) to the screws securing the oil pickup screen and install the screen (**Figure 249**).

21. Make sure the sealing surfaces on the oil sump and crankcase are clean and free of old gasket residue. Install a new gasket as shown in **Figure 250** and install the oil sump. Gradually and evenly tighten all the oil sump bolts in a crisscross pattern. Torque the bolts to 1.0 mkg (7.0 ft.-lb.).

22. Turn the engine over and install the bolt securing the upper crankcase (**Figure 251**). Torque the bolt as specified for the lower crankcase bolts.

> *NOTE*
> *At this point the engine can be installed in the frame to complete the assembly. The frame makes an ideal holding fixture.*

23. Install the external seal retainer on models so equipped (**Figure 252**). Fold over the tabs to secure the retainer bolts.

24. Install the bearing retainer as shown in **Figure 253**. Apply a small amount of blue Loctite (Lock N' Seal No. 2114) to the retainer screws before installing them.

25. Install the clutch and gearshift components as outlined in Chapter Five.

NOTE
If the alternator rotor/starter clutch assembly was removed during engine disassembly, perform Steps 26-28. If the clutch assembly was not removed, proceed to Step 29.

26. Wipe the tapered end of the crankshaft clean with contact cleaner or lacquer thinner.

27. Place 2 equally sized blocks of wood under a piston to keep the crankshaft from turning. Install the rotor/starter clutch assembly on the crankshaft. Torque the retaining bolt to 9.0-10.0 mkg (65-72.5 ft.-lb.).

28. If the starter clutch assembly was disassembled or the rollers fell out during disassembly, refer to **Figure 226** and perform the following:

a. Torque the Allen bolts securing the starter clutch to the rotor body to 1.5-2.0 mkg (11.0-14.5 ft.-lb.).

b. Place the alternator rotor on a clean surface and install a spring and plunger (push piece) into the starter clutch. Hold the plunger in position with a small wire or drill bit inserted through the hole in the unit as shown in **Figure 227**.

c. Slide the roller in the assembly and gently withdraw the wire or drill bit until the spring tension holds the roller in place (**Figure 228**). Repeat for the other rollers.

29. Hold the starter idler gear in position and install the idler gear shaft (**Figure 254**).
30. Apply a thin film of Suzuki Bond No. 4, or equivalent, approximately 1 in. on each side of the crankcase seams (**Figure 255**).

> *CAUTION*
> *Carefully examine the magnets in the alternator rotor. Remove all foreign objects, metal filings, etc., that may have been picked up by the magnets. A small, unnoticed piece of metal "trash" stuck to the magnets could cause serious and expensive alternator damage.*

31. Carefully install a new engine cover gasket so that the small holes in the gasket are correctly aligned with the oil groove in the crankcase (**Figure 256**). Install the left engine cover.
32. Ensure that the O-ring and spring-loaded plunger are correctly positioned and install the gear indicator switch. Make sure the switch and alternator wires are correctly routed as shown in **Figure 257**.
33. Install the starter motor and the starter motor cover.

OIL PUMP

The oil pump fitted on GS400 and GS425 engines is a high volume, low-pressure unit. The oil pump used on GS450 engines is a high-pressure unit. The high oil pressure is necessary to provide adequate lubrication for the insert type bearings used on GS450 engines.

The pump is not repairable and should be carefully cleaned, inspected and/or replaced if the engine is undergoing a complete rebuild.

If abnormal oil pump pressure is suspected, have the pressure checked by a dealer, as a special gauge is required to perform the task.

Removal/Installation

1. To gain access to the oil pump refer to Chapter Five and perform *Clutch Removal*.
2. On GS400 and GS425 engines remove the screws securing the pump and remove the pump (**Figure 258**). The screws can usually be removed without having to remove the pump gear.

4

3. On GS450 engines perform the following:
   a. Remove the circlip securing the pump gear (**Figure 259**).
   b. Remove the drive pin and thrust washer from the pump shaft (**Figure 260**).
   c. Remove the screws securing the pump to the crankcase and remove the pump.

4. Remove and discard the O-rings from the oil pump passages (**Figure 261**).

5. Installation is the reverse of these steps. Use new O-rings in the oil passages.

Disassembly/Inspection/Assembly

The following procedure is provided to determine the overall wear of the oil pump. The pump is not repairable and must be replaced if any tolerance is greater than specified.

1. Remove the screw and 2 pins securing the pump body together (**Figure 262**).

2. Gently tap on the pump shaft to separate the pump components.

3. Push the shaft back through the pump body. Disassemble the pump inner and outer rotors from the pump body.

4. Clean the pump components in solvent. Carefully examine the pump body for wear or signs of damage (**Figure 263**).

5. Assemble the 2 pump rotors with the punch marks positioned as shown in **Figure 264**. Carefully examine the rotors for signs of excessive wear or damage.

6. Install the pump rotors into the pump body. The chamfered edge of the rotor is positioned toward the inside of the pump.

7. Use a feeler gauge and measure the clearance between the inner and outer rotors (**Figure 265**). The clearance limit is 0.2 mm (0.008 in.).

8. Measure the outer rotor clearance as shown in **Figure 266**. The clearance limit is 0.25 mm (0.010 in.).

9. Use a straight edge with a feeler gauge and measure the pump side clearance (**Figure 267**). The clearance must not exceed 0.15 mm (0.006 in.).

10. When reassembling the pump, use blue Loctite (Lock N' Seal No. 2114) on the screw securing the pump assembly.

CAM CHAIN TENSIONER

Removal/Installation

NOTE
*If the engine is still installed in the motorcycle, it is necessary to remove the carburetors to gain access to the tensioner assembly. Refer to Chapter Six and perform **Carburetor Removal**.*

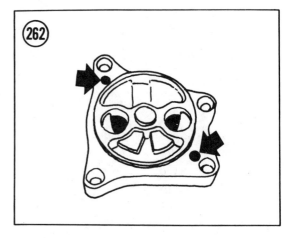

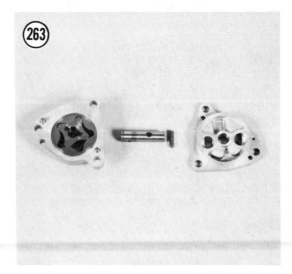

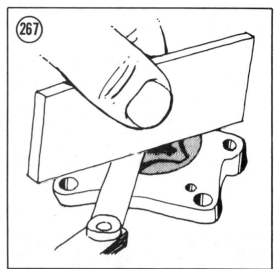

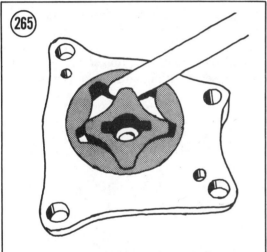

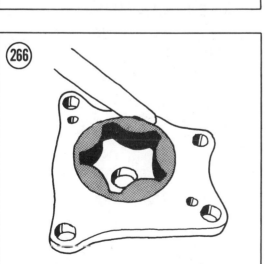

1. Loosen the locknut securing the lockscrew and tighten the lockscrew to hold the tensioner plunger (**Figure 268**).

2. Remove the bolts securing the tensioner to the cylinder and remove the tensioner assembly (**Figure 269**).

3. Before installing the tensioner, completely compress the spring-loaded plunger and secure it with the lockscrew.

4. Make sure the gasket is installed on the tensioner assembly and install the assembly to the cylinder block. Torque the mounting bolts to 0.6-0.8 mkg (4.5-6.0 ft.-lb.).

5. Loosen the locknut securing the lockscrew and back off the lockscrew 1/4 turn to allow the spring-loaded plunger to move in against the internal chain tensioner. Tighten the locknut to secure the lockscrew.

NOTE
Do not back out the lockscrew more than 1/2 turn or the spring-loaded plunger may become disengaged from the tensioner body. If this should occur, it will be necessary to remove the tensioner assembly and reinstall the plunger into the tensioner body.

Disassembly/Assembly

Refer to **Figure 270** for this procedure.
1. Loosen the locknut securing the lockscrew and remove the lockscrew from the tensioner body.
2. Remove the plunger, spring and O-ring.
3. Clean the parts in solvent and inspect the plunger and tensioner body for damage or excessive wear. Replace the worn parts as necessary.
4. Install a new O-ring on the lockscrew. Oil the O-ring and lockscrew and install the lockscrew a few turns into the tensioner body.
5. Apply molybdenum lubricant such as Bel-Ray Moly Lube to the plunger. Install the spring and plunger in the tensioner body. Make sure that the flat spot on the plunger coincides with the position of the lockscrew. Move the plunger in and out several times to make sure that it moves freely without sticking or binding.
6. Fully compress the plunger and secure the compressed position with the lockscrew.

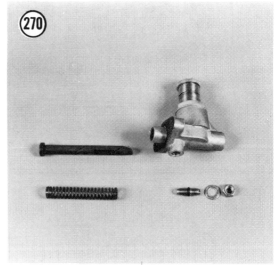

Table 1 ENGINE TORQUE SPECIFICATIONS

Item	mkg	ft.-lb.
Camshaft cover bolts	0.9-1.0	6.5-7.0
Ignition advance governor	1.3-2.3	9.5-16.5
Cylinder head nut	3.5-4.0	25.5-29.0
Cylinder head bolt	0.7-1.1	5.0-8.0
Camshaft bearing cap bolts	0.8-1.2	6.0-8.5
Camshaft sprocket bolt	0.9-1.2	6.5-8.5
Cam chain tensioner bolts	0.6-0.8	4.5-6.0
Cam chain adjuster locknut	0.9-1.4	6.5-10.0
Alternator rotor bolt	9.0-10.0	65.0-72.5
Starter clutch Allen bolts	1.5-2.0	11.0-14.5
Connecting rod nuts	3.0-3.4	21.5-25.0
Crankcase bolts (GS450)		
Bolts 1-8	2.0-2.4	14.5-17.0
Bolts 9-12	0.9-1.3	6.5-9.5
Crankcase bolts (all other models)		
6 mm	1.0	7.0
8 mm	2.0	14.5
Starter motor bolts	0.4-0.7	3.0-5.0
Oil pan bolts	1.0	7.0
Oil pressure sensor	1.3-1.7	9.5-12.5
Clutch sleeve hub nut	4.0-6.0	29.0-43.5
Clutch spring bolt	0.4-0.6	3.0-4.5
Drive sprocket nut	5.0-7.0	36.0-51.0
Oil filter cover nut	0.6-0.8	4.5-6.0
Exhaust crossover clamp	0.9-1.3	6.5-10.0
Muffler bracket bolt	2.7-4.3	19.5-31.0
Spark plugs	1.5-2.0	11.0-14.0
Engine mounting bolts		
8 mm	2.0-3.0	14.5-21.5
10 mm	3.0-3.7	21.5-27.0
Front foot rest mounting bolts		
8 mm	1.5-2.5	11.5-18.0
10 mm	2.7-4.3	19.5-31.0
Rear foot rest mount bolts	2.7-4.3	19.5-31.0

Table 2 CAMSHAFT SPECIFICATIONS

	Standard	Service limit
GS400B lobe height		
Intake	36.265-36.295 mm (1.4278-1.4289 in.)	36.150 mm (1.4232 in.)
Exhaust	35.735-35.765 mm (1.4069-1.4081 in.)	35.600 mm (1.4016 in.)
GS400C lobe height		
Intake	36.485-36.515 mm (1.4364-1.4376 in.)	36.370 mm (1.4319 in.)
Exhaust	36.085-36.115 mm (1.4209-1.4219 in.)	35.950 mm (1.4154 in.)

(continued)

Table 2 CAMSHAFT SPECIFICATIONS (cont.)

GS425 lobe height		
Intake	36.485-36.515 mm	36.190 mm
	(1.4364-1.4376 in.)	(1.4248 in.)
Exhaust	36.085-36.115 mm	35.790 mm
	(1.4209-1.4219 in.)	(1.4019 in.)
GS450 lobe height		
Intake	36.782-36.812 mm	36.490 mm
	(1.4481-1.4493 in.)	(1.4366 in.)
Exhaust	36.283-36.313 mm	35.990 mm
	(1.4285-1.4296 in.)	(1.4169 in.)
Camshaft deflection (runout)		
	—	0.10 mm
		(0.004 in.)
Camshaft journal clearance		
GS400, GS425	0.020-0.054 mm	0.150 mm
	(0.0008-0.0021 in.)	(0.0059 in.)
GS450	0.032-0.066 mm	0.150 mm
	(0.0013-0.0026 in.)	(0.0059 in.)
Camshaft journal diameter (all models)		
	21.959-21.980 mm	—
	(0.8661-0.8667 in.)	
Camshaft bearing cap inside diameter		
GS400	21.959-21.980	—
	(0.8645-0.8654 in.)	
GS425	22.000-22.013	—
	(0.8661-0.8667 in.)	
GS450	22.012-22.025	—
	(0.8666-0.8671 in.)	

Table 3 VALVE SPECIFICATIONS

Item	Standard	Service limit
Valve stem deflection (runout)	—	0.05 mm
		(0.02 in.)
Valve head deflection (radial runout)	—	0.03 mm
		(0.001 in.)
Valve-to-guide clearance		
Intake (all models)	0.025-0.055 mm	0.090 mm
	(0.0009-0.0022 in.)	(0.0035 in.)
Exhaust (GS400)	0.030-0.060 mm	0.100 mm
	(0.0012-0.0024 in.)	(0.0039 in.)
Exhaust (GS425, GS450)	0.040-0.070 mm	0.100 mm
	(0.0016-0.0028 in.)	(0.0039 in.)
Valve stem diameter (GS400)		
Intake	6.965-6.980 mm	—
	(0.2742-0.2748 in.)	
Exhaust	6.955-6.970 mm	—
	(0.2738-0.2744 in.)	

(continued)

Table 3 VALVE SPECIFICATIONS (cont.)

Valve stem diameter (GS425, GS450)		
Intake	6.960-6.975 mm (0.2740-0.2746 in.)	—
Exhaust	6.945-6.960 mm (0.2734-0.2740 in.)	—
Valve seat width	1.0-1.2 mm (0.04-0.05 in.)	—
Valve spring free length (GS400, GS425)		
Inner	—	33.8 mm (1.33 in.)
Outer	—	41.5 mm (1.63 in.)
Valve spring free length (GS450)		
Inner	—	35.5 mm (1.40 in.)
Outer	—	40.5 mm (1.59 in.)

Table 4 GS400 PISTON AND CYLINDER SPECIFICATIONS

	Standard	Limit
Piston pin bore	16.002-16.008 mm (0.6300-0.6302 in.)	16.080 mm (0.6331 in.)
Piston pin diameter	15.995-16.000 mm (0.6297-0.6299 in.)	15.960 mm (0.6283 in.)
Piston diameter	64.945-64.960 mm (2.5569-2.5575 in.)	64.880 mm (2.5512 in.)
Piston measuring point (from skirt)	15 mm (0.6 in.)	
Cylinder inner diameter	65.000-65.015 mm (2.5591-2.5596 in.)	65.100 mm (2.5630 in.)
Piston-to-cylinder clearance	0.050-0.060 mm (0.0020-0.0024 in.)	0.120 mm (0.0047 in.)
Cylinder distortion	—	0.10 mm (0.004 in.)

Table 5 GS425 PISTON AND CYLINDER SPECIFICATIONS

	Standard	Limit
Piston pin bore	16.002-16.008 mm (0.6300-0.6302 in.)	16.080 mm (0.6331 in.)
Piston pin diameter	15.995-16.000 mm (0.6297-0.6299 in.)	15.960 mm (0.6283 in.)
Piston diameter	66.945-66.960 mm (2.6356-2.6362 in.)	66.880 mm (2.6331 in.)
Piston measuring point (from skirt)	15 mm (0.6 in.)	
Cylinder inner diameter	67.000-67.015 mm (2.6378-2.6384 in.)	67.080 mm (2.6410 in.)
Piston-to-cylinder clearance	0.050-0.060 mm (0.0020-0.0024 in.)	0.120 mm (0.0047 in.)
Cylinder distortion	—	0.10 mm (0.004 in.)

Table 6 GS450 PISTON AND CYLINDER SPECIFICATIONS

	Standard	Limit
Piston pin bore	18.002-18.008 mm (0.7087-0.7090 in.)	18.030 mm (0.7098 in.)
Piston pin diameter	17.995-18.000 mm (0.7085-0.7087 in.)	17.980 mm (0.7079 in.)
Piston diameter	70.945-70.960 mm (2.7931-2.7937 in.)	70.880 mm (2.7905 in.)
Piston measuring point (from skirt)	15 mm (0.6 in.)	
Cylinder inner diameter	71.000-71.015 mm (2.7951-2.7959 in.)	71.080 mm (2.7984 in.)
Piston-to-cylinder clearance	0.050-0.060 mm (0.0020-0.0024 in.)	0.120 mm (0.0047 in.)
Cylinder distortion	—	0.10 mm (0.004 in.)

Table 7 PISTON RING SPECIFICATIONS

	Standard	Limit
Ring-to-groove clearance		
Top ring	0.020-0.055 mm (0.0008-0.0022 in.)	0.180 mm (0.0071 in.)
Middle ring	0.020-0.060 mm (0.0008-0.0024 in.)	0.150 mm (0.0059 in.)
Ring thickness		
Top ring	1.175-1.190 mm (0.0463-0.0469 in.)	1.100 mm (0.0433 in.)
Middle ring	1.170-1.190 mm (0.0461-0.0469 in.)	1.100 mm (0.0433 in.)
Ring groove width		
Top ring	1.21-1.23 mm (0.047-0.048 in.)	1.30 mm (0.0512 in.)
Middle ring	1.21-1.23 mm (0.047-0.048 in.)	1.30 mm (0.0512 in.)
Oil ring	2.51-2.53 mm (0.099-0.100 in.)	2.60 mm (0.1024 in.)
Ring end gap		
Top and middle rings	0.10-0.30 mm (0.004-0.012 in.)	0.7 mm (0.03 in.)
Ring free end gap		
Top ring and middle rings		
GS400 models	Approx. 8 mm (0.31 in.)	6 mm (0.24 in.)
GS425 models	Approx. 9 mm (0.35 in.)	7.2 mm (0.28 in.)
Top rings (GS450 models)		
"N" type	Approx. 9 mm (0.35 in.)	7.2 mm (0.28 in.)
"R" type	Approx. 9 mm (0.35 in.)	7.2 mm (0.28 in.)
(continued)		

Table 7 PISTON RING SPECIFICATIONS (cont.)

Middle rings (GS450 models)		
"N" type	Approx. 9.5 mm (0.37 in.)	7.6 mm (0.30 in.)
"R" type	Approx. 9 mm (0.35 in.)	7.2 mm (0.28 in.)

Table 8 CONNECTING ROD SPECIFICATIONS (GS450 ENGINES)

	Standard	Service limit
Small end inside diameter	18.006-18.014 mm (0.7089-0.7092 in.)	18.040 mm (0.7102 in.)
Piston pin outside diameter	17.995-18.000 mm (0.7085-07087 in.)	17.980 mm (0.7079 in.)
Big end width	22.95-23.00 mm (0.904-0.906 in.)	—
Big end side clearance	0.10-0.20 mm (0.004-0.008 in.)	0.30 mm (0.012 in.)
Big end bearing clearance	0.024-0.048 mm (0.0009-0.0019 in.)	0.080 mm (0.0031 in.)
Crankshaft crank pin (rod journal) width	23.10-23.15 mm (0.909-0.911 in.)	—
Crankshaft crank pin (rod journal) outside diameter	33.976-34.000 mm (1.3376-1.3386 in.)	—

Table 9 CRANKSHAFT SPECIFICATIONS (GS450 ENGINES)

	Standard	Service Limit
Crankshaft runout	—	0.05 mm (0.0020 in.)
Crankshaft thrust bearing thickness	2.95-2.98 mm (0.116-0.117 in.)	2.85 mm (0.112 in.)
Crankshaft and balancer shaft bearing clearance	0.020-0.044 mm (0.0008-0.0017 in.)	0.080 mm (0.0031 in.)
Crank pin (rod journal) outside diameter	33.976-34.000 mm (1.3376-1.3386 in.)	—
Crankshaft main bearing journal outside diameter	31.976-32.000 mm (1.2589-1.2598 in.)	—
Balancer shaft bearing journal outside diameter	31.984-32.000 mm (1.2592-1.2598 in.)	—

Table 10 CONNECTING ROD BEARING SELECTION (1980-1981 GS450 Engines)

	Crank pin code		
	1 33.992-34.000 mm (1.3383-1.3386 in.)	2 33.984-33.992 mm (1.3380-1.3383 in.)	3 33.976-33.984 mm (1.3376-1.3380 in.)
Connecting rod code 1 37.000-37.008 mm (1.4567-1.4570 in.)	Green	Black	Brown
2 37.008-37.016 mm (1.4570-1.4573 in.)	Black	Brown	Yellow
Bearing color code/thickness **Color/Suzuki part No.**	**Bearing thickness**		
Green/12164-44100-010	1.484-1.488 mm (0.0584-0.0586 in.)		
Black/12164-44100-020	1.488-1.492 mm (0.0586-0.0587 in.)		
Brown/12164-44100-030	1.492-1.496 mm (0.0587-0.0589 in.)		
Yellow/12164-44100-040	1.496-1.500 mm (0.0589-0.0591 in.)		
None/12164-44100-025	undersized 0.25 mm		
None/12164/44100-050	undersized 0.50 mm		

Table 11 CONNECTING ROD BEARING SELECTION (1982-ON GS450 Engines)

	Crank pin code		
	1 33.992-34.000 mm (1.3383-1.3386 in.)	2 33.984-33.992 mm (1.3380-1.3383 in.)	3 33.976-33.984 mm (1.3376-1.3380 in.)
Connecting rod code 1 37.000-37.008 mm (1.4567-1.4570 in.)	Green	Black	Brown
2 37.008-37.016 (1.4570-1.4573 in.)	Black	Brown	Yellow
Color/Suzuki part No.	**Bearing thickness**		
Green/12164-44100-010	1.484-1.488 mm (0.0584-0.0586 in.)		
Black/12164-44100-020	1.488-1.492 mm (0.0586-0.0587 in.)		
Brown/12164-44100-030	1.492-1.496 mm (0.0587-0.0589 in.)		
Yellow/12164-44100-040	1.496-1.500 mm (0.0589-0.0591 in.)		
None/12164-44100-025	undersized 0.25 mm		
None/12164-44100-050	undersized 0.50 mm		

Table 12 CRANKSHAFT AND BALANCER SHAFT BEARING SELECTION (1980-1981 GS450 Engines)

Crankshaft and balancer shaft bearing journal code		
A	B	C
31.992-32.000 mm	31.984-31.992 mm	31.976-31.984 mm
(1.2595-1.2598 in.)	(1.2592-1.2595 in.)	(1.2589-1.2592 in.)
Crankcase journal code		
A		
35.000-35.008 mm	Green	Black	Brown
(1.3780-1.3783 in.)			
B		
35.008-35.016 mm	Black	Brown	Yellow
(1.3783-1.3786 in.)			

Bearing color code/thickness Color/Suzuki part No.	Bearing thickness
Green/12229-44100-010	1.486-1.490 mm (0.0585-0.0587 in.)
Black/12229-44100-020	1.490-1.494 mm (0.0587-0.0588 in.)
Brown/12229-44100-030	1.494-1.498 mm (0.0588-0.0590 in.)
Yellow/12229-44100-040	1.498-1.502 mm (0.0590-0.0591 in.)
None/12229-44100-025	undersized 0.25
None/12229-44100-050	undersized 0.50

4

Table 13 CRANKSHAFT AND BALANCER SHAFT BEARING SELECTION (1982-ON GS450 Engines)

Crankshaft and balancer shaft bearing journal code		
A	B	C
31.992-32.000 mm	31.984-31.992 mm	31.976-31.984 mm
(1.2595-1.2598 in.)	(1.2592-1.2595 in.)	(1.2589-1.2592 in.)
Crankcase journal code		
A		
35.000-35.008 mm	Green	Black	Brown
(1.3780-1.3783 in.)			
B		
35.008-35.016 mm	Black	Brown	Yellow
(1.3783-1.3786 in.)			

Bearing color code/thickness Color/Suzuki part No.	Bearing thickness
Green/12229-44100-010	1.486-1.490 mm (0.0585-0.0587 in.)
Black/12229-44100-020	1.490-1.494 mm (0.0587-0.0588 in.)
Brown/12229-44100-030	1.494-1.498 mm (0.0588-0.0590 in.)
Yellow/12229-44100-040	1.498-1.502 mm (0.0590-0.0591 in.)
None/12229-44100-025	undersized 0.25
None/12229-44100-050	undersized 0.50

CHAPTER FIVE

CLUTCH, TRANSMISSION AND KICKSTARTER

This chapter provides maintenance procedures for the clutch, transmission (including gearshift mechanism) and the kickstarter.

All clutch components and some gearshift and kickstarter components can be removed with the engine installed in the motorcycle. To remove the transmission and the internal components of the kickstarter and gearshift mechanism, it is necessary to remove and disassemble the engine. Refer to Chapter Four for *Engine Removal* and *Lower End Disassembly* procedures.

CLUTCH

Cable Replacement

1. Pull up rubber boot and loosen locknut securing cable adjuster (**Figure 1**). Screw in adjuster to provide maximum cable slack.
2. Remove pinch bolt securing gearshift lever and remove lever (**Figure 2**). Bolt must be removed completely, not just loosened.
3. Use a hammer driven impact tool and loosen 5 screws securing sprocket cover (**Figure 3**). Remove screws and lift off cover.
4. Straighten tab inside clevis that retains the cable end and slide cable end out of clevis (**Figure 4**).

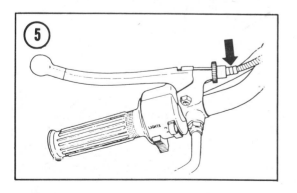

5. Disconnect cable from clutch lever (**Figure 5**).

6. Remove adjuster screw from sprocket cover and remove old cable.

7. Route new cable exactly as old cable. Secure cable to frame with securing clamp located under fuel tank. It may be necessary to remove fuel tank (Chapter Six) to gain access to cable clamp.

8. Connect both ends of cable and install sprocket cover.

9. Install gearshift lever and perform *Clutch Adjustment* as outlined in Chapter Three.

Clutch Removal/Installation

Special preparation should be made before performing a complete clutch removal. A special holding tool or access to an impact wrench (air or electric) is necessary to remove the nut securing the clutch sleeve hub. Read the following procedure first to determine what option is best suited for your situation. Refer to **Table 1** for clutch component torque specifications.

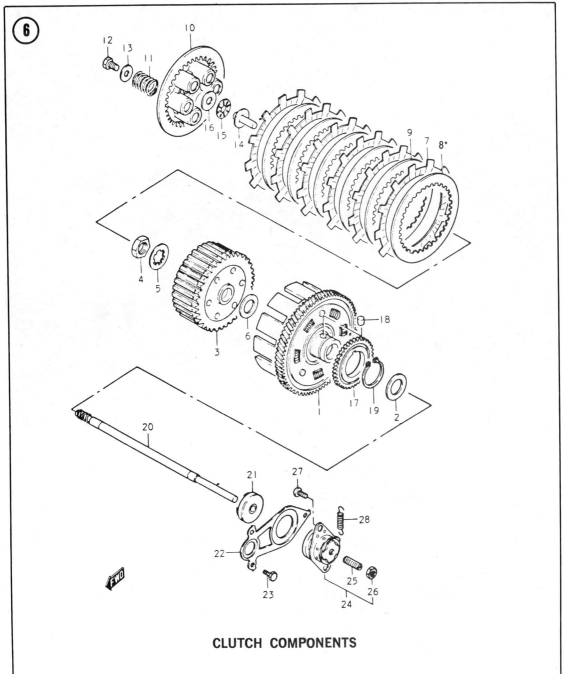

CLUTCH COMPONENTS

1. Primary driven gear
2. Washer
3. Sleeve hub
4. Nut
5. Washer
6. Washer
7. Drive plate
8. Driven No. 1 plate*
9. Driven No. 2 plate
10. Pressure disc

11. Spring
12. Bolt
13. Washer
14. Push piece
15. Bearing
16. Washer
17. Oil pump drive gear
18. Pin
19. Circlip

20. Pushrod
21. Oil seal
22. Oil seal holder
23. Bolt
24. Release screw assembly
25. Adjusting screw
26. Nut
27. Screw
28. Spring

(*)GS400 and 425 models only

Refer to **Figure 6** for this procedure.
1. Place the motorcycle on the centerstand.
2. Remove the oil filler cap.
3. Place a drain pan under the engine and remove the drain plug. See **Figure 7** for GS400 and GS425 models. See **Figure 8** for GS450 models. Allow several minutes for the oil to drain completely.
4. Remove the screws securing the ignition cover and remove the cover (**Figure 9**).
5. Remove the bolts securing the kickstart lever and remove the lever (**Figure 10**). The bolt must be completely removed, not just loosened.

6. On GS400 and GS425 models, perform the following:

a. Remove the wires from the breaker points (**Figure 11**). Note that the black wire connects to the right cylinder points and the white wire to the left cylinder points.
b. Remove the screws securing the breaker point plate to the engine cover.
c. Carefully spread the breaker points and slide the plate off the advance governor shaft. Note how the ignition wiring is routed.

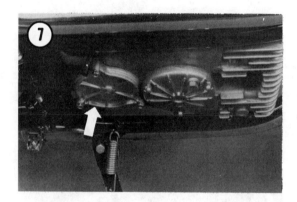

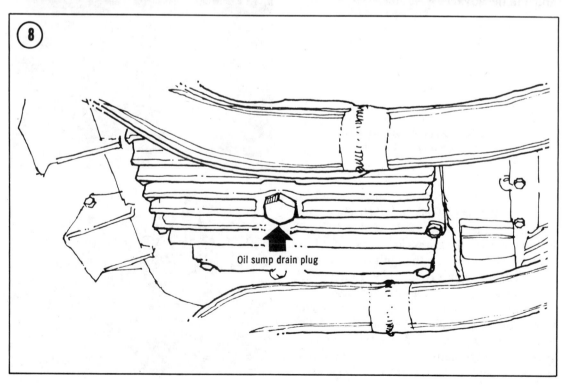

Oil sump drain plug

7. On GS450 models, perform the following:

  a. Remove the screws securing the signal generator unit (**Figure 12**). Note that the upper mark on the plate is aligned with the mark on the engine cover (**Figure 13**).

  b. Remove the signal generator unit. Note how the ignition wiring is routed.

  c. Disconnect the wire from the oil pressure switch.

8. Remove the bolt securing the advance governor (**Figure 14**).

9. Carefully remove the advance governor mechanism (**Figure 15**). Note how the drive pin of the end of the crankshaft engages the notch in the advance governor.

NOTE
To keep the crankshaft from turning while loosening the advance governor bolt, shift the transmission into gear and press on the rear brake pedal. If the cylinder block is removed, the crankshaft can be held by placing 2 wooden blocks between a piston and the engine crankcase.

10. Use a hammer-driven impact tool to loosen all the screws securing the right engine cover. Identify the location of the different length screws as the screws are removed. Make sure the screws inside the ignition recess are removed. See **Figure 16** for GS400 and GS425 models and **Figure 17** for GS450 models.

11. Gently tap around the edge of the cover with a soft-faced mallet to help break the cover loose from the engine and remove the cover. Have a few rags ready as some oil is bound to run out. Remove and discard the old gasket.

CAUTION
Do not attempt to pry the cover loose with a screwdriver or similar object, or the sealing surface on the cover and/or the engine will be damaged.

12. Work in a crisscross pattern and gradually and evenly loosen 6 bolts securing pressure disc. Remove bolts and springs (**Figure 18**).

13. Remove pressure disc (**Figure 19**).

14. Remove release bearing assembly (**Figure 20**).

15. Pull out pushrod (**Figure 21**).

16. Remove clutch drive and driven plates. On GS400 and GS425 models, the No. 1 driven plate next to sleeve hub is thicker than the other driven plates (**Figure 22**). If only plate replacement or inspection is desired, further disassembly is unnecessary.

17. Use a chisel and fold back tab on locking washer (**Figure 23**).

> *NOTE*
> *To remove the nut securing the sleeve hub, it is necessary to use a special tool or air impact wrench. A simple tool can be purchased or locally fabricated. To build such a tool, weld a rod to an old steel driven plate as shown in **Figure 24**.*

18. Slide clutch housing tool over sleeve hub and use a piece of pipe over steel rod end to boost leverage. Hold sleeve hub with tool and loosen hub nut.

19. Remove hub nut and washer. Remove sleeve hub (**Figure 25**). Remove washer located behind sleeve hub (**Figure 26**).

20. Remove clutch housing/primary driven gear assembly (**Figure 27**).

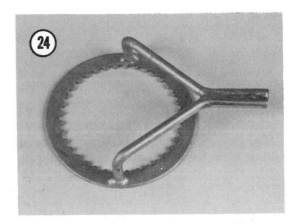

21. Remove thrust washer next to bearing (**Figure 28**). Note that washer may have stuck to clutch housing assembly.

22. Installation is the reverse of these steps. Keep the following points in mind:

a. Ensure that clutch housing/primary driven gear is fully meshed with drive gear (**Figure 29**). Hold in on clutch housing and rotate oil pump gear slightly until pump gear is engaged with drive gear on back of clutch housing.

b. Install washer between clutch housing and sleeve hub (**Figure 26**).

c. Hold sleeve hub with special tool and torque hub nut to 4.0-6.0 mkg (29.0-43.2 ft.-lb.).

d. Fold over the locking tab to secure hub nut (**Figure 30**).

e. On GS400 and GS425 models, install No. 1 driven clutch plate first. The No. 1 plate is slightly thicker than the other steel driven plates and does *not* have a small "0" mark on plate surface. Install remaining plates alternately.

f. Install bolts securing pressure disc (**Figure 31**). Torque bolts evenly in a crisscross pattern to 0.4-0.6 mkg (2.9-4.3 ft.-lb.). See **Figure 32**.

CAUTION
If it is necessary to replace a clutch retaining bolt, always use a Suzuki replacement bolt. They are especially hardened for that application. Using an incorrect bolt may cause clutch failure and subsequent damage.

g. Use a new gasket when installing right engine cover.

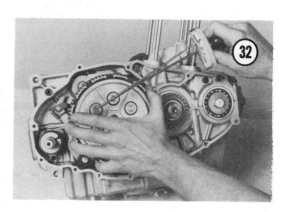

h. When installing advance governor ensure that slot engages pin on end of crankshaft (**Figure 33**). Align slot on hex washer with dogs on advance governor (**Figure 34**). Torque advance governor bolt to 1.3-2.3 mkg (9.5-16.5 ft.-lb.). See **Figure 35**.

NOTE
Check that spring-loaded advance weights move freely without binding or tight spots. If advance weights are not free, it may be necessary to remove hex washer and very lightly dress down surface of washer with a file.

i. When installing breaker plate align mark on plate with mark on upper screw hole (**Figure 36**). This provides a preliminary setting for ignition timing.

j. Refer to Chapter Three and add engine oil, perform *Clutch Adjustment* and *Contact Breaker Point and Timing Adjustments*.

Inspection

Refer to **Table 2** for clutch component specifications.

1. Measure the free length of the clutch springs as shown in **Figure 37**. Replace any springs that are not within the limits specified in **Table 2**. It is generally recommended that all springs be replaced as a set if any one is not within the specified tolerance.

2. Measure the drive plate claw width as shown in **Figure 38**. Replace any drive plates worn beyond the service limits specified in **Table 2**.

3. Measure the thickness of the clutch drive plates as shown in **Figure 39**. Replace any plates worn beyond the specified service limits.

4. Measure each driven plate for distortion with a feeler gauge on a piece of plate glass as shown in **Figure 40**. Replace any plate that is warped beyond the limits specified in **Table 2**.

5. Carefully examine the bushing in the clutch housing/primary driven gear assembly (**Figure 41**). Replace the assembly if the bushing is worn or damaged.

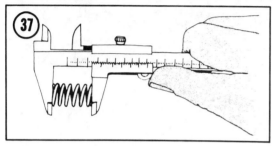

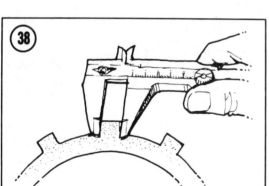

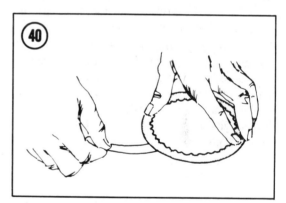

6. Check the condition of the clutch housing (**Figure 42**). Deep grooves on the housing edges caused by the drive plates will prevent proper clutch operation. Replace the clutch housing if deep grooves are present.

7. Examine the springs (**Figure 43**) in the clutch housing. Replace the housing if the springs appear damaged or distorted.

8. Examine the clutch release bearing assembly (**Figure 44**). Replace worn or damaged components.

9. Inspect the sleeve hub (**Figure 45**) for damage or signs of excessive wear. Replace the sleeve hub if deep notches are present where the clutch plates slide on the hub grooves.

10. Check the pressure disc (**Figure 46**) for signs of excessive wear or damage. Replace if defective.

11. Roll the clutch pushrod (**Figure 47**) on a smooth surface to check for bends or other damage. Replace the pushrod if necessary.

12. Remove the circlip securing the oil pump drive gear (**Figure 48**).

13. Carefully examine the drive gear (**Figure 49**) and the pin on the clutch hub (**Figure 50**) for signs of wear or damage. Replace the drive gear if the gear teeth are worn or damaged. Replace the clutch housing if the drive pin shows signs of excessive wear or fatigue.

14. Install the drive gear with the shoulder on the gear positioned toward the clutch housing as shown in **Figure 51**.

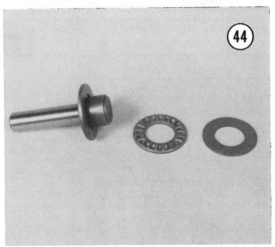

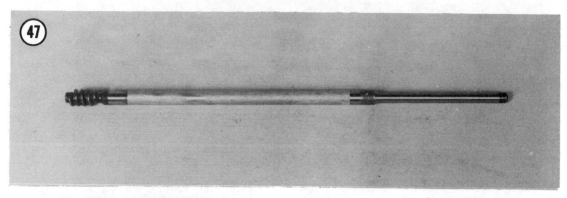

TRANSMISSION

Transmission service requires that the engine be removed and the crankcase separated. Refer to *Engine Removal* and *Lower End Disassembly* in Chapter Four. It is not necessary to remove the crankshaft for transmission repair.

The drive dogs on 2nd and 6th driven gears supplied as Suzuki replacement parts have been slightly modified. This change affects spare parts for all GS400, GS425 and GS450 models. If a new 2nd gear is installed, the new style 6th driven gear must also be installed as the shift dogs on these gears must mate exactly. The new 2nd gear is also fitted with a shouldered bushing; therefore, the washer (item 19, **Figure 52**) is not used when the new style parts are installed.

Removal/Installation

Refer to **Figure 52** for this procedure.
1. Remove and disassemble engine as outlined in Chapter Four.
2. Carefully lift out drive shaft gear set (**Figure 53**). Note positions of shift forks in gears.
3. Lift out countershaft gear set (**Figure 54**).
4. Perform *Inspection*. If gear or bearing replacement is required, refer the task to an authorized dealer. Certain gears and bearings are a press fit and require special tools and expertise for removal and installation.

NOTE
If gear replacement is required due to excessive wear, it is recommended that shift forks be removed and inspected. Refer to **Gearshift Removal***.*

5. Installation is the reverse of these steps. Keep the following points in mind:

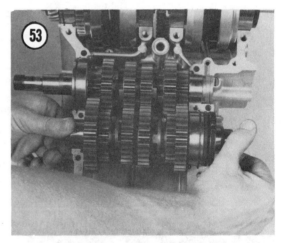

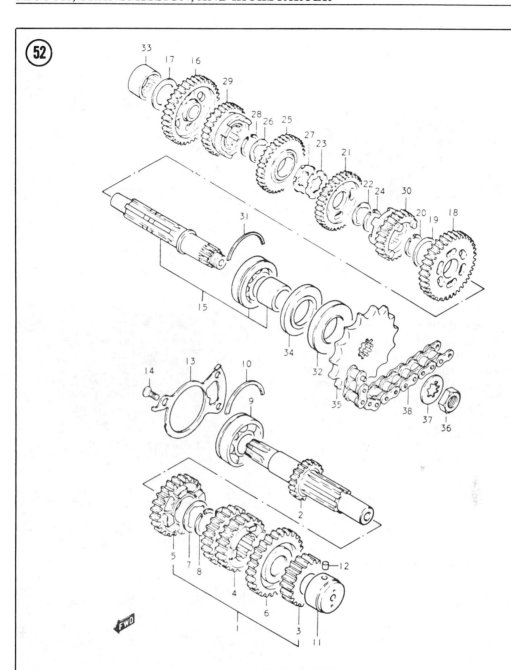

TRANSMISSION

1. Countershaft assembly	11. Left-hand bearing	21. 3rd driven gear	31. C-ring
2. Countershaft	12. Pin	22. Washer	32. Oil seal
3. 2nd drive gear	13. Bearing holder	23. Lockwasher	33. Right-hand bearing
4. 3rd drive gear	14. Screw	24. Circlip	34. Oil seal
5. 5th drive gear	15. Drive shaft set	25. 4th driven gear	35. Engine sprocket
6. 6th drive gear	16. 1st driven gear	26. Washer	36. Nut
7. Washer	17. Washer	27. Lockwasher	37. Lockwasher
8. Circlip	18. 2nd driven gear	28. Circlip	38. Drive chain
9. Right-hand bearing	19. Washer	29. 5th driven gear	
10. C-ring	20. Circlip	30. 6th driven gear	

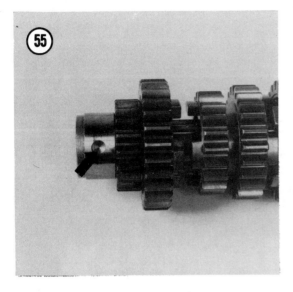

a. Indentation on countershaft end bearing (**Figure 55**) must engage dowel in crankcase. Position bearing so holes are lined up nearly perpendicular to crankcase sealing surface (**Figure 56**). Rotate bearing slightly until indentation engages dowel.

b. Ensure that locating pin on countershaft bearing is positioned in notch in crankcase (**Figure 57**).

c. Position bearing locating pins on drive shaft bearings in notches in crankcase (**Figure 58**).

d. Ensure that shift forks are properly positioned in transmission gears.

e. Perform *Engine Lower End Assembly* as outlined in Chapter Four.

Inspection

> *CAUTION*
> *If a gear must be replaced, always replace the gear it mates with, as wear patterns have developed on the gears. If both gears in a "set" are not replaced at the same time, the newly replaced gear may wear excessively and cause additional damage.*

> *NOTE*
> *If gear replacement is required, it is recommended that the corresponding gearshift forks also be replaced. Refer to* **Gearshift** *in this chapter.*

1. Clean and carefully inspect all gears for burrs, chips or roughness on the teeth.

2. Closely examine all bearings for wear, missing rollers or cracks in the races (**Figure 59**).

3. Carefully check all the gear engagement dogs. See **Figure 60** for inside dogs and **Figure 61** for outside dogs. Both gears in a "dog set" must be replaced if the engagement dogs are damaged or rounded on the corners. Worn or rounded engagement dogs will cause the transmission to jump out of gear or shift improperly.

4. Set up a dial indicator to measure the gear back lash. This can be performed with the gears installed in the engine as shown in **Figure 62** or on V-blocks as shown in **Figure 63**. Record the actual gear back lash and refer to **Table 3** for standard and service limit specifications. Replace the mating gears as a "set" if any exceed the specified back lash limits.

5

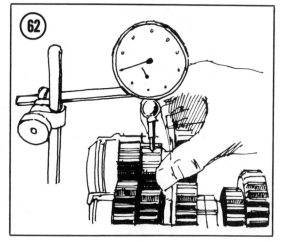

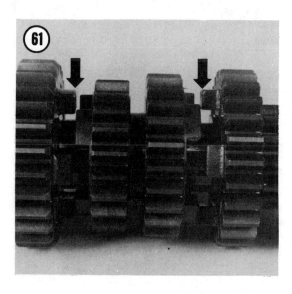

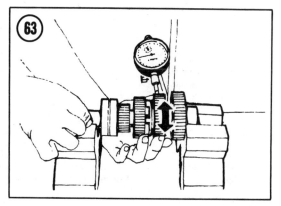

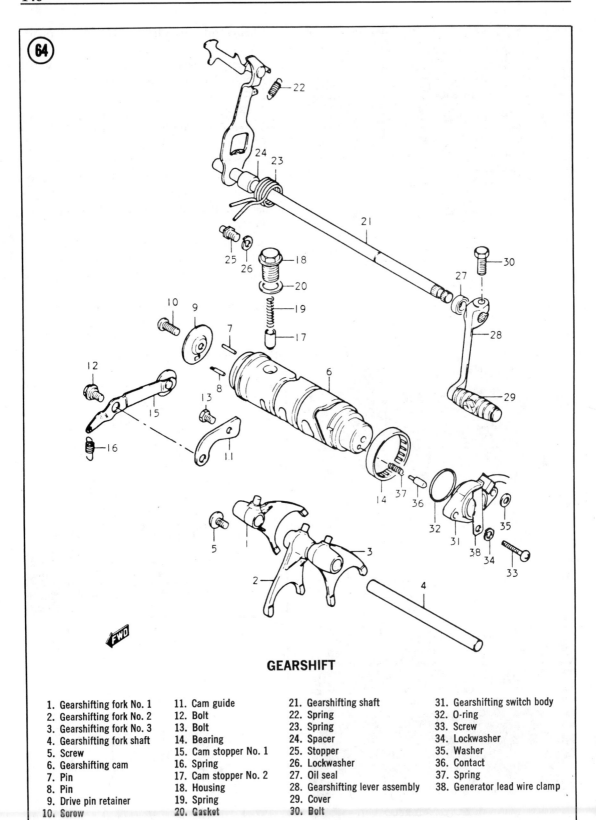

GEARSHIFT

1. Gearshifting fork No. 1
2. Gearshifting fork No. 2
3. Gearshifting fork No. 3
4. Gearshifting fork shaft
5. Screw
6. Gearshifting cam
7. Pin
8. Pin
9. Drive pin retainer
10. Screw

11. Cam guide
12. Bolt
13. Bolt
14. Bearing
15. Cam stopper No. 1
16. Spring
17. Cam stopper No. 2
18. Housing
19. Spring
20. Gasket

21. Gearshifting shaft
22. Spring
23. Spring
24. Spacer
25. Stopper
26. Lockwasher
27. Oil seal
28. Gearshifting lever assembly
29. Cover
30. Bolt

31. Gearshifting switch body
32. O-ring
33. Screw
34. Lockwasher
35. Washer
36. Contact
37. Spring
38. Generator lead wire clamp

GEARSHIFT

Gearshift repair work, except for the shifting cam and shift forks, can be carried out with the engine in the motorcycle. To remove the shifting cam and shift forks, it is necessary to remove the engine and separate the crankcase halves.

Removal/Installation

Refer to **Figure 64** for this procedure.

1. Perform *Clutch Removal.*
2. Remove shouldered bolt securing No. 1 cam stopper (**Figure 65**).
3. Disconnect spring and remove cam stopper (**Figure 66**).
4. Disengage spring loaded shifting pawl on upper portion of gearshift shaft and remove shaft from engine (**Figure 67**).
5. Remove screw securing drive pin retainer and remove retainer (**Figure 68**).
6. Remove drive pins from end of gear shifting cam (**Figure 69**). Note that one drive pin has a machined flat spot (**Figure 70**).

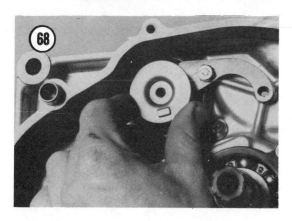

7. Remove bolt securing cam guide and re-move guide (**Figure 71**).

> *NOTE*
> *Further disassembly is not required except for gearshifting cam and shift forks. If shifting cam and shift fork removal is desired, it is necessary to remove and disassemble the engine. Refer to **Engine Removal** and **Lower End Disassembly** as outlined in Chapter Four. If further disassembly is not required, proceed to Step 14.*

8. Remove transmission gear sets as outlined under *Transmission Removal*.

9. Use a hammer driven impact tool and re-move locking screw securing shift fork shaft (**Figure 72**).

10. Slide out shift fork shaft and remove shifting forks (**Figure 73**). Note the location of each shifting fork to aid installation. Forks are not interchangeable and must be installed ex-actly as removed.

11. Unscrew No. 2 cam stopper housing and remove cam stopper with spring (**Figure 74**).

12. Remove spring loaded switch contact and spring from end of shifting cam (**Figure 75**).

13. Carefully slide out gearshifting cam. See **Figure 76**.

14. Perform *Inspection*.

15. Installation is the reverse of these steps. Keep the following points in mind:

CAUTION
Use Loctite Lock N' Seal No. 2114 or equivalent on all fasteners securing gearshift components. A loose fastener can cause serious engine damage.

a. Install shifting cam, shift fork shaft, shifting shaft, and forks. Refer to **Figure 77** and position forks in order shown with dowel ends engaged in shifting cam grooves. Secure shift fork shaft with locking screw. See **Figure 72**.

b. Install transmission gearsets as outlined under *Transmission Installation*. Assemble crankcase halves as outlined in Chapter Four.

c. Rotate countershaft and drive shaft by hand to determine if gears are in neutral. Each shaft must rotate independently of the other. If not in neutral, rotate countershaft and gradually turn shifting cam until neutral position is located. Install No. 2 cam stopper to hold shifting cam in neutral position.

d. Install cam guide and install drive pin with machined flat as shown in **Figure 78**.

e. Install other 5 drive pins and install drive pin retainer to hold pins in place. Cut away portion of retainer must line up over machined drive pin (**Figure 79**).

f. Install the gearshift shaft as shown in **Figure 80**.

g. Install No. 1 cam stopper as shown in **Figure 81** and secure with shouldered bolt. Ensure that cam stopper moves freely on shouldered bolt and spring tension is sufficient to hold cam stopper against drive pins.

> *CAUTION*
> *Temporarily install gearshift lever on shift shaft. Rotate transmission countershaft by hand and upshift and downshift transmission through each gear. Ensure that each gear engages and shift mechanism works freely without binding or sticking. Investigate and correct shifting malfunctions before continuing engine assembly.*

h. Perform *Clutch Installation.*

Inspection

1. Clean all of the gearshift components in clean solvent.
2. Examine cam guide and drive pin retainer for damage or excessive wear (**Figure 82**).
3. Roll gearshift shaft on a smooth flat surface and check for bends or distortion. Examine spring loaded shifting pawl for excessive wear or damage. Ensure that spring on shaft is positioned as shown in **Figure 83**.
4. Check No. 1 cam stopper and shouldered bolt for wear or damage and replace if necessary (**Figure 84**).
5. Examine No. 2 cam stopper components and replace if worn or damaged (**Figure 85**).

6. Carefully inspect grooves in shifting cam for excessive wear or roughness (**Figure 86**).
7. Measure thickness of shift forks (**Figure 87**) and replace if worn excessively. Standard dimension for forks is 5.3-5.4 mm (0.208-0.212 in.). Service limit is 5.2 mm (0.205 in.).

> *CAUTION*
> *It is recommended that marginal shift forks be replaced. Worn forks can cause the transmission to slip out of gear, leading to more serious and expensive damage.*

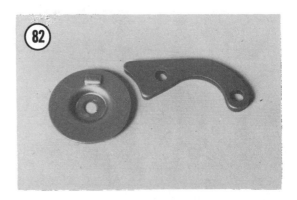

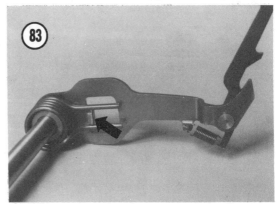

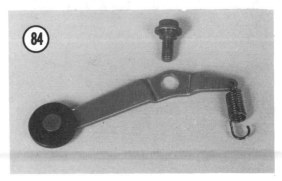

8. Slide shift forks on fork shaft and make sure forks slide freely, but without excessive play (**Figure 88**).

9. Inspect shifting cam bearing (**Figure 89**) for damaged or worn rollers.

CAUTION
The shifting cam bearing is a press fit in crankcase. Do not attempt to remove bearing for inspection or bearing damage will result. If replacement is necessary, refer task to an authorized dealer.

KICKSTARTER

To remove entire kickstarter assembly it is necessary to remove and disassemble the engine. The kickstarter return spring can be replaced with the engine installed in the motorcycle.

Removal/Installation

Refer to **Figure 90** for this procedure.

NOTE
Some early model machines developed a kickstarter spring problem that prevented the kickstarter lever from returning to the full upright position. Perform the applicable Suzuki engineered modification to prevent the kickstarter lever return problem.

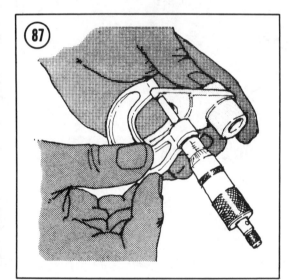

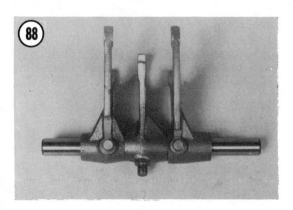

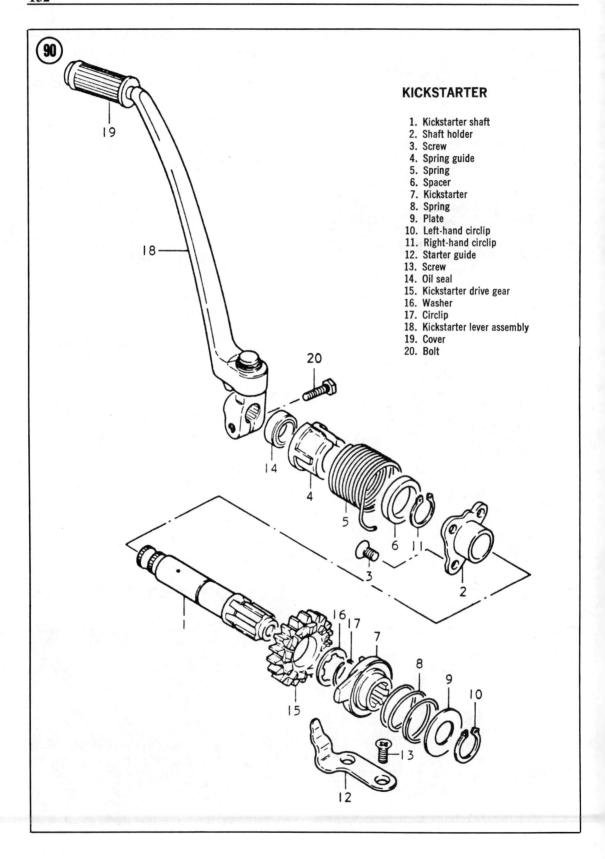

KICKSTARTER

1. Kickstarter shaft
2. Shaft holder
3. Screw
4. Spring guide
5. Spring
6. Spacer
7. Kickstarter
8. Spring
9. Plate
10. Left-hand circlip
11. Right-hand circlip
12. Starter guide
13. Screw
14. Oil seal
15. Kickstarter drive gear
16. Washer
17. Circlip
18. Kickstarter lever assembly
19. Cover
20. Bolt

a. On GS400B models, engine Nos. 10001 to 19272, delete the spacer behind the spring guide. Replace original spring guide with a new spring guide (part No. 26221-44000). Add 1.5 mm washer (part No. 08211-20282) between spring guide and clutch cover. If clutch cover must be replaced, install new style clutch cover (part No. 11340-44001) with new spring guide but *without* 1.5 mm washer.

b. On GS400B models, engine Nos. 19900 to 21755, and GS400X models, engine Nos. 10001 to 12738, install 1.5 mm washer (part No. 08211-20282) between spring guide and clutch cover unless clutch cover must be replaced. If cover must be replaced, use new style clutch cover (part No. 11340-44001) *without* 1.5 mm washer.

1. If it is only necessary to replace kickstarter return spring, perform *Clutch Removal* procedure, Steps 1 through 11, to gain access to return spring.

To gain access to other kickstarter components, perform *Engine Removal* and *Engine Lower End Disassembly* as outlined in Chapter Four.

2. Remove flat washer on models so equipped. Pull out and remove return spring guide. See **Figure 91**.

3. Use pliers to disengage spring end from kickstarter shaft (**Figure 92**). Note that spring is positioned in hole closer to engine. Unhook spring end from crankcase and remove spring.

4. Remove spacer from shaft (**Figure 93**) on models so equipped.

5. Use circlip pliers and remove circlip securing kickstarter shaft (**Figure 94**).

6. Use hammer driven impact tool and loosen 3 screws securing shaft holder. Remove screws and shaft holder (**Figure 95**).

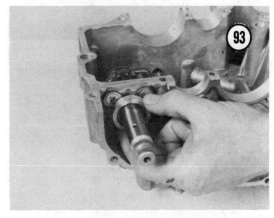

CAUTION
Screws securing shaft holder are 12 mm
long. Screws securing bearing retainer
behind clutch housing are 16 mm long.
Take care that different length screws
are not mixed up.

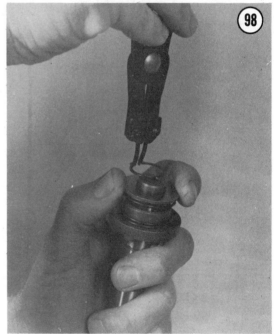

7. Remove 2 screws and remove starter guide (**Figure 96**).

8. Slide shaft assembly out of drive gear and remove from crankcase (**Figure 97**). Lift out drive gear.

9. If further disassembly of kickstarter shaft components is required, remove circlip from end of shaft (**Figure 98**).

10. Perform *Inspection*.

11. Installation is the reverse of these steps. Keep the following points in mind:

a. If kickstarter shaft was disassembled, ensure that punch marks on shaft and kickstarter are aligned when components are assembled (**Figure 99**).

b. Use Loctite Lock N' Seal No. 2114 or equivalent on screws securing starter guide and shaft holder.

c. Ensure that circlip is installed on shaft (**Figure 94**).

d. Before installing shaft return spring, rotate shaft fully clockwise against starter guide to preset shaft position.

e. Make sure return spring end is hooked in crankcase and rotate spring counterclockwise until free end can be installed in shaft hole (**Figure 100**).

Inspection

1. Carefully examine starter drive gear (**Figure 101**) for damaged teeth and excessive wear.
2. Check return springs for signs of cracking or metal fatigue and replace if necessary.
3. Examine starter shaft for twisted splines or other signs of damage.
4. Inspect starter guide for excessive wear and replace if necessary.

Tables are on the following page.

Table 1 TORQUE SPECIFICATIONS

Item	mkg	ft.-lb.
Clutch sleeve hub nut	4.0-6.0	29-43
Clutch spring bolt	0.4-0.6	3-5
Neutral cam stopper	1.8-2.8	13-20

Table 2 CLUTCH SPECIFICATIONS

Item	Standard	Limit
Clutch spring free length		
GS400 models	38.4 mm (1.51 in.)	36.5 mm (1.44 in.)
GS425, GS450 models	40.4 mm (1.59 in.)	38.4 mm (1.52 in.)
Drive plate thickness		
GS425 models	2.65-2.95 mm (0.104-0.116 in.)	2.35 mm (0.093 in.)
GS400, GS450 models	2.9-3.1 mm (0.114-0.122 in.)	2.6 mm (0.102 in.)
Drive plate claw width		
GS400, GS425 models	11.8-12.0 mm (0.46-0.47 in.)	11.0 mm (0.43 in.)
GS450 models	15.8-16.0 mm (0.62-0.63 in.)	15.0 mm (0.59 in.)
Driven plate thickness		
GS400, GS425 1st plate	1.6 (0.062 in.)	—
GS400, GS425 remaining 5 plates	2.0 (0.078 in.)	—
GS450 models	1.54-1.66 mm (0.061-0.065 in.)	—
Driven plate distortion (all models)	—	0.10 mm (0.004 in.)

Table 3 GEAR BACKLASH SPECIFICATIONS

Gear	Standard	Limit
1st, 2nd, 3rd, and 4th	0-0.05 mm (0-0.002 in.)	0.1 mm (0.004 in.)
5th and 6th	0-0.10 mm (0-0.004 in.)	0.15 mm (0.006 in.)

FUEL AND EXHAUST SYSTEMS

For correct operation, a gasoline engine must be supplied with fuel and air mixture in proper proportion by weight. A mixture in which there is an excess of fuel is said to be rich. A lean mixture is one which contains an insufficient amount of fuel. It is the function of the carburetor to supply the correct fuel/air mixture to the engine under all operating conditions.

This chapter includes removal and maintenance for the fuel tank, fuel valve, carburetors, and exhaust system. Carburetor adjustments are outlined in Chapter Three.

FUEL TANK AND FUEL VALVE

Fuel Tank Removal/Installation

1. Place fuel valve in ON position and disconnect fuel line from fuel valve.

2. Disconnect vacuum hose from carburetor (**Figure 1**).

3. Remove bolt securing rear of tank to frame (**Figure 2**).

4. Lift up on rear of tank and slide tank back to disengage front rubber mounting pads (**Figure 3**). Make sure rubber washers on mounting bolt are not lost (**Figure 4**).

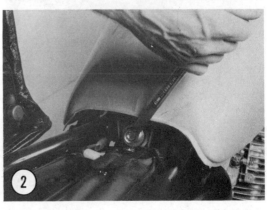

5. Installation is the reverse of these steps. Lightly lubricate the tank mounting pads with rubber lubricant or WD-40 to aid in tank installation.

Fuel Valve Removal/Installation

1. Remove fuel tank.
2. Turn valve to PRIME position and drain fuel into a suitable container.
3. Remove 2 bolts securing fuel valve and carefully remove valve. Take care that strainer is not damaged.
4. Refer to **Figure 5** if valve disassembly is required for cleaning and/or repair.
5. Installation is the reverse of these steps. Ensure that sealing O-ring is properly positioned on valve before valve is secured to tank.

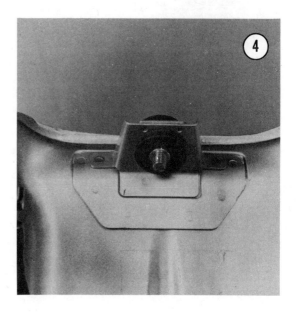

CARBURETORS

All models are equipped with twin Mikuni BS 34 carburetors. These carburetors are equipped with diaphragm actuated throttle valves that are controlled by engine vacuum.

> *NOTE*
> *All models **manufactured** after January 1, 1978, are engineered to meet stringent E.P.A. (Environmental Protection Agency) regulations. The carburetors are flow tested and preset at the factory for maximum performance within E.P.A. regulations. Altering carburetor jet needle and air screw preset adjustments is forbidden by law. Failure to comply with E.P.A. regulations may result in heavy fines.*

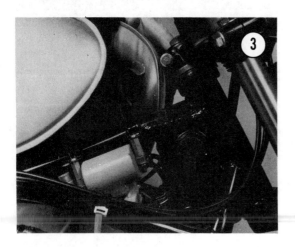

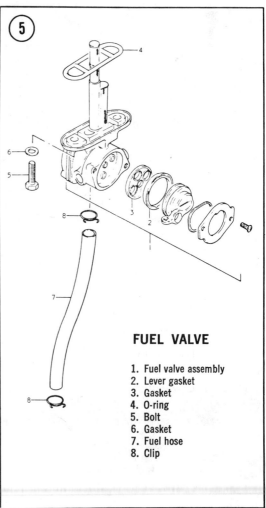

FUEL VALVE

1. Fuel valve assembly
2. Lever gasket
3. Gasket
4. O-ring
5. Bolt
6. Gasket
7. Fuel hose
8. Clip

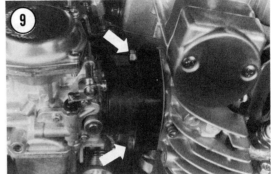

Removal/Installation

1. Remove the fuel tank.

2. Loosen the locknut securing the throttle cable adjusters (**Figure 6**) and slacken the cables. Disconnect the cable ends from the carburetors.

3. Loosen the clamp screws securing each carburetor to the air box and intake flange (**Figure 7**).

4. Remove the strap securing the carburetor vent hoses to the frame (**Figure 8**).

5. On GS400 and GS425 models, perform the following:

    a. Remove the bolts securing each carburetor mounting flange (**Figure 9**).

    b. Use a hammer and a small piece of wood (such as a dowel) and gently tap the large spacer from between the cylinder head and the carburetor flange (**Figure 10**).

    c. Hold the carburetors back against the air box and remove the mounting flanges from the carburetors as shown in **Figure 11**.

    d. Slide the carburetors forward out of the air box and remove the carburetors.

6. On GS450 models, perform the following:

    a. Remove the strap securing the battery and remove the battery (**Figure 12**).

    b. Remove the screws securing the air box to the frame. See **Figure 13** for the left side and **Figure 14** for the right side.

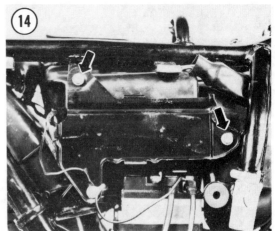

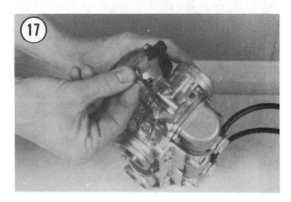

   c. Shift the air box back as far as possible and disengage the carburetors from the air box.

   d. Pull the carburetors back out of the intake flanges and remove the carburetors.

7. Installation is the reverse of these steps. Keep the following points in mind:

   a. On GS400 and GS425 models, ensure that the gaskets are correctly installed between the spacers and the cylinder head.

   b. Lightly lubricate the carburetor mounting flanges with WD-40 or equivalent lubricant to ease carburetor installation.

   c. Adjust the throttle cables and carburetors as outlined in Chapter Three.

Disassembly/Assembly

Refer to **Figure 15** for this procedure.

1. Loosen set screws securing choke levers to choke shaft (**Figure 16**). Ensure that set screws are loosened enough for screw points to clear indentations in choke shaft.

2. Remove screw from choke lever and remove lever (**Figure 17**). Note location of spring washer and spacer ring.

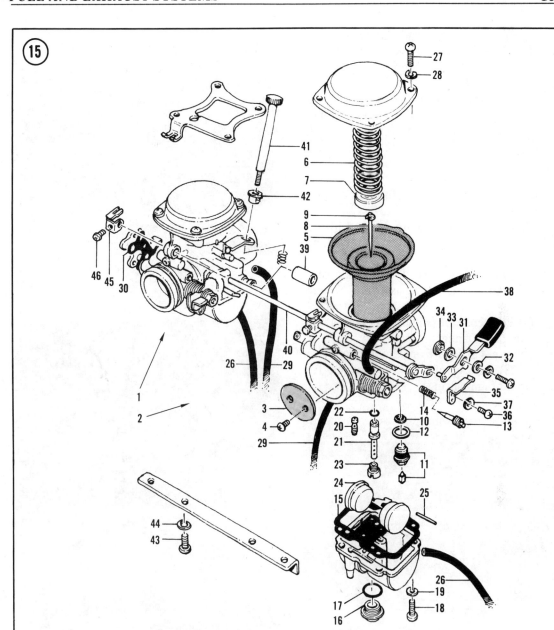

CARBURETOR

1. Right-hand carburetor assembly	13. Pilot air screw	25. Float pin
2. Left-hand carburetor assembly	14. Spring	26. Hose
3. Throttle valve	15. Float chamber gasket	27. Screw
4. Screw	16. Drain plug	28. Lockwasher
5. Diaphragm assembly	17. O-ring	29. Hose
6. Spring	18. Screw	30. Gasket
7. Plate	19. Lockwasher	31. Choke lever
8. Spring clip	20. Pilot jet	32. Washer
9. Jet needle	21. Needle jet	33. Spring washer
10. Screen	22. O-ring	34. Spring ring
11. Needle valve	23. Main jet	35. Spring plate
12. Gasket	24. Float	36. Screw

37. Lockwasher
38. Hose
39. Hose
40. Choke shaft
41. Throttle adjuster
42. Bushing
43. Screw
44. Lockwasher
45. Lever
46. Screw

3. Pull out choke shaft (**Figure 18**) and remove both shaft levers (**Figure 19**).

4. Remove 4 screws and remove upper carburetor bracket (**Figure 20**).

5. Remove screws securing carburetor to lower bracket. Carefully separate carburetors and observe how throttle linkage is fitted (**Figure 21**). Ensure that fuel hose is not damaged when carburetors are separated (**Figure 22**).

6. Remove 4 screws and carefully lift off float chamber (**Figure 23**).

7. Slide out float pin (**Figure 24**) and lift out float. Remove the float chamber gasket (**Figure 25**).

8. Use a socket wrench to loosen, then carefully remove needle valve assembly (**Figure 26**).

9. Lift out needle jet (**Figure 27**) taking care not to damage O-ring.

10. Remove 4 screws from diaphragm cover (**Figure 28**), and carefully lift off cover. Remove diaphragm spring.

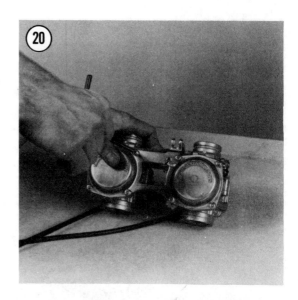

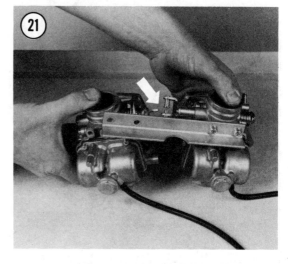

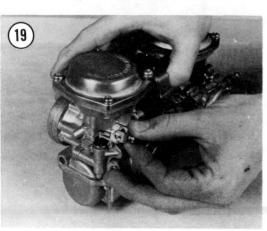

11. Lift up and remove diaphragm assembly as shown in **Figure 29**.

> *CAUTION*
> *Exercise great care when removing diaphragm assembly so that diaphragm is not damaged. Do not lose or damage jet needle with nylon plate inside diaphragm assembly.*

12. Remove choke plunger assembly. See **Figure 30**.

6

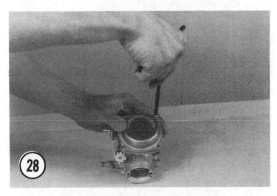

13. Remove screws securing choke plunger body to carburetor and remove plunger body (**Figure 31**). Remove gasket.

14. Unscrew and carefully remove pilot air screw (**Figure 32**).

15. Remove pilot jet from float chamber (**Figure 33**).

> *CAUTION*
> *Screwdriver blade must fit pilot jet slot exactly or jet will be damaged when removed.*

16. Remove drain plug from bottom of float chamber to gain access to main jet. Remove main jet (**Figure 34**).

17. Perform *Cleaning and Inspection.*

18. Assembly is the reverse of these steps. Keep the following points in mind:

   a. Make sure O-ring is properly positioned on float chamber drain plug (**Figure 35**).

   b. Ensure that choke plunger assembly is installed in correct order (**Figure 36**).

   c. When installing diaphragm assembly, ensure that 2 tabs on diaphragm are correctly positioned as shown in **Figure 37**.

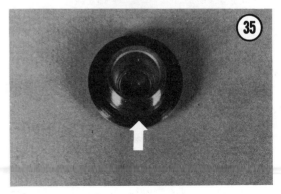

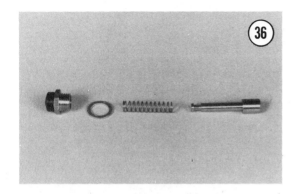

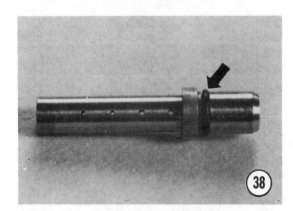

d. Before installing needle jet make sure O-ring is installed (**Figure 38**).

e. Use a caliper or a locally fabricated gauge and measure the float level, without the float chamber gasket, as shown in **Figure 39**. Make sure that the spring-loaded pin on the needle valve is not compressed by the float arm. The correct float level for all models is 25.6-27.6 mm (1.01-1.14 in.). The correct float level for GS450 models is 21.4-23.4 mm (0.84-0.92 in.). If the level is not correct, carefully bend the tang on the float arm until the specified level is achieved.

f. On 1977 and earlier models, *gently* turn in the pilot air screw until it bottoms, then back out the screw approximately one turn as a preliminary adjustment.

CAUTION
Do not overtighten the pilot air screw or the screw will be grooved or scored. Even the slightest damage will affect carburetor performance.

Cleaning and Inspection

1. Thoroughly clean and dry all parts. If special carburetor cleaner is used, do not immerse any gaskets or O-rings or they will be destroyed.

2. Blow out all passages and jets with compressed air. Do not use wire to clean any orifices; wire will enlarge them.

3. Carefully examine screen on end of float needle seat (**Figure 40**). Carefully remove and clean screen if necessary.

4. Examine cone on needle valve and replace valve and seat if it is scored or pitted.

5. Check the taper on the pilot air screw (**Figure 41**) and replace screw if it is grooved or scored.

6. Inspect the rubber seating surface on choke plunger (**Figure 42**) and replace plunger if seat is deeply grooved or damaged.

7. Carefully examine jet needle (**Figure 43**) and replace needle if scored or grooved. Note position of spring clip on needle.

HIGH ALTITUDE ADJUSTMENT
(1982-ON)

E.P.A. approved main jets are available for machines operated at elevations 4,000 ft. and higher. All high altitude carburetor parts must be installed by a Suzuki dealer to avoid violation of E.P.A. regulations.

EXHAUST SYSTEM

Removal/Installation

1. Remove the bolts securing each exhaust pipe flange and slide the flange down the pipe (**Figure 44**).

2. Remove the bolts securing each muffler mounting bracket to the frame (**Figure 45** and **Figure 46**).

3. Loosen the clamp bolts securing each side of the crossover pipe, on models so equipped.

4. Slide the exhaust pipe out of the cylinder head and remove the pipe and muffler as a unit (**Figure 47**).

5. If muffler removal is desired, loosen each clamp securing the muffler to the exhaust pipe and slide the muffler off the pipe. It is usually necessary to twist the muffler back and forth to break it loose from the exhaust pipe.

6. Installation is the reverse of these steps. Keep the following points in mind:

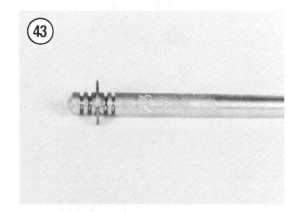

a. Slide the exhaust pipes into the cylinder ports and install the rear muffler mounting bolts to secure the rear of the exhaust system.

b. Leave all mounting bolts loose at this time so the exhaust system can be shifted around as it is secured.

c. Hold the exhaust pipes into the cylinder ports and secure the pipes with the flanges. Tighten the bolts finger-tight at this time.

d. Tighten the bolts securing the mufflers to the frame. Torque the bolts to 2.7-4.3 mkg (20-31 ft.-lb.).

e. Make sure all the exhaust pipe flanges are correctly positioned and the exhaust pipes are correctly aligned. Torque the flange bolts to 1.5-2.0 mkg (11-15 ft.-lb.). Torque the clamp bolts securing the crossover pipe to 0.9-1.4 mkg (7-10 ft.-lb.).

CHAPTER SEVEN

ELECTRICAL SYSTEM

The electrical system consists of the following subsystems:
a. Charging system
b. Starting system
c. Ignition system
d. Lighting system

Complete wiring diagrams are included at the end of the book.

CHARGING SYSTEM

The charging system consists of the battery, alternator, rectifier and regulator. See **Figure 1** for all 1978 and earlier models and **Figure 2** for all 1979 and later models.

The alternator generates an alternating current (AC) which the rectifier converts to direct current (DC). The regulator maintains the voltage going to the battery and the load (lights, ignition, etc.) at a constant level regardless of the variations in engine speed and load.

On 1979 and later models, the rectifier and regulator are combined in one unit. If either function of the unit fails, the entire unit must be replaced. On all 1978 and earlier models, the rectifier and regulator are separate units.

Whenever a charging system trouble is suspected, make sure the battery is fully charged and in good condition before beginning any tests. Make sure all connections are clean and tight.

**Charging System Output Test
(1978 and Earlier Models)**

1. Raise the seat and remove the left side cover. Refer to **Figure 3** and disconnect the yellow wire from the regulator to isolate it from the circuit.
2. Connect the white/green wire from the alternator to the white/red wire from the rectifier.

*NOTE
For U.S. and Canadian models, remove the screw securing the headlamp switch lock cap (**Figure 4**) and turn off the headlamp for this test.*

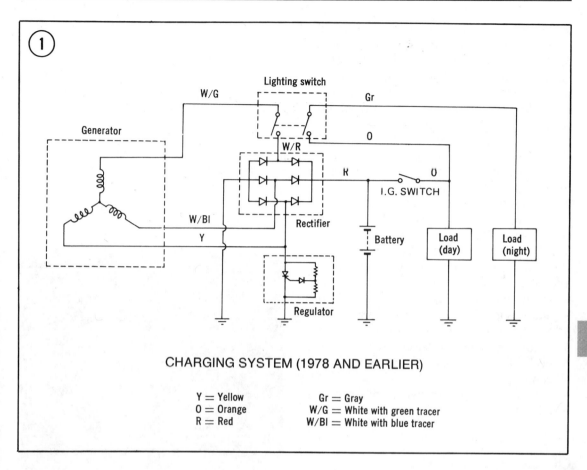

CHARGING SYSTEM (1978 AND EARLIER)

Y = Yellow
O = Orange
R = Red

Gr = Gray
W/G = White with green tracer
W/Bl = White with blue tracer

7

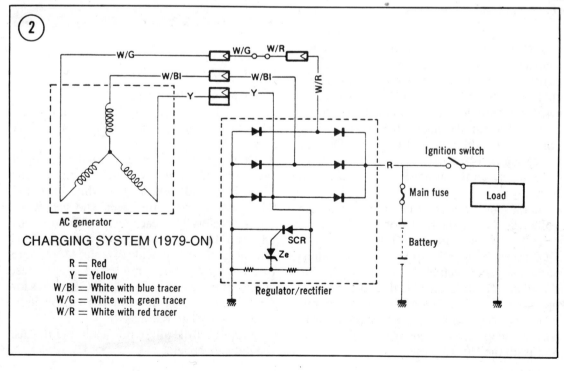

CHARGING SYSTEM (1979-ON)

R = Red
Y = Yellow
W/Bl = White with blue tracer
W/G = White with green tracer
W/R = White with red tracer

3. Make sure all lights are switched *off* (this is a no-load test). Start and run the engine at 5,000 rpm. With a voltmeter, check the voltage between the red rectifier wire and ground. If the voltmeter indicates 16.5 volts DC or more, the alternator and the rectifier are good; proceed to the next step to check the regulator. If the voltmeter indication is less than 16.5 volts DC, either the alternator or rectifier may be defective. Refer to *Rectifier Test*. If the rectifier tests good, the alternator is defective.

4. Shut off the engine and reconnect the wiring in the normal manner. Make sure the light switch is still *off*. Start the engine and run it at 5,000 rpm. With a voltmeter, check the voltage between the positive (+) lead of the battery and a good ground on the frame. If the voltmeter indication is 14-15.5 volts DC, the regulator is good. If the voltage is less than 14 or more than 15.5, the regulator is defective.

5. Before replacing any defective components, recheck all voltages as described to make sure all connections were correct.

6. Install the headlamp switch lock cap and install the left side cover.

Charging System Output Test (1979 and Later Models)

1. Remove the left side cover. Pull back the rubber boot on the main battery lead connected to the starter relay. Connect the positive (+) lead of a voltmeter to the red (+) lead on the starter relay (**Figure 5**). Connect the negative (-) lead to a good ground on the frame.

2. Start and run the engine at 5,000 rpm. The voltmeter should indicate 14-15 volts DC. An indication of 14-15 volts DC signifies that all charging system components are operating correctly.

3. If the voltmeter indicates more than 15.5 volts DC, replace the regulator/rectifier.

4. If the voltmeter indicates less than 14 volts DC, either the regulator/rectifier or the alternator may be defective. Perform the *No-load Alternator Test* to determine if the alternator is operating correctly. If the no-load test is satisfactory, replace the regulator/rectifier to correct the low voltage condition.

5. Install the left side cover.

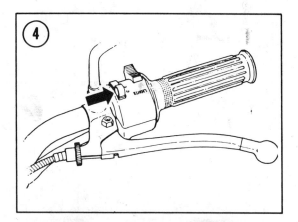

No-load Alternator Test (1979 and Later Models)

1. Remove the left side cover.

2. Open the large wire boot and disconnect the white/blue, white/green and yellow alternator wires.

3. Refer to **Figure 6** and alternately connect the leads of an AC voltmeter between the white/blue and yellow, the white/blue and white/green, and white/green and yellow alternator leads. With each test connection, start and run the engine at 5,000 rpm. The AC voltmeter should indicate 75 volts AC or more (65 volts for GS425 models) for each test connection. Less than 75 volts AC (65 volts for GS425 models) on any test connection indicates a faulty alternator.

4. Reconnect the alternator leads and replace the left side cover.

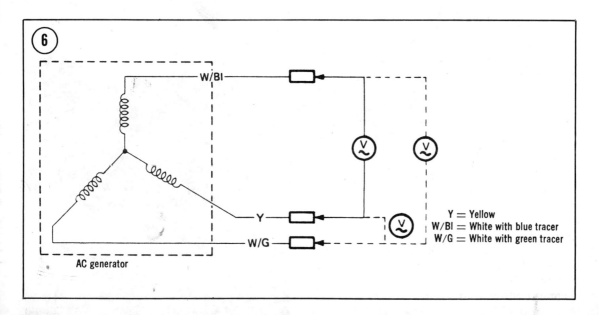

(6)

W/Bl

Y

W/G

AC generator

Y = Yellow
W/Bl = White with blue tracer
W/G = White with green tracer

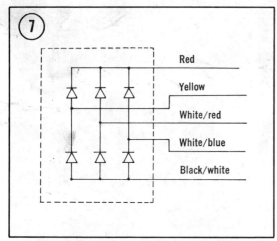

(7)

Red

Yellow

White/red

White/blue

Black/white

Rectifier Test
(1978 and Earlier Models)

Refer to **Figure 7** for this procedure.

The 6 diodes in the rectifier are the electrical equivalent of one-way valves; they permit current to flow in a forward direction and prevent it from flowing in the reverse direction—if they are functioning correctly.

A VOM as described in Chapter One or a continuity tester is required for the following test.

> *CAUTION*
> *Do not run engine with rectifier leads disconnected or electrical system damage will occur.*

7

1. Disconnect all leads from the rectifier.
2. Connect negative lead of tester to ground terminal (black/white) and connect positive lead of tester to yellow, white/red, and white/blue wires one at a time in sequence. Continuity must be indicated for each wire. If continuity is not present on any of the wires, replace the rectifier. If continuity is present, proceed to next step.
3. Connect tester positive lead to black/white wire and negative lead to yellow, white/red, and white/blue wire one at time. *No* continuity should be present. If continuity on any wires is present, replace the rectifier. If all checks at this point are satisfactory, check other 3 diodes using red wire as ground, first with negative tester lead on red wire and then the positive lead. Replace the rectifier if any diodes are faulty.

Alternator Stator
Removal/Installation

1. Drain engine oil as outlined in Chapter Three.
2. Use hammer driven impact tool and loosen screws holding left engine cover (**Figure 8**). Remove screws, cover, and gasket. Note location of different length screws. Keep a few rags handy as some oil is bound to run out when cover is removed.

CAUTION
Do not pry cover loose with a screwdriver or cover, and/or crankcase damage may result. Cover is held tight by magnetic attraction of alternator rotor. A strong pull is required to overcome magnetic field.

3. Remove screws securing stator to engine case and remove stator (**Figure 9**). Note how wiring is routed.

4. Installation is the reverse of these steps. Ensure that rubber grommet in engine cover is correctly positioned.

Alternator Rotor
Removal/Installation

The alternator rotor is a permanent magnet unit. Rotor removal is usually only necessary during engine disassembly or if motorcycle has been damaged in an accident. Because special tools are required for rotor removal, it is recommended that the task be performed by an authorized dealer.

Rectifier Removal/Installation
(1978 and Earlier Models)

Refer to **Figure 10** for this procedure.

1. Remove left side cover.

2. Disconnect rectifier leads. Unscrew rectifier attaching screw and remove rectifier.

3. Installation is the reverse of these steps. Make certain that leads are connected correctly.

Regulator Removal/Installation
(1978 and Earlier Models)

Refer **Figure 11** for this procedure.
1. Remove left side cover.
2. Disconnect regulator lead and remove attaching screws; remove the regulator.
3. Installation is the reverse of these steps. Make sure screws are tight and lead connection is clean and tight.

Regulator/Rectifier Unit Removal/
Installation (1979 and Later Models)

1. Remove the left side cover.
2. Disconnect the regulator/rectifier unit leads.
3. Remove the screws securing the unit to the frame and remove the unit (**Figure 12**).
4. Installation is the reverse of these steps. Ensure that the leads are connected securely.

STARTING SYSTEM

The starting system consists of a starter motor and starting relay (solenoid). Refer to **Figure 13** for a schematic of starting system.

Before checking for suspected trouble in the starting system, ensure that all connections are clean and tight. Make certain that the battery is in good condition, with correct electrolyte level and fully charged.

If the system is functioning correctly, the relay (**Figure 14**) will make a single audible "clack" when the starter button is pressed and the motor will begin to turn at once.

If the relay makes no sound and the motor does not turn, and if the battery is fully charged, an open circuit in the relay coil is likely. It must be replaced.

If the relay chatters when the button is pressed and the motor does not turn, there may be a bad ground connection. The relay contacts may be faulty, or the motor may have an internal open circuit. In such a case, the problem should be referred to a dealer for thorough testing.

Starter Motor
Removal/Installation

1. Refer to Chapter Four and remove cam chain tensioner.
2. Remove bolts securing starter motor cover and remove cover (**Figure 15**).
3. Disconnect starter wire from starter motor and remove motor (**Figure 16**).
4. Installation is the reverse of these steps.

Starter Relay
Removal/Installation

1. Remove left side cover.
2. Remove battery and starter motor leads from relay. Unplug yellow/green relay wire.
3. Remove 2 screws securing relay (**Figure 14**) and remove relay.
4. Installation is the reverse of these steps. Ensure that mounting screws and electrical connections are tight.

IGNITION SYSTEM

All 1979 and earlier models are fitted with a breaker point system (**Figure 17**). All 1980 and later models are fitted with an electronic ignition system (**Figure 18**).

The breaker point system consists of 2 coils with condensers, 2 contact breaker point sets and 2 spark plugs. The Kokusan electronic breakerless ignition system utilizes the same type of ignition coils and spark plugs, however, the breaker points and condensers are replaced with a signal generator and an igniter unit. The signal generator, mounted in place of the breaker points, generates pulses which are routed to the igniter unit. The igniter unit amplifies the pulses and triggers the output of the ignition coils.

7

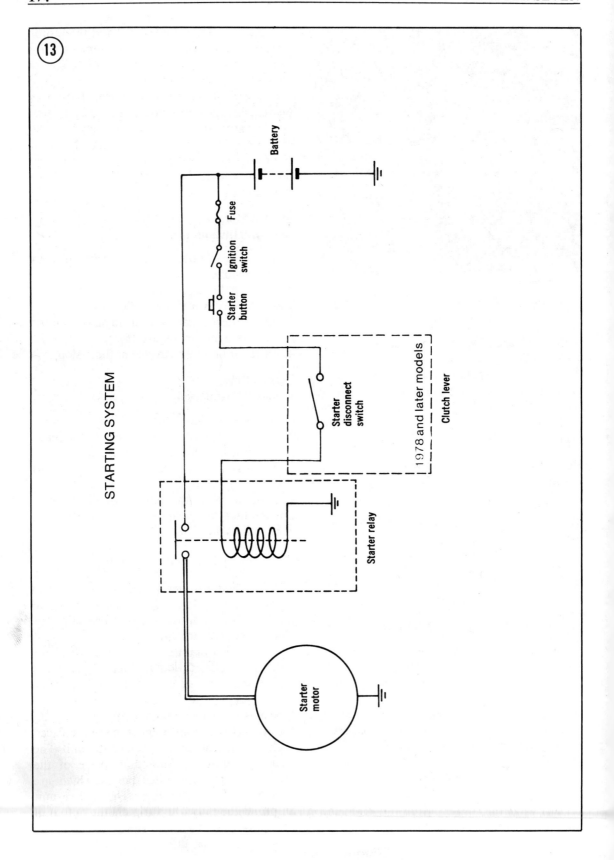

⑬

STARTING SYSTEM

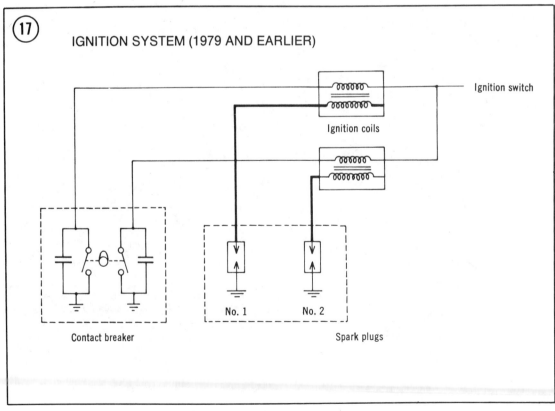

IGNITION SYSTEM (1979 AND EARLIER)

Ignition switch

Ignition coils

Contact breaker

No. 1   No. 2

Spark plugs

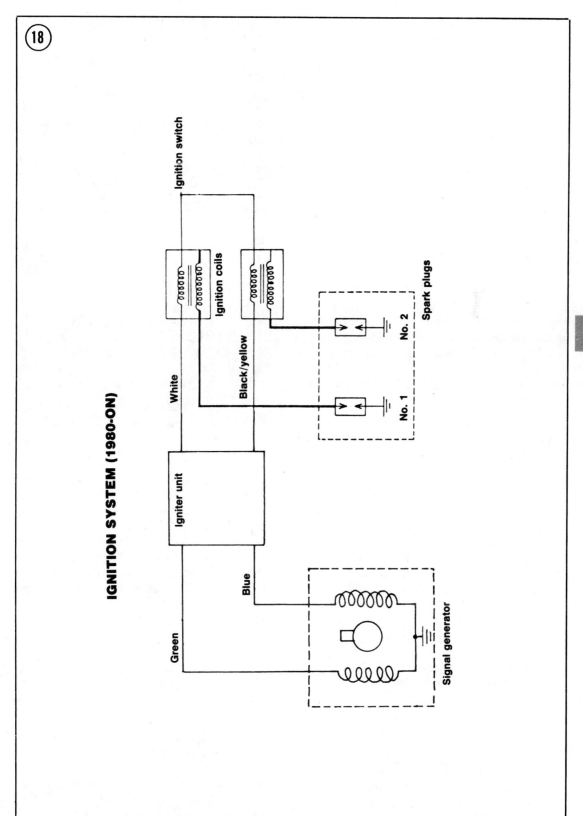

7

Ignition timing on the electronic ignition system is pre-set and non-adjustable, therefore, it requires no periodic maintenance. Periodic maintenance for the breaker point ignition system is outlined under *Tune-up* in Chapter Three.

On 1983 and later models, the ignition system incorporates an electronic advance circuit. Mechanical advance weights are no longer used. Test procedures for the electronic ignition system parts remain the same as for earlier models.

Signal Generator Test

1. Remove the left side cover to gain access to the signal generator wires (**Figure 19**).
2. Disconnect both signal generator wires.
3. Connect an accurate ohmmeter between each wire and ground (**Figure 20**). The ohmmeter indication must be 60-80 ohms for each wire or the signal generator unit is defective.
4. Reconnect the wires and replace the left side cover.

Igniter Unit Test

1. Carefully remove the spark plug leads from each spark plug. Remove the spark plugs and reconnect the spark plug leads. Lay both spark plugs against the cylinder head so that each plug is grounded on the head.
2. Remove the left side cover and disconnect both signal generator wires (**Figure 19**).
3. Turn on the motorcycle ignition.

> *NOTE*
> *This test utilizes the 1 1/2 volt battery in the ohmmeter to simulate the pulse from the signal generator. A 1 1/2 volt power source, such as a dry cell battery, can also be used for this test.*

> *CAUTION*
> *Ensure that the polarity is observed for this test or the igniter unit will be destroyed. The negative lead connects to the black/white wire (on the igniter unit) and the positive lead connects to the green/white or green/red wires (on the igniter unit).*

4. Set the ohmmeter to the R1 scale and connect the negative (–) lead to the black/white lead on the igniter unit.
5. Connect the ohmmeter positive (+) lead to either signal generator wire terminal on the igniter unit connector. This simulates the pulse from one-half of the signal generator. As the positive lead is connected to the igniter unit terminal, one spark plug should fire. When the positive lead is connected to the other igniter unit terminal, the other spark plug should fire. If both spark plugs are properly grounded and one or both fail to fire, replace the igniter unit.
6. Install both spark plugs. Reconnect the igniter unit wires and install the left side cover.

Signal Generator Removal/Installation

1. Remove the 3 screws securing the ignition cover and remove the cover (**Figure 21**). Take care not to damage the cover gasket.

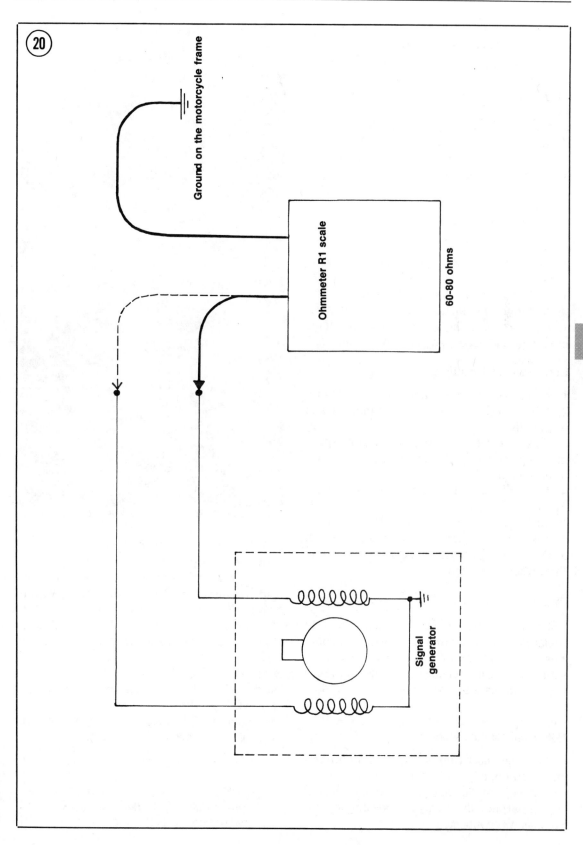

2. Remove the left side cover and disconnect both signal generator wires (**Figure 19**).

3. Remove the screws securing the signal generator unit (**Figure 22**) and remove the generator unit. Note how the wiring is routed along the engine sump.

4. Installation is the reverse of these steps. Ensure that the signal generator leads are connected properly and the wiring is routed correctly in the retaining clips.

Igniter Unit
Removal/Installation

1. Remove the left side cover.

2. Disconnect the leads from the igniter unit (**Figure 23**).

3. Remove the screws securing the igniter unit to the mounting bracket and remove the unit.

4. Installation is the reverse of these steps. Ensure that all leads are properly connected.

Coil Removal/Installation

1. Refer to Chapter Six and remove fuel tank.

2. Disconnect orange/white primary leads from coils.

3. Disconnect high-tension leads from spark plugs—grasp the spark plug caps, not the wires, to pull them off.

4. Unscrew nuts from coil mounts and remove coils along with high-tension leads (**Figure 24**).

5. Installation is the reverse of these steps. Make sure high-tension leads are routed to their respective cylinders.

Coil Test

The easiest test for a suspected coil is to replace it with a coil that is known to be good. For instance, if one of the cylinders is operating satisfactorily, interchange the coils and see if the symptoms move to the opposite cylinder.

Condenser Test
(1979 and Earlier Models)

The condenser can be tested with an ohm-meter equipped with a battery of 12 volts or less. An ohmmeter equipped with a battery of higher output will destroy a good condenser as soon as it is connected.

1. Connect one lead of ohmmeter to metal case of condenser.

2. Touch other ohmmeter lead to condenser lead. If condenser is good, ohmmeter will at first indicate a very low resistance, then start climbing higher and higher. It may reach infinity. Touch condenser lead to the case to discharge it.

3. If meter drops to a low value and stays there, or climbs only slightly, condenser is shorted. If needle never drops to a low value, but remains high, the condenser is open. In either case, replace the condenser.

NOTE
Condensers are mounted at the rear of each coil. Condenser leads must be cut and soldered to test or replace condensers.

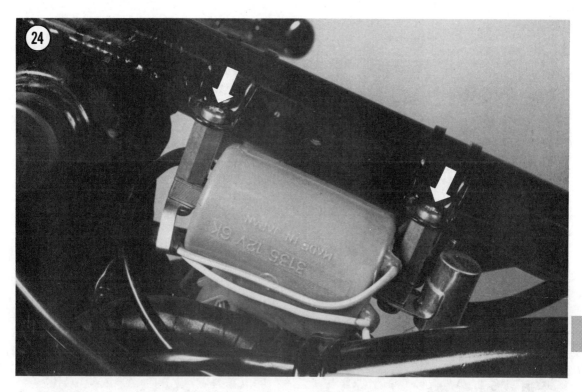

Breaker Points and Spark Plugs

Breaker point and spark plug maintenance is outlined in Chapter Three.

BATTERY SERVICE

Removal/Installation

1. Open the seat and remove the right side cover to gain access to the battery.
2. Remove the rubber strap securing the battery (**Figure 25**).
3. Disconnect the leads—negative first, then positive. On GS450 models, disconnect the positive battery lead from the starter motor. Remove the battery from the box.
4. Clean top of battery with a solution of baking soda and water. Scrub off any stubborn deposits with a wire brush and rinse battery with clear water. Dry it thoroughly.

> *CAUTION*
> *Keep cleaning solution out of battery cells or electrolyte will be severely weakened.*

5. Clean battery leads with a stiff wire brush.

6. Inspect battery case for cracks. If any are found, battery should be replaced. Its condition will deteriorate rapidly and leaking electrolyte will damage painted, plated, and polished surfaces as well as electrical insulation.
7. If battery is in good condition, install it and connect the leads, positive first, then ground.
8. Coat terminals with petroleum jelly, such as Vaseline.
9. Check electrolyte level and top off if necessary. Add only distilled water, never electrolyte.
10. Install battery and secure with rubber strap. Make sure battery cables are connected securely.

Testing

Hydrometer testing is the best way to check battery condition. Use a hydrometer with numbered graduations from 1.100 to 1.300 rather than one with color-coded bands. To use the hydrometer, squeeze the rubber ball, insert the tip in the cell and release the ball. Draw enough electrolyte to float the weighted float inside the hydrometer. Note the number in line with surface of the electrolyte; this is the spe-

cific gravity for this cell. Return the electrolyte to the cell from which it came.

The specific gravity of the electrolyte in each battery cell is an excellent indication of that cell's condition. A fully charged cell will read 1.260-1.280, while a cell in acceptable condition may read from 1.230-1.250. A weak cell reads from 1.200-1.220 and anything below 1.160 is discharged.

Specific gravity varies with temperature. For each 10° that electrolyte exceeds 80° F, add 0.004 to the reading indicated on the hydrometer. Subtract 0.004 for each 10° below 80° F.

If the cells test in the poor range, the battery requires recharging. The hydrometer is useful for checking the progress of the charging operation. **Table 1** shows approximate state of charge.

Charging

CAUTION
Always disconnect both battery connections before charging equipment.

The battery can be charged while installed in the motorcycle; however, it is so easily removed after the leads have been disconnected that it is not worth the risk of damaging the motorcycle finish with electrolyte during charging. Charge it only in a well-ventilated area.

WARNING
Make certain open flames and cigarettes, etc., are kept away from battery during charging. Highly explosive hydrogen gas is formed during charging. Never arc terminals to check the condition of charge; the resulting spark could ignite the gas.

1. Connect charger: positive-to-positive and negative-to-negative. See **Figure 26**.
2. Remove caps from cells and check electrolyte level. Correct level, if necessary, by adding only distilled water. Leave caps off during charging.
3. If charger output is variable, select a low rate (1.5-3 amps), turn on charger, and allow battery to charge as long as possible. If it is

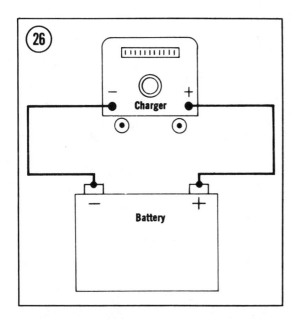

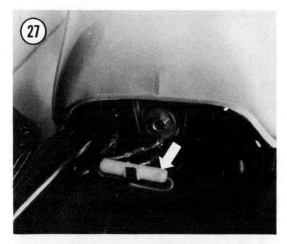

severely discharged, as long as 8 hours may be required to charge it completely.

4. When charging is complete, test it with a hydrometer. If specific gravity level is satisfactory, wait an hour and test it again. If specific gravity is still correct, battery is fully charged and in good condition. If specific gravity level drops between tests, it is likely that one or more cells are sulfated. In such a case, the battery should be replaced as soon as possible.

MAIN FUSE

There is a single main fuse in the battery positive lead. On GS400 and GS425 models, the fuse is located under the seat as shown in **Figure 27**. On GS450 models, the fuse is located behind the left-hand side cover (**Figure 28**).

If a fuse blows, find out the reason for the failure before replacing it. Usually the trouble is a short circuit in the wiring caused by worn insulation or a disconnected wire touching the frame.

> *CAUTION*
> *Never substitute tin foil or wire for a fuse. Never use a higher amperage fuse than specified. An overload could result in a fire and loss of the motorcycle.*

LIGHTING SYSTEM

The lighting system consists of the headlamp (with two filaments for high-beam and low-beam operation), the taillamp, stoplamp, directional signals, and warning and indicator lamps. **Table 2** lists replacement bulbs for these components.

Headlamp Removal/Installation

1. Loosen 3 lockscrews securing headlamp rim (**Figure 29**) and pull rim out from the top.
2. Unplug connector from rear of headlamp.
3. Remove clips securing lamps into rim (**Figure 30**) and remove lamp.
4. Installation is the reverse of these steps. Perform *Headlamp Adjustment*.

Headlamp Adjustment

Adjust the headlamp beam horizontally and vertically according to the motor vehicle regulations in your area.

To adjust it horizontally, turn the screw (A, **Figure 31**). To adjust it vertically, loosen the mounting bolts on either side, move the headlight body as required and tighten the bolts (B, **Figure 31**).

Taillamp Replacement

A single bulb functions as a taillamp, stoplamp, and license plate illumination lamp. If only one of the 2 filaments fail, the bulb must be replaced. To replace it, remove the lens and turn the bulb counterclockwise to unlock it, clockwise to lock the new bulb into the socket.

Directional Signal
Lamp Replacement

To replace any of the 4 directional signal lamps, remove the lens, turn the bulb counterclockwise to unlock it, and turn the new bulb clockwise to lock it into the socket. When installing the lens, do not tighten the screws so tightly that the lens cracks.

Front Stoplamp Switch
Removal/Installation

The front stoplamp switch is actuated by the front brake lever. Refer to **Figure 32** for this procedure.

1. Remove 2 screws securing switch cover to brake lever assembly.

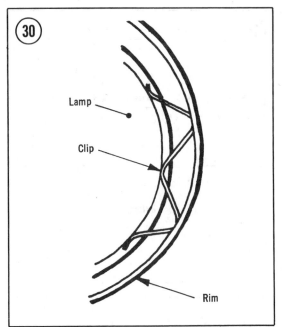

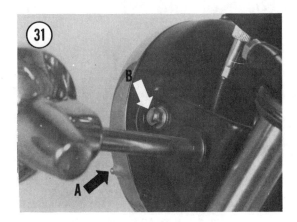

2. Carefully lift off switch housing. Do not lose the spring-loaded switch contact in the switch body. Replace brass switch contact if worn.

3. Installation is the reverse of these steps. Make sure small spring is installed beneath brass contact (**Figure 33**). Holes in switch cover are slightly elongated to allow for switch adjustment.

Rear Stoplamp Switch
Removal/Installation

Refer to **Figure 34** for this procedure.

1. Remove return spring from switch plunger.

2. Pull back rubber boot. Disconnect switch wires.

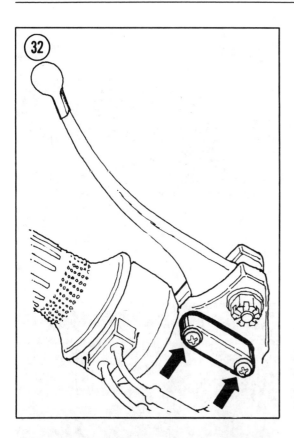

3. Remove locknut securing switch to frame and remove switch.

4. Installation is the reverse of these steps. Adjust switch locknuts so that stoplamp comes on when brake pedal is pressed.

Gearshift Indicator Switch Test

1. Remove pinch bolt securing gearshift lever and remove lever.

2. Remove screws securing engine sprocket cover (**Figure 35**) and remove cover.

3. Remove 2 screws securing switch to end of gearshift cam (**Figure 36**). Make sure spring-loaded plunger is not lost (**Figure 37**).

7

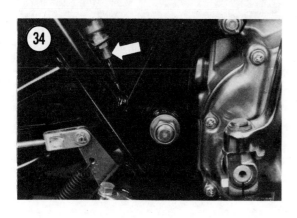

4. Perform switch test as follows:
   a. Turn on ignition switch and, with a jumper wire, manually ground each terminal on indicator switch.
   b. If gear indications are not correct, remove fuel tank as outlined in Chapter Six and disconnect indicator switch harness (**Figure 38**).
   c. Perform continuity test on indicator switch harness and replace if continuity is not present on each terminal.
   d. If continuity is present on switch terminals, check wiring connections on instrument panel indicator light. If wiring is in good condition, replace indicator light.

5. Switch installation is the reverse of removal. Ensure that O-ring is properly positioned behind switch (**Figure 37**).

Horn Removal/Installation

To remove horn, disconnect two wires and remove bolt securing horn to frame (**Figure 39**). When installing horn, ensure that rubber bushings are properly located on horn bracket.

Directional Lamp Relay
Removal/Installation

1. Remove the left side cover.
2. Remove the connector from the relay. See **Figure 40** for the early style relay and **Figure 41** for the later style relay.
3. Remove the relay from the mounting plate.
4. Installation is the reverse of these steps.

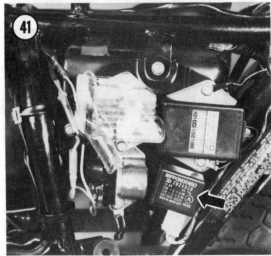

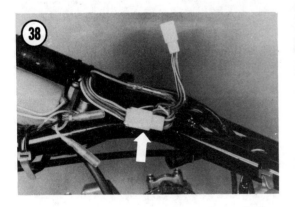

INSTRUMENTS

All models are fitted with an instrument cluster which includes a tachometer, speedometer gear position lights and warning lights. Some models are fitted with a fuel gauge.

Instrument Cluster
Removal/Installation

Refer to **Figure 42** for this procedure.
1. Remove the fuel tank as described in Chapter Six.
2. Remove the headlamp assembly.

3. Disconnect the instrument assembly wiring connectors located inside the headlamp housing.
4. Disconnect the speedometer and tachometer cables (**Figure 43**).
5. Remove the bolts securing the instrument cluster to the mounting bracket (**Figure 44**). Carefully note the location of rubber washers, grommets and cable straps. Remove the instrument cluster.

6. Installation is the reverse of these steps. Ensure that all wiring connectors and cables are properly connected.

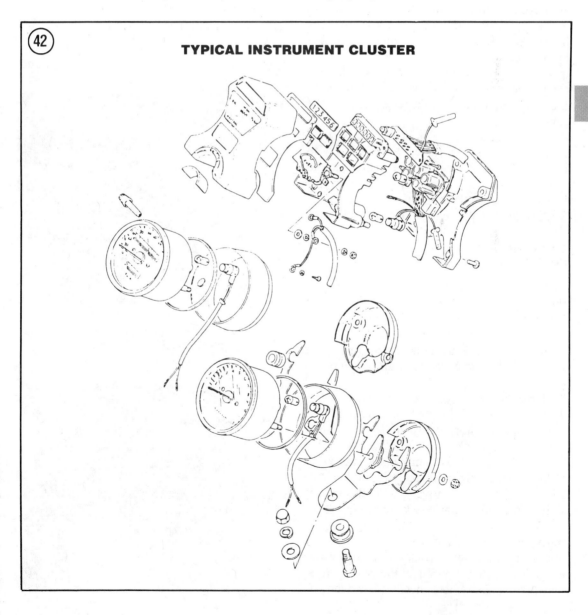

(42) **TYPICAL INSTRUMENT CLUSTER**

7

Instrument Cluster
Disassembly/Assembly

Refer to **Figure 42** for this procedure.
1. Remove the instrument cluster as described in this chapter.
2. Remove the screws securing the rear cover to the center instrument cluster and remove the cover.
3. Remove the nuts securing the mounting bracket to the instrument cluster and remove the bracket.
4. To isolate a defective indicator bulb or wiring fault, perform continuity tests on the applicable circuits as shown in **Figure 45**.
5. To replace indicator bulbs in the instrument cluster, carefully pull the rubber bulb holder out of the panel.
6. On models so equipped, to replace the fuel gauge, remove the nuts securing the gauge to the instrument panel and carefully lift out the gauge.
7. To gain access to an indicator bulb in the tachometer or speedometer it is necessary to remove the nuts securing the instrument to the mounting bracket and remove the instrument from the housing.
8. Assembly is the reverse of these steps.

Fuel Gauge Test
(Models So Equipped)

Perform the following test to determine if the fuel tank sending unit or the fuel gauge in the instrument cluster is defective.
1. Remove the left-hand side cover.
2. Disconnect the fuel tank sensing unit wires near the left-hand edge of the air box and fuel tank.
3. Turn the motorcycle ignition on.
4. Use a jumper wire such as a straightened paper clip to short between the fuel gauge leads (not the tank sending unit leads). If the fuel gauge needle fails to move, the gauge unit or the wiring harness is defective. If the fuel gauge needle does move, the tank sending unit or the wiring harness is defective.
5. To determine if the fuel gauge or the wiring harness is defective, use a jumper wire and ground the yellow/black lead. If the fuel gauge needle does not move, the gauge unit is defective. Extreme needle movement

indicates a fault in the wiring or connectors.
6. To determine if the tank sending unit or the wiring harness is defective, use an accurate ohmmeter and measure the resistance between the tank sending unit leads. A large unstable resistance indication signifies a defective sending unit. A normal resistance of approximately 1-20 ohms (depending on the level of fuel in the tank) signifies the fault lies in the wiring or connectors. An indication of approximately 100-120 ohms is for an empty tank.

Fuel Gauge Unit
Removal/Installation
(Models So Equipped)

The fuel gauge is housed in the instrument cluster. To replace the gauge unit, remove and

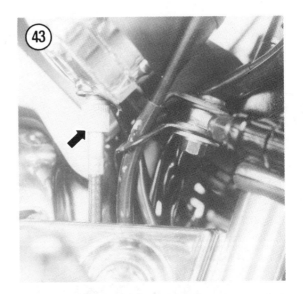

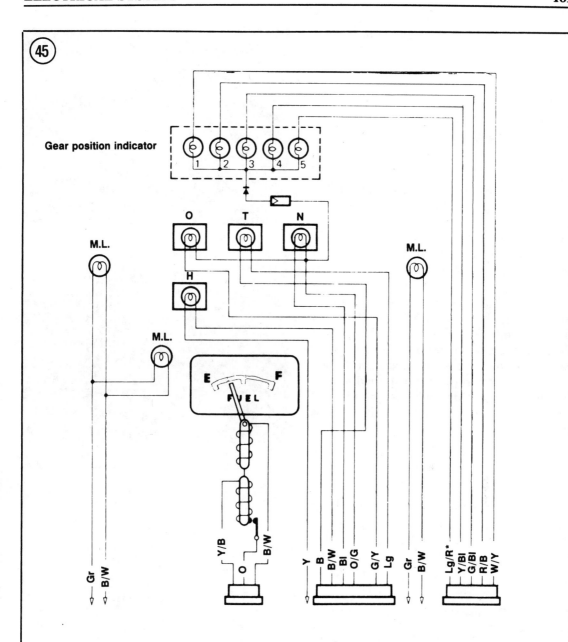

"L" MODEL INSTRUMENT CLUSTER
WIRING DIAGRAM

M.L.-Meter light
O-Oil pressure indicator
T-Turn signal indicator
N-Neutral indicator
H-High beam indicator

*G/R on 1983 GS450 ED models

disassemble the instrument cluster as described in this chapter.

Fuel Tank Sending Unit Removal/Installation (Models So Equipped)

1. Remove the fuel tank as described in Chapter Six.
2. Turn the fuel tank over and carefully drain any remaining gasoline into a suitable container.
3. Remove the screws securing the half-moon shaped fuel drain plate and gasket to gain access to the sending unit.
4. Remove the bolts securing the sending unit to the fuel tank (**Figure 46**). Carefully remove the sending unit. Remove the wires from the unit if it is to be replaced.
5. Installation is the reverse of these steps. Ensure that the sending unit gasket is in good condition and properly positioned before installing the sending unit. Secure the fuel drain plate hose and sending unit wires as shown in **Figure 47**.

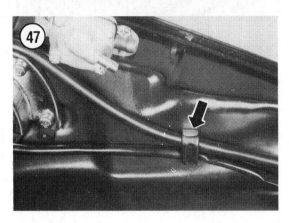

SIDESTAND SWITCH

Certain 1983 and later models are equipped with a sidestand switch and warning light to indicate when the sidestand is in the down position.

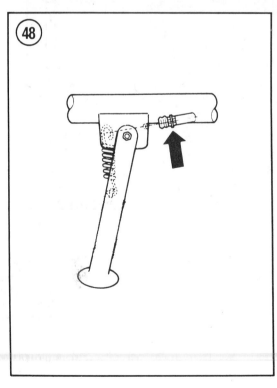

Switch Replacement/Adjustment

Refer to **Figure 48** for this procedure.
1. Disconnect the wires connecting the sidestand switch to the main wiring harness.
2. Disconnect the switch spring from the sidestand.
3. Unscrew the locknuts securing the switch to the motorcycle frame and remove the switch.
4. Installation is the reverse of these steps. Adjust the position of the switch in the frame so that the warning light comes on when the sidestand is down and goes off when the sidestand is up.

Table 1   STATE OF CHARGE

Specific Gravity	State of Charge
1.110-1.130	Discharged
1.140-1.160	Almost discharged
1.170-1.190	One-quarter charged
1.200-1.220	One-half charged
1.230-1.250	Three-quarters charged
1.260 1.280	Fully charged

Table 2   LAMP RATINGS

	Watts
Headlamp*	
High beam	50
Low beam	35
Meter lamp	3.4
Turn signal indicator lamp	3.4
High beam indicator lamp	3.4
Oil pressure indicator lamp	3.4
Neutral indicator lamp	3.4
Turn signal lamp	23
Rear combination lamps	
Tail and parking	8 (3 cp)
Stop	23 (32 cp)

*US and Canadian GS400 models use a 40/30 watt sealed beam unit.

7

FRONT SUSPENSION AND STEERING

This chapter includes repair and service procedures for the front wheel, steering components, and forks. Front brake repair is outlined in Chapter Ten.

FRONT WHEEL

Removal/Installation

1. Place motorcycle on centerstand and support engine with a block (**Figure 1**) so front wheel is clear of the ground.

2. Unscrew and disconnect speedometer cable (**Figure 2**).

3. Remove cotter pin from axle nut and loosen nut.

4. On models equipped with drum brakes, disconnect front brake cable as follows:

    a. Remove the cotter pin from the cable end (**Figure 3**).

    b. Remove adjuster nut and disconnect cable from brake lever (**Figure 4**).

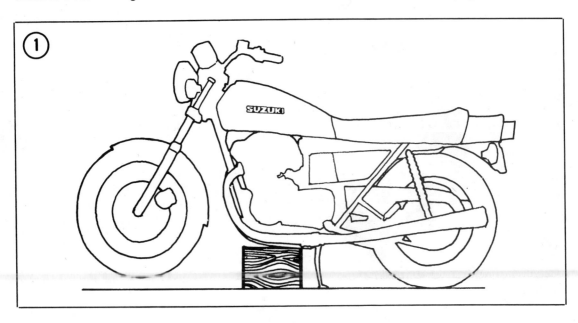

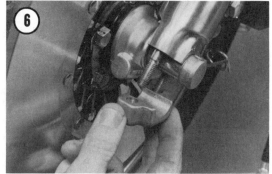

c. Disengage cable from brake backing plate retainer (**Figure 5**).

5. Remove nuts securing both axle holders and remove holders (**Figure 6**). Remove front wheel.

NOTE
Do not actuate the front disc brake with the front wheel removed, or the brake pads may be pushed out of the caliper body. If this should occur, refer to Chapter Ten and compress the pad and piston back into the caliper body.

6. Installation is the reverse of these steps. Keep the following points in mind:

a. Assemble the axle and wheel components as shown in **Figure 7** or **Figure 8**.
b. Position the speedometer drive unit as shown in **Figure 9**.
c. Lift the front wheel into place and install the axle holder nuts finger-tight. Make sure that the space between the holder and fork leg is equal on both sides as shown in **Figure 10**.
d. Torque the axle nut and axle holder nuts as specified in **Table 1**.

CAUTION
Insert a screwdriver shaft or drift through the hole in the axle shaft head to prevent the axle from turning while tightening the axle nut. If the axle should turn while the nut is tightened, the speedometer drive unit may be damaged.

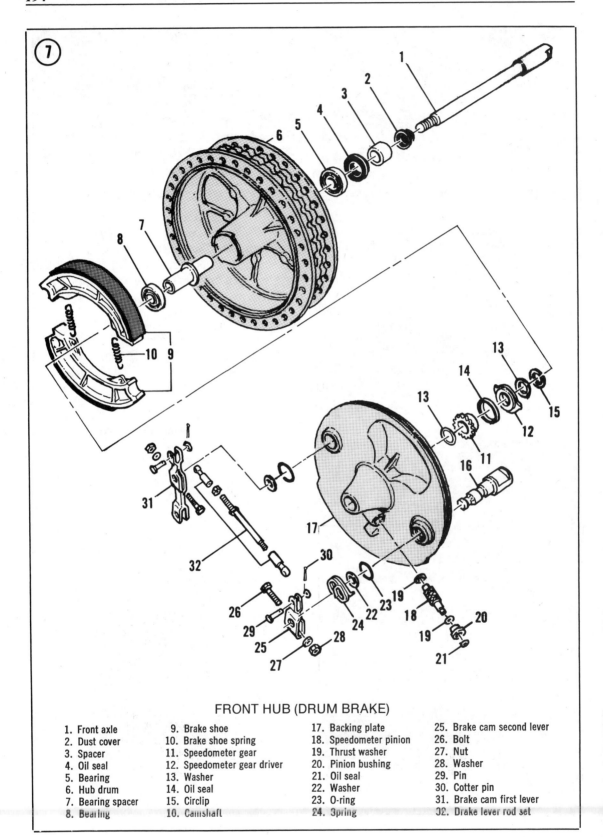

FRONT HUB (DRUM BRAKE)

1. Front axle
2. Dust cover
3. Spacer
4. Oil seal
5. Bearing
6. Hub drum
7. Bearing spacer
8. Bearing
9. Brake shoe
10. Brake shoe spring
11. Speedometer gear
12. Speedometer gear driver
13. Washer
14. Oil seal
15. Circlip
16. Camshaft
17. Backing plate
18. Speedometer pinion
19. Thrust washer
20. Pinion bushing
21. Oil seal
22. Washer
23. O-ring
24. Spring
25. Brake cam second lever
26. Bolt
27. Nut
28. Washer
29. Pin
30. Cotter pin
31. Brake cam first lever
32. Brake lever rod set

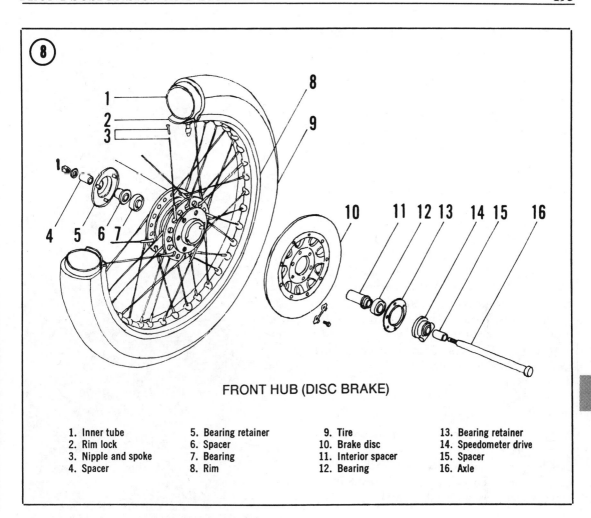

8

FRONT HUB (DISC BRAKE)

1. Inner tube
2. Rim lock
3. Nipple and spoke
4. Spacer
5. Bearing retainer
6. Spacer
7. Bearing
8. Rim
9. Tire
10. Brake disc
11. Interior spacer
12. Bearing
13. Bearing retainer
14. Speedometer drive
15. Spacer
16. Axle

8

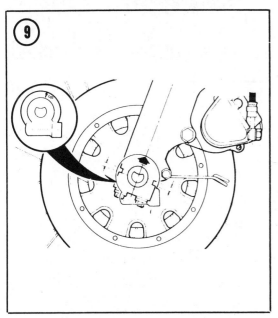

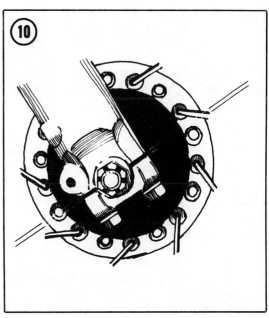

e. When connecting the speedometer cable, make sure the slot in the cable end (**Figure 11**) engages the blade in the speedometer drive unit.

f. On drum brake models, perform *Front Brake Adjustment* as outlined in Chapter Three.

Disassembly

Refer to **Figure 7** or **Figure 8** for this procedure.

1. Unscrew axle nut and remove axle. On disc brake models, axle is removed with the speedometer drive. On drum brake models, remove axle with brake backing plate (**Figure 12**). Note the location of axle spacers.

2. On disc brake models, straighten lock tabs on disc bolts. Unscrew bolts and remove the disc. Remove right bearing cover.

3. Tap the bearings out of the hub with a long, soft drift. Collect the spacers.

Inspection

1. Inspect brake components as described in Chapter Ten.

2. Clean hub inside and out with solvent. Clean bearing covers, axle, and speedometer drive. Clean spacers inside and out.

CAUTION
Do not clean bearings in solvent. They are sealed and permanently lubricated.

3. Turn each bearing by hand and check it for smoothness and play. It should turn smoothly and quietly. Replace bearings if they are questionable.

4. Inspect axle for runout (**Figure 13**). If runout exceeds 0.25 mm (0.010 in.), replace the axle. *Do not* attempt to straighten it.

5. Measure the axial and radial runout of the wheel with a dial indicator as shown in **Figure 14**. Maximum runout in either direction is 2.0 mm (0.08 in.).

NOTE
If a dial indicator is not available, a simple gauge can be improvised as shown in Figure 15.

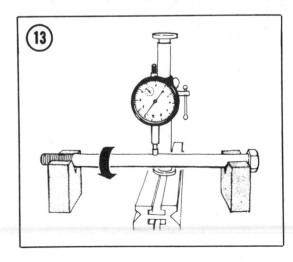

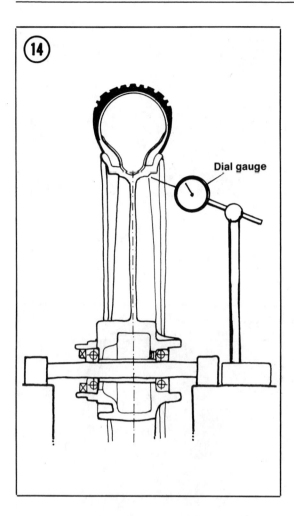

Dial gauge

6. If the runout on a spoke wheel is excessive, refer to *Spoke Wheels* and attempt to true the wheel.

7. If the runout on an alloy wheel is excessive, check the wheel bearings and/or replace the wheel. The stock Suzuki alloy wheel cannot be repaired; it must be replaced.

Assembly

Refer to **Figure** 7 or **Figure** 8 for this procedure.

1. Pack inside of hub with grease. Grease spacers inside and out.

2. Install left bearing in the hub using a driver or socket that is only fractionally smaller in diameter than outer bearing race. This is essential so that force required to drive the bearing into the hub is applied only to the outer race.

3. Install interior spacer through inside of hub. Shoulder on spacer rests against left bearing inner race.

4. Install the right bearing, spacer, and bearing retainer.

5. Install the disc. Tighten bolts to 1.5-2.5 mkg (11-18 ft.-lb.) and bend lock tabs against bolt heads.

6. Install speedometer drive so that tangs on the drive unit line up with slots in the hub. Perform *Front Wheel Installation.*

8

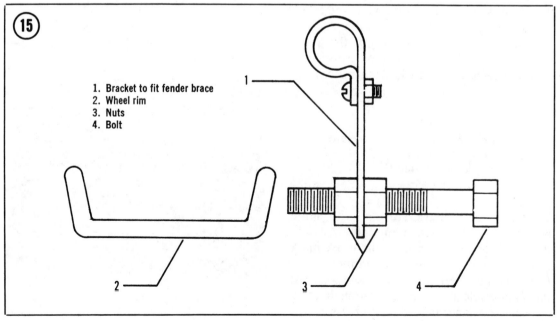

1. Bracket to fit fender brace
2. Wheel rim
3. Nuts
4. Bolt

WHEEL BALANCING

An unbalanced wheel can adversely affect the handling of the motorcycle as well as make the machine very uncomfortable to ride.

Wheels are relatively easy to balance without special equipment. Most dealers or motorcycle accessory shops carry an assortment of balance weights that can be crimped on the spokes as shown in **Figure 16**. Alloy wheels will accept standard automotive type weights or adhesive weights designed for automobile "mag" wheels. Buy a couple of each weight available. If the weights are unused they can usually be returned.

Many dealers now have high-speed spin balancing services available. This type of balancing is very fast and accurate. Have your wheels balanced by the high-speed spin method if such services are available.

Before attempting to balance a wheel, make sure the wheel bearings are in good condition and properly lubricated. If balancing is to be performed with the wheels still installed on the motorcycle, ensure that the brakes do not drag. A brake that drags will prevent the wheel from turning freely, resulting in an inaccurate wheel balance. Before the rear wheel can be balanced, the drive chain must be removed.

1. Rotate the wheel slowly and allow it to come to rest by itself. Make a chalk mark on the tire at the 6 o'clock position and rotate the wheel as before, several times, noting the position of the chalk mark each time the wheel comes to rest. If the wheel stops at different positions each time, the wheel is balanced.

NOTE
*If desired, the wheel may be removed from the motorcycle and supported on a stand as shown in **Figure 17**.*

2. If the chalk mark stops at the same position—6 o'clock—each time, add weight to the 12 o'clock position until the chalk mark stops at a different position each time.

3. Install the wheel, if removed, and road test the motorcycle on a smooth, straight road. Repeat the balance procedure if necessary.

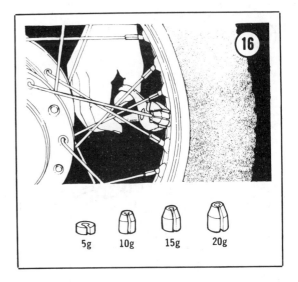

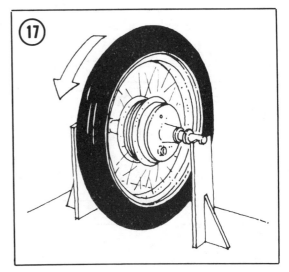

SPOKE WHEELS

Spokes should be routinely checked for tightness. The "tuning fork" method for checking spoke tightness is simple and works well. Tap each spoke with a spoke wrench or the shank of a screwdriver and listen to the tone. A correctly tightened spoke will emit a clear, ringing tone, while a loose spoke will sound flat. All of the spokes in a correctly tightened wheel will emit tones of similar pitch but not necessarily the same precise tone.

Bent, broken or stripped spokes should be replaced as soon as they are detected, as they can cause the destruction of an expensive hub.

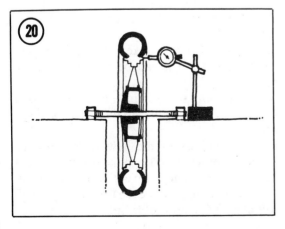

NOTE
Most professional motorcycle mechanics use and recommend the Rowe Products spoke wrench (Figure 18). It will not round off the square edges of the spoke nipples and fits virtually all sizes of spokes.

Runout Adjustment (Truing)

1. To measure the runout of the rim, support the wheel in a stand as shown in **Figure 19** or support the motorcycle so that the wheel being checked is free of the ground.
2. Install a dial indicator (**Figure 20**) or locally fabricated runout indicator (**Figure 15**). Adjust the position of the bolt until it just clears the rim.
3. Rotate the rim and note whether the clearance between the rim and the indicator increases or decreases. Mark the tire with chalk or crayon at areas where the clearance is large or small. Maximum runout on the edge and/or the face of the rim is 2.0 mm (0.08 in.).
4. To pull or "true" the rim, tighten spokes which terminate on the same side of the hub and loosen the spokes which terminate on the opposite side of the hub as shown in **Figure 21**. In most cases, only a slight amount of adjustment is necessary. After adjustment, rotate the rim and make sure that another area of the rim has not been pulled out of true. Continue adjustment and checking until runout does not exceed 2.0 mm (0.08 in.). Be patient and thorough, adjusting the position of the rim a little at a time.

NOTE
If rims can not be trued within 2.0 mm (0.08 in.) of edge or face runout, the rim is damaged and must be replaced. Unless you are experienced in wheel lacing, this task is best left to a dealer or motorcycle shop experienced in wheel repair.

5. Always tighten spokes gradually and evenly in a crisscross pattern on one side of the hub then the other. One-half to one turn should be sufficient; do not overtighten.
6. After tightening spokes, always check the runout to make sure that the rim has not been pulled out of true.

8

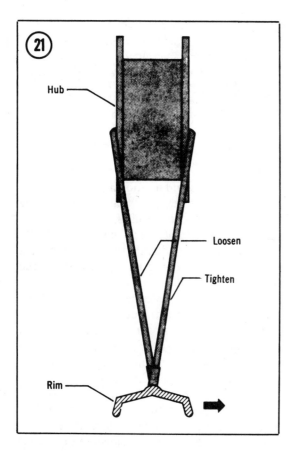

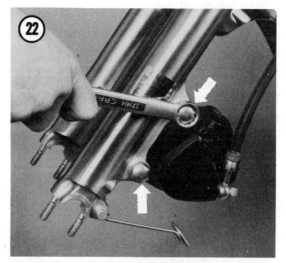

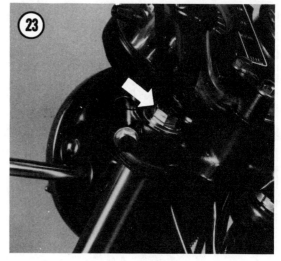

Spoke Replacement

A stripped or broken spoke can usually be replaced with the tire still installed on the wheel, providing the spoke nipple is in good condition. If the nipple is damaged or more than 2 or 3 spokes need replacing, the tire must first be removed from the wheel. If several spokes need replacing, the rim is also probably damaged. Unless you are skilled in wheel lacing and rim replacement, this task is best left to a dealer or motorcycle shop skilled in wheel repair.

To replace one or two damaged spokes with the tire still mounted, perform the following procedure.

1. Inflate the tire to at least 30 psi to help hold the spoke nipple in the rim.

2. Unscrew the nipple from the damaged or broken spoke. If the old spoke is not broken, press the nipple into the rim far enough to free the end of the damaged spoke. Take care not to push the nipple back into the rim. Remove the old spoke.

3. Trim the threaded end of the new spoke so that it is about 2 or 3 threads shorter than the old spoke. This permits the new spoke to stretch without the risk of puncturing the inner tube.

4. Install the new spoke into the hub and gently bow it so it can be inserted into the nipple.

5. Tighten the spoke nipple until the tone of the new spoke is similar to the other spokes in the wheel.

6. The tightness of the new spoke must be checked frequently. The spoke will stretch and must be retightened several times before it takes a final "set". Make the first check after 30 minutes to one hour of riding.

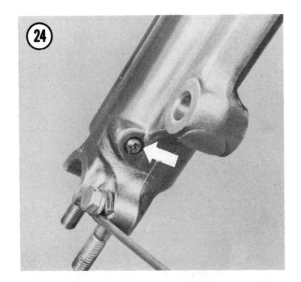

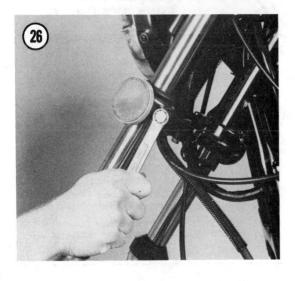

FRONT FORK

Removal/Installation

1. Remove the front wheel as outlined under *Front Wheel Removal*.

2. On disc brake models, remove the bolts securing the brake caliper (**Figure 22**) and remove the caliper. Support the caliper from the handlebars with a piece of wire or Bungee cord. Do not allow the caliper to hang by the hose.

3. Remove the fender bolts and remove the fender.

4. If the fork is being removed for disassembly, perform the following:

   a. Loosen the fork cap bolts (**Figure 23**).
   b. Remove the drain screw (**Figure 24**) and drain the oil from each fork leg. Allow several minutes for the forks to drain completely.

5. Loosen the upper and lower pinch bolts securing each fork leg (**Figure 25** and **Figure 26**). Pull down and remove each fork leg.

6. Installation is the reverse of these steps. Torque the fork pinch bolts and fork cap bolts as specified in **Table 1**.

Disassembly/Assembly

Refer to **Figure 27A** for this procedure.

NOTE
Preparation should be made prior to starting the disassembly as an impact tool (air or electric) or a special holding tool is necessary to remove the Allen retaining bolt in the bottom of each fork leg. The Allen bolt is secured with a thread locking compound (such as Loctite) and is often difficult to remove because the damper rod will turn inside the fork tube. Have a local dealer remove the Allen bolts with an impact tool or with an Allen wrench and the special holding tool. Use Suzuki part No. 09940-34561 (Attachment "D") inside the fork tube to hold the damper rod. Attachment "D" can be used with the Suzuki handle (Suzuki part No. 09940-34520) or with one or two long 3/8 inch drive socket extensions.

1. Remove the front fork as outlined in this chapter.

8

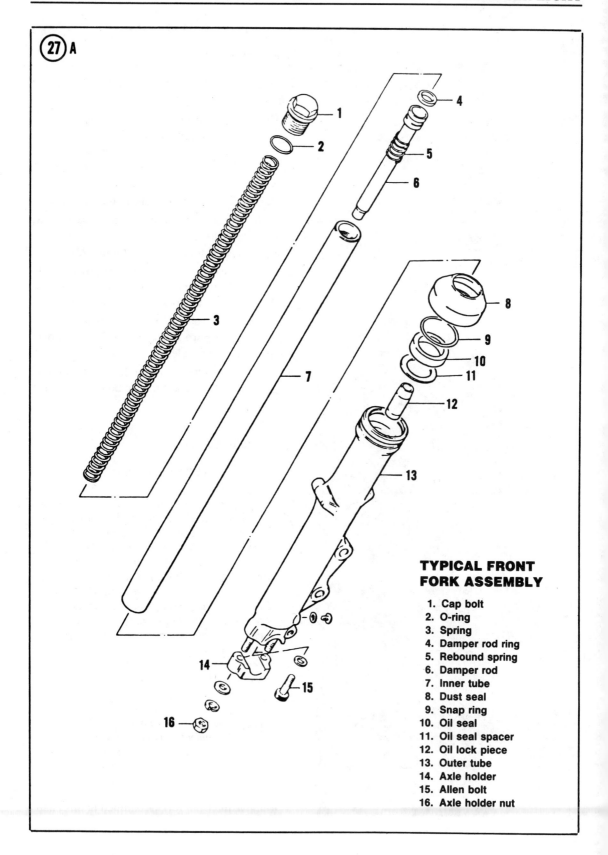

㉗ A

**TYPICAL FRONT
FORK ASSEMBLY**

1. Cap bolt
2. O-ring
3. Spring
4. Damper rod ring
5. Rebound spring
6. Damper rod
7. Inner tube
8. Dust seal
9. Snap ring
10. Oil seal
11. Oil seal spacer
12. Oil lock piece
13. Outer tube
14. Axle holder
15. Allen bolt
16. Axle holder nut

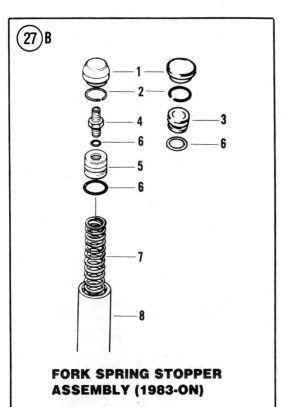

FORK SPRING STOPPER ASSEMBLY (1983-ON)

1. Rubber fork cap
2. Snap ring
3. Spring stopper (without air valve)
4. Air valve
5. Spring stopper (with air valve)
6. O-ring
7. Fork spring
8. Fork inner tube

2A. On 1977-1981 models, remove the fork cap bolt (**Figure 27A**) from the inner tube.

2B. On 1983-on models, refer to **Figure 27B** and perform the following:

   a. Remove the rubber cap from the top of each fork tube.

   b. On models equipped with air valves (**Figure 28**), carefully bleed off the fork air pressure.

   c. Carefully press down against the spring stopper and remove the snap ring securing the stopper (A, **Figure 28**). Remove the spring stopper. Take care not to damage the O-ring (B, **Figure 28**).

3. Remove the spring spacer on models so equipped.

4. Remove the fork springs (**Figure 29**).

5. Tip up the fork tube and drain the fork oil. Stroke the fork several times over a drain pan to pump out all the remaining oil. Let the fork tube drain for several minutes.

6. Use the special holding tools or an impact tool and remove the Allen bolt from the bottom of the fork outer tube (**Figure 30**).

8

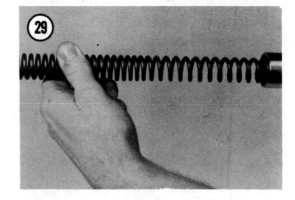

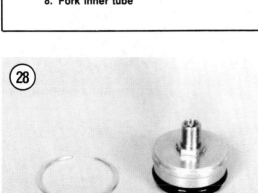

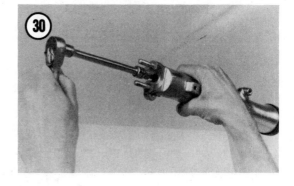

7. Slide out and remove the inner tube from the outer tube (**Figure 31**).

8. Remove the oil lock piece from the end of the damper rod (**Figure 32**).

> *NOTE*
> *The oil lock piece is often stuck to the bottom of the outer tube. Make sure the piece is not lost.*

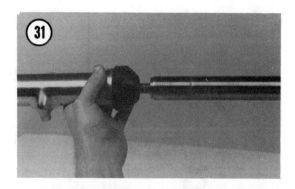

9. Tip up the inner tube and slide out the damper rod assembly complete with the rebound spring (**Figure 33**).

10. Remove the rebound spring from the damper rod (**Figure 34**).

11. Carefully pry off and remove the fork dust boot (**Figure 35**).

12. Remove the snap ring securing the oil seal (**Figure 36**).

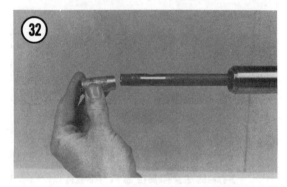

> *NOTE*
> *On some model forks, it may be necessary to use snap ring pliers to remove the snap ring securing the oil seal.*

13. Lift out and remove the seal retaining washer on models so equipped.

14. Carefully pry out the old seal with a large blade screwdriver or tire tool as shown in **Figure 37**. Pad the edge of the outer fork tube with a rag or piece of aluminum to prevent damage to the fork tube.

15. Perform *Inspection.*

16. Assembly is the reverse of these steps. Keep the following points in mind:

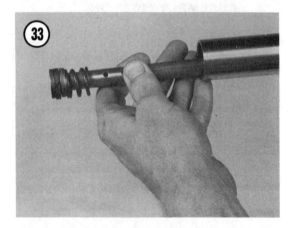

  a. Ensure that all fork components are clean and dry. Wipe out the seal bore before installing the new oil seal. Lightly oil the inner and outer tubes and damper rod assembly before assembling the parts. Apply a light film of grease to the outer edge and lips of each fork seal before installing the seals.

  b. Install the new oil seal (open end down) and tap the seal into position with a seal driver or suitably sized socket (**Figure 38**).

  c. Install the seal retaining washer (on models so equipped) and secure the seal with the snap ring.

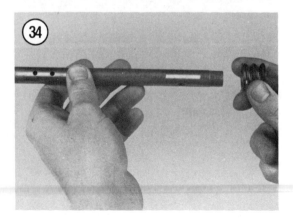

d. Make sure the rebound (top-out) spring is installed on the damper rod before installing the rod in the inner fork tube.

NOTE
Temporarily install the fork springs and the fork cap bolt. The tension of the fork springs will keep the damper rod extended through the end of the fork tube and ease fork assembly.

e. Apply blue Loctite (242) to the Allen retaining bolt before installing the bolt. Ensure that the washer is fitted to the bolt. Torque the bolt to 1.5-2.5 mkg (11-18 ft.-lb.).

f. Install the dust cover over the seal.

17. Remove the fork springs. Refer to **Table 2** and add the specified amount and type of fork oil to each fork tube. Use a graduate or a baby bottle (**Figure 39**) to ensure the oil amount is correct for each fork tube. Oil level can also be measured from the top of the fork tube. Use an accurate ruler or the Suzuki oil level gauge (part No. 09943-74111) to ensure the oil level is as specified in **Table 2**. The oil level must be measured with the forks completely compressed and without springs.

NOTE
An oil level measuring device can be locally fabricated as shown in Figure 40. Fill the fork with a few cc's more than the required amount of oil. Position the hose clamp on the top edge of the fork tube and draw out the excess

8

oil. Oil is sucked out until the level reaches the small diameter hole. A precise oil level can be achieved with this simple device.

18. Install the fork spring and the spring spacer, if so equipped. Make sure the closer coils on the spring are pointed down.

19A. On 1977-1981 models, ensure the O-ring on the fork cap is in good condition and install the fork cap. Tighten the fork cap to 1.5-3.0 mkg (11-22 ft.-lb.).

19B. On 1982-on models, ensure the O-ring (B, **Figure 28**) is in good condition. Lightly oil the O-ring and install the spring stopper in the fork tube. Press down on the stopper until the snap ring groove is exposed and install the snap ring to secure the spring stopper. Ensure that the snap ring is fully engaged in the groove in the fork tube.

Inspection

1. Thoroughly clean all parts in solvent and dry them completely. Lightly oil and assemble the inner and outer fork tubes, then slide the tubes together. Check for looseness, noise or binding. Replace any defective parts.

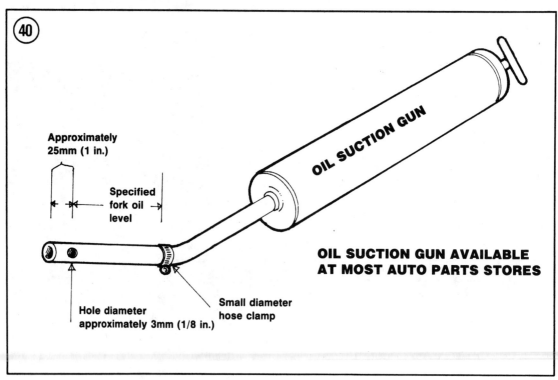

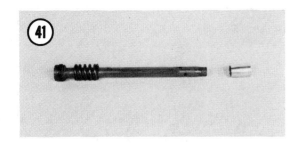

2. Carefully examine the area of the inner fork tube that passes through the fork seal. Any scratches or roughness on the tube in this area will damage the oil seal. If the inner fork tube is scratched or pitted it should be replaced.

3. Inspect the damper rod assembly for damage or roughness (**Figure 41**). Check for signs of galling, deep scores or excessive wear. Replace the parts as necessary. Make sure all the oil passages are clean and free of any sludge or oil residue.

4. Inspect the dust cover on the fork tube for holes or abrasive damage. A damaged cover may allow dirt and moisture to pack up next to the fork seal. Packed in dirt can scratch the surface of the fork tubes as well as damage the fork seal. Install new dust covers if any damage exists.

5. Accurately measure the fork springs. If any spring is shorter than the length specified in **Table 2** replace both springs as a set.

STEERING HEAD

The steering head should be disassembled periodically and the bearings packed with new grease. All 1979 and earlier models use 18 uncaged ball bearings in each of the upper and lower bearing races. All 1980 and later models are equipped with tapered roller bearings in both upper and lower bearing races.

Use a good heavy grade of grease such as wheel bearing grease when lubricating the bearings, since on 1979 and earlier models, the grease is also used to hold the bearing balls in position during installation.

Disassembly/Lubrication/Assembly

Refer to **Figure 42** or **Figure 43** for this procedure.

1. Remove the front forks.
2. Remove the fuel tank as outlined in Chapter Six to avoid possible damage to the tank.
3. Loosen the pinch bolt securing the large steering stem bolt or nut (**Figure 44**).
4. Remove the large steering stem bolt or nut (**Figure 45**).
5. Lift up on the handlebars and lift off the upper steering stem head.
6. Remove the steering stem nut and lift off the dust cover. Use a locally improvised tool similar to **Figure 46** or Suzuki special tool part No. 09940-14910 to remove the stem nut. If care is exercised, a hammer and punch may also be used to tap off the nut (**Figure 47**).
7. On 1979 and earlier models, remove the upper bearing outer race. On 1980 and later models, lift out the upper roller bearing.
8. The entire steering stem can now be partially withdrawn from the frame. On 1979 and earlier models, place a container under the steering head to catch any ball bearings that may fall out. To lubricate the bearings, further disassembly is unnecessary.

NOTE
To completely remove the steering stem it is necessary to remove the brake hose, disconnect the speedometer and tachometer cables, cable and wire retainers, directional light wiring and all other components secured to the lower steering stem bracket.

9. Assembly is the reverse of disassembly. Keep the following points in mind:
   a. Pack the upper and lower roller bearings with heavy duty grease.
   b. On 1979 and earlier models, ensure that 18 bearing balls are installed in each bearing race.
   c. On 1980 and later models, use the Suzuki special tool (part No. 09940-14910) or equivalent and temporarily torque the steering stem nut

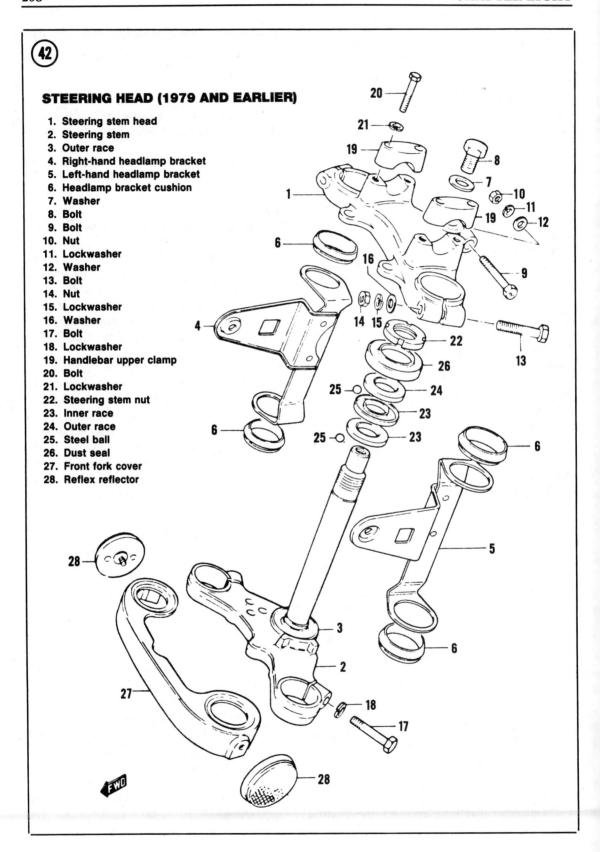

㊷

STEERING HEAD (1979 AND EARLIER)

1. Steering stem head
2. Steering stem
3. Outer race
4. Right-hand headlamp bracket
5. Left-hand headlamp bracket
6. Headlamp bracket cushion
7. Washer
8. Bolt
9. Bolt
10. Nut
11. Lockwasher
12. Washer
13. Bolt
14. Nut
15. Lockwasher
16. Washer
17. Bolt
18. Lockwasher
19. Handlebar upper clamp
20. Bolt
21. Lockwasher
22. Steering stem nut
23. Inner race
24. Outer race
25. Steel ball
26. Dust seal
27. Front fork cover
28. Reflex reflector

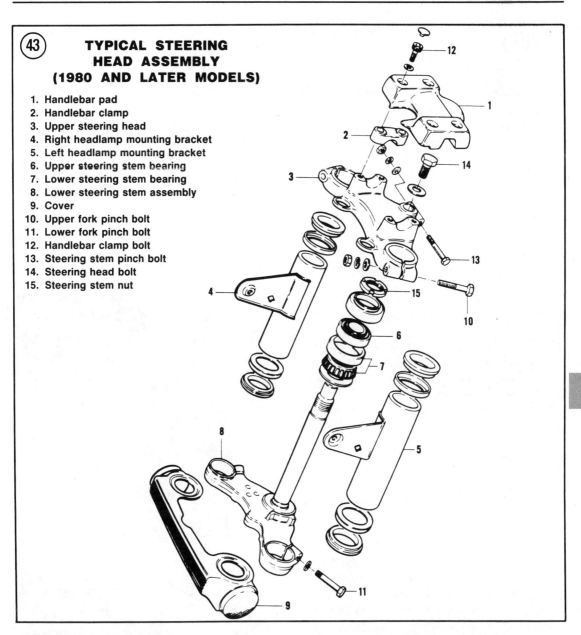

(43) **TYPICAL STEERING
HEAD ASSEMBLY
(1980 AND LATER MODELS)**

1. Handlebar pad
2. Handlebar clamp
3. Upper steering head
4. Right headlamp mounting bracket
5. Left headlamp mounting bracket
6. Upper steering stem bearing
7. Lower steering stem bearing
8. Lower steering stem assembly
9. Cover
10. Upper fork pinch bolt
11. Lower fork pinch bolt
12. Handlebar clamp bolt
13. Steering stem pinch bolt
14. Steering head bolt
15. Steering stem nut

8

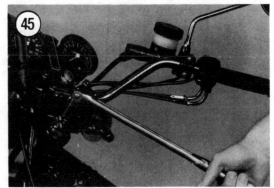

to 4.0-5.0 mkg (29-36 ft.-lb.) to seat the roller bearings. Turn the steering lock-to-lock a few times to ensure that the movement is smooth without excessive play. Back off the steering stem nut approximately 1/4 turn.

d. On 1979 and earlier models, tighten the steering stem nut fully to seat the bearing balls. Back off the nut just enough for smooth steering movement without any perceptible free play.

e. Install the large steering stem nut or bolt and torque to 3.6-5.2 mkg (26-38 ft.-lb.). Check that the steering stem moves easily and smoothly from side-to-side and no vertical play is present. Readjust the steering stem nut if necessary.

f. Torque the steering stem pinch bolt to 1.5-2.5 mkg (11-18 ft.-lb.).

g. If the lower steering bracket was removed, install all wire and cable retainers and the brake hose. Bleed the brakes as outlined in Chapter Ten if any brake hoses were opened.

Inspection

1. Clean the bearing races and bearings with solvent.

2. Check the frame welds around the steering head for cracks and fractures. If any are found, have them repaired by a competent frame shop or welding service.

3. Check the bearings for pitting, scratches or signs of corrosion. If they are less than perfect, replace them as a set.

4. Check the races for pitting, galling and corrosion. If any of these conditions exist, replace the races. See the applicable bearing replacement procedure.

5. Check the steering stem for cracks, damage or wear.

Steering Head Adjustment

1. Place the motorcycle on the centerstand and place a block under the engine until the front wheel is clear of the ground. Grasp each fork leg at the lower end and attempt to move the front end back and forth. If any fore and

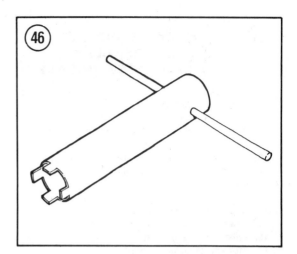

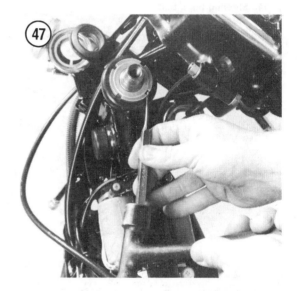

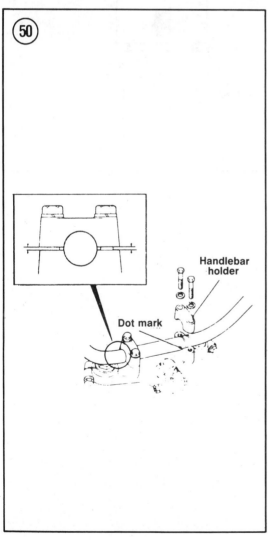

Handlebar holder

Dot mark

aft movement of the front end is detected, the steering stem locknut will have to be adjusted.

2. Loosen the pinch bolt securing the steering stem head bolt or nut (**Figure 44**) and loosen the head bolt or nut (**Figure 45**).

3. Use the Suzuki spanner wrench (part No. 09940-10122) or equivalent and adjust the steering stem locknut (**Figure 48**) until all play is removed from the steering head, yet the front end turns freely from side to side, under its own weight. If the Suzuki spanner is not available the steering locknut can be gently tapped with a hammer and a punch or screwdriver. Take care not to damage the locknut.

4. Torque the steering stem head bolt or nut and the steering stem pinch bolt as specified in **Table 1**.

Handlebar Removal/Installation

1. If the handlebars are to be replaced, it is necessary to remove the clutch lever, front master cylinder and throttle grip.

2. Remove the bolts securing the handlebar clamps and remove the handlebars. On GS450 models, remove the plugs covering the handlebar Allen bolts (**Figure 49**).

3. Install the handlebar with the dot and handlebar clamps equally positioned as shown in **Figure 50**. Torque the clamp bolts to 1.2-2.0 mkg (9-15 ft.-lb.).

4. Install the clutch lever, front master cylinder and throttle grip if removed.

Bearing Race Replacement (1979 and Earlier Models)

1. Insert a hardwood dowel or brass drift into the steering head as shown in **Figure 51** and tap around the race to drive it out. Do the same with the opposite race.

2. Install new races by tapping them into the steering head with a hardwood block (**Figure 52**). Make sure the races are seated squarely before tapping them into place. Tap them in until they are fully seated in the steering head.

3. Use 2 screwdrivers and carefully pry off the lower race from the lower steering stem. Carefully tap a new race into place with a wooden block.

8

Bearing Replacement
(1980 and Later Models)

Several special tools and considerable expertise are required to replace the steering head bearings and bearing races. It is recommended that this task be referred to an authorized dealer who is equipped with the necessary tools.

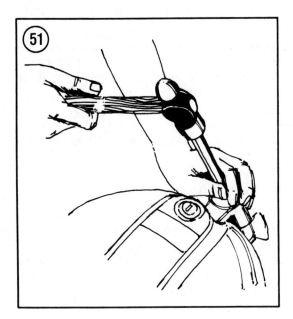

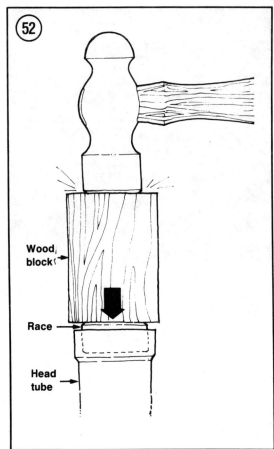

Table 1 FRONT SUSPENSION TORQUE SPECIFICATIONS

Item	mkg	ft.-lb.
Front axle nut	3.6-5.2	26-38
Front axle holder nut	1.5-2.5	11-18
Front caliper mounting bolt	2.5-4.0	18-29
Upper fork pinch bolt	2.0-3.0	15-22
Lower fork pinch bolt	2.5-4.0	18-29
Steering stem pinch bolt	1.5-2.5	11-18
Steering stem head bolt or nut	3.6-5.2	26-38
Handlebar clamp bolt	1.2-2.0	9-15
Fork cap bolts	1.5-3.0	11-22
Brake disc mounting bolt	1.5-2.5	11-18

Table 2 FRONT FORK SPECIFICATIONS

Recommended fork oil	SAE 10, 20 or 30 weight fork oil or 50:50 mix with ATF (automatic transmission fluid)		
Fork oil capacity	**cc**	**U.S. oz.**	**Imp. oz.**
GS400	145	4.9	5.1
GS425L	160	5.4	5.6
GS450N, C	145	4.9	5.1
GS450LZ	189	6.4	6.7
GS450EZ	178	6.0	6.3
GS450TZ	181	6.1	6.4
GS450TXZ	143	4.8	5.0
GS450ED			
Right leg	165	5.6	5.8
Left leg	187	6.3	6.6
GS450TXD	155	5.2	5.5
GS450LD, LF, LG, LH	277	9.4	9.8

Fork oil level*	**9mm**	**in.**	
GS400	187	7.1	
GS425L,	173	6.8	
GS425E	187	7.1	
GS450LZ	117	4.6	
GS450EZ	131	5.6	
GS450TZ	125	4.9	
GS450TXZ, TXD	208	8.2	
GS450ED	190	7.5	
GS450LD, LF, LG, LH	118.5	4.7	

(continued)

Table 2 FRONT FORK SPECIFICATIONS (cont.)

Fork spring length (service limit) mm		in.
GS400, GS425	486	19.1
GS450E, T	496	19.5
GS450L	506	19.9
GS450LZ	503	19.8
GS450LD	504	19.84
GS450TD	493	19.41
GS450LF, LG, LH	505	19.88

* Measure the oil level from the top of the fork leg with the fork leg held vertical, the spring removed and the fork leg completely compressed.

CHAPTER NINE

REAR SUSPENSION

This chapter includes repair and replacement procedures for the rear wheel and rear suspension components. Rear brake repair is outlined in Chapter Ten.

REAR WHEEL

Removal/Installation

1. Place motorcycle on centerstand. If desired, remove mufflers as outlined in Chapter Six to provide better access to rear wheel components.
2. Remove cotter pin securing axle nut. See **Figure 1**.
3. Remove axle nut and washer (**Figure 2**).
4. Remove adjuster nut from brake rod (**Figure 3**) and disengage rod from brake lever. Do not lose brake lever pivot pin (**Figure 4**).
5. Remove snap clip or cotter pin securing torque link nut (**Figure 5**).
6. Remove nut securing brake torque link (**Figure 6**) and disengage link from brake backing plate.
7. Loosen locknut on chain adjuster bolt and back out bolt (**Figure 7**).

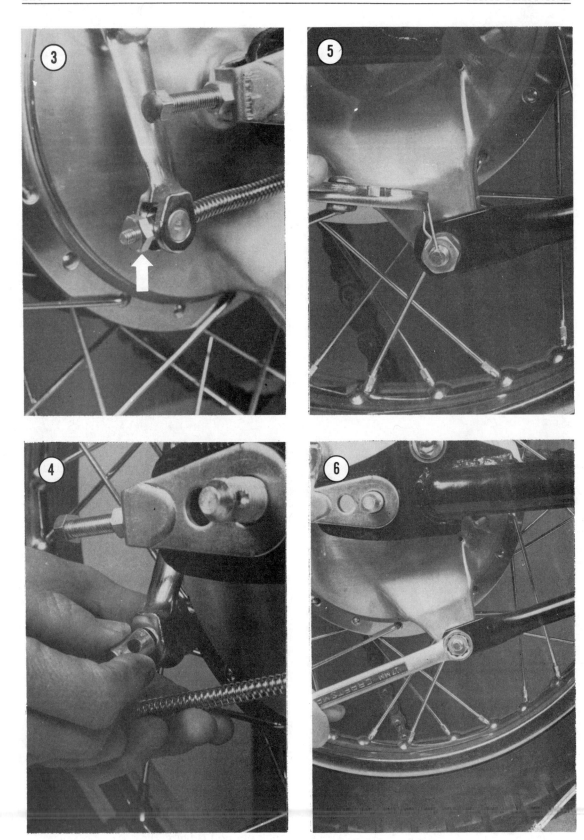

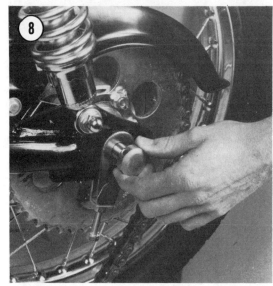

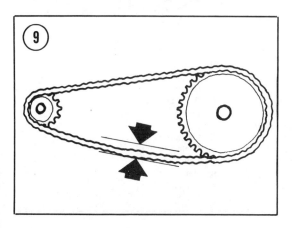

8. Swing chain adjusters down and push rear wheel as far forward as possible to gain maximum chain slack. Pull out axle (**Figure 8**). Disengage chain from rear sprocket and remove rear wheel.

9. Installation is the reverse of these steps. Keep the following points in mind:

a. Turn both chain adjuster bolts gradually and equally and check the chain deflection (slack) between the sprockets as shown in **Figure 9**. The chain slack should be 15-20 mm (5/8-13/16 in.) for GS400 models, and 20-30 mm (13/16-1 3/16 in.) for all other models.

b. Make sure that the index marks on the adjusters are aligned equally on both sides (**Figure 10**).

c. Torque the rear axle nut and torque link nut as specified in **Table 1**. Secure both nuts with new cotter pins or snap clips.

d. Adjust the rear brake adjuster nut to provide approximately 20-30 mm (3/4-1 3/16 in.) free play at the brake pedal.

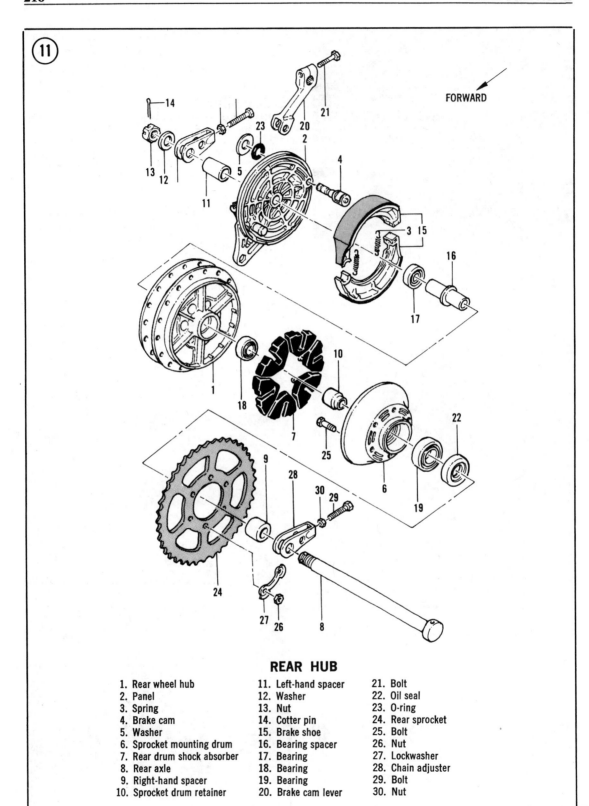

REAR HUB

1. Rear wheel hub
2. Panel
3. Spring
4. Brake cam
5. Washer
6. Sprocket mounting drum
7. Rear drum shock absorber
8. Rear axle
9. Right-hand spacer
10. Sprocket drum retainer

11. Left-hand spacer
12. Washer
13. Nut
14. Cotter pin
15. Brake shoe
16. Bearing spacer
17. Bearing
18. Bearing
19. Bearing
20. Brake cam lever

21. Bolt
22. Oil seal
23. O-ring
24. Rear sprocket
25. Bolt
26. Nut
27. Lockwasher
28. Chain adjuster
29. Bolt
30. Nut

Disassembly/Assembly

Refer to **Figure 11** for this procedure.

1. Remove rear wheel.

2. Lift out sprocket drum and remove drum retainer (spacer). See **Figure 12**.

3. Remove the 6 rubber shock absorbers (**Figure 13**).

4. Fold back locking tabs securing 6 sprocket nuts (**Figure 14**). Remove nuts and bolts and remove the sprocket.

5. Assembly is the reverse of these steps. Secure sprocket bolts with locking tabs. Inspect brake components as outlined in Chapter Ten.

Inspection

1. Rotate bearings by hand and check for roughness. If bearings turn smoothly, they need not be removed. However, if roughness is apparent, drive the sealed bearings out of the hub from the inside using a soft drift, or from the outside with a bearing puller.

2. Check sprocket for wear and replace it if teeth show signs of undercutting (**Figure 15**).

3. Check axle for straightness (**Figure 16**). If delflection is greater than 0.25 mm (0.010 in.), replace the axle.

9

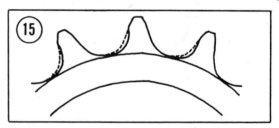

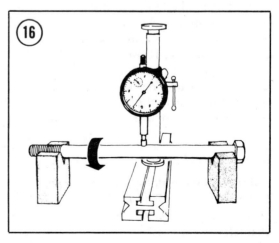

4. Check for bent, broken, or loose spokes. Replace any that are bent or broken and tighten loose spokes so that all spokes will have an equal "ring" when tapped with a wrench. Refer to *Spoke Adjustment* in Chapter Eight.

Wheel Balancing

Refer to *Wheel Balancing* as outlined in Chapter Eight.

SUSPENSION UNITS

The rear suspension units (spring/shock absorber assemblies) are non-repairable items. If units fail to dampen adequately, replace them as a set.

Removal/Installation

1. Place motorcycle on the centerstand and set the spring preload to the softest position.
2. Remove upper and lower mounting nuts and washers (**Figure 17 and Figure 18**) and remove suspension units.

> *NOTE*
> *Remove and install one unit at a time; the unit that remains in place will maintain the correct relationship between the top and bottom mounts and make the job easier.*

3. Installation is the reverse of these steps. Torque upper and lower mounting nuts to 2.0-3.0 mkg (15-22 ft.-lb.).

SWINGING ARM

The swinging arm pivot is equipped with pressed-in needle bearings. If correctly maintained (periodic cleaning, greasing, and adjustment), these bearings should last the life of the motorcycle. However, if they must be replaced, the swinging arm should be removed and entrusted to a dealer; a special puller is required to remove the bearings and it is unlikely that you would ever use it more than once.

Removal/Installation

Refer to **Figure 19** for this procedure.
1. Perform *Rear Wheel Removal* and *Suspension Unit Removal* as outlined in this chapter.

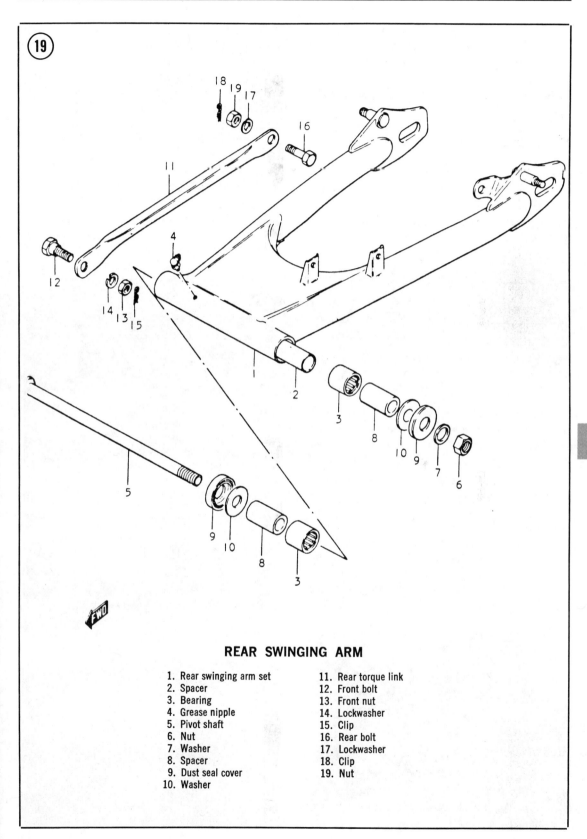

REAR SWINGING ARM

1. Rear swinging arm set
2. Spacer
3. Bearing
4. Grease nipple
5. Pivot shaft
6. Nut
7. Washer
8. Spacer
9. Dust seal cover
10. Washer
11. Rear torque link
12. Front bolt
13. Front nut
14. Lockwasher
15. Clip
16. Rear bolt
17. Lockwasher
18. Clip
19. Nut

2. Remove nut securing swinging arm pivot bolt and remove bolt (**Figure 20**).

3. Remove dust cover and washer (**Figure 21**) from each side of swinging arm.

4. Remove inner bearing race (spacer). See **Figure 22**.

5. Check condition of needle bearings (**Figure 23**) and replace them if they are worn, galled, or feel rough. Refer bearing replacement to a dealer.

6. Installation is the reverse of these steps. Grease pivot bolt and bearings before installation. Install pivot bolt from the left side and torque nut as specified in **Table 1**.

SPROCKET REPLACEMENT

Rear sprocket removal is outlined under *Rear Wheel Disassembly*. Remove engine drive sprocket as described in *Engine Removal*, Chapter Four.

DRIVE CHAIN

Drive chain care is very important. The chain and sprockets should be cleaned, inspected, and adjusted at least every 1,000 km (600 miles). If chain or sprocket wear is evident, they must be replaced as a set. An excessively stretched chain will cause severe vibration and will be difficult if not impossible to adjust properly.

Since the chain is a continuous type (no master link) a great deal of work would be involved in removing it just for cleaning.

An alternative method of cleaning is to use the high-pressure hose at a coin-operated car wash or use detergent and water with a small brush. Clean all exterior grit and dirt from the chain and drive the motorcycle briefly (no more than 2 miles). This warms the chain and throws off the trapped moisture. Thoroughly lubricate the chain with a spray chain lubricant. Strictly follow the manufacturer's instructions for its use. Keep the chain lubricated at all times to avoid stiff links, rust and corrosion, and excessive wear.

To remove chain, it is necessary to remove the swinging arm and chain guard. Refer to *Swinging Arm Removal*. Adjust chain as outlined under *Drive Chain Adjustment and Lubrication* in Chapter Three.

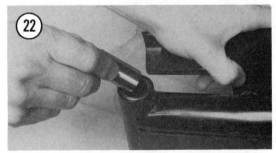

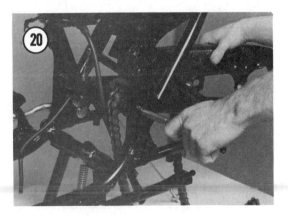

Table 1   REAR SUSPENSION TORQUE SPECIFICATIONS

Item	mkg	ft.-lb.
Rear sprocket nut	2.5-4.0	18-29
Swinging arm pivot nut		
GS400, GS425 models	5.0-8.0	36-58
GS450 models	5.0-5.8	36-42
Shock absorber nut	2.0-3.0	15-22
Rear axle nut		
GS400, GS425	8.5-11.5	62-83
GS450	5.0-8.0	36-58
Torque link nut	2.0-3.0	15-22

9

CHAPTER TEN

BRAKES

All models are equipped with a drum rear brake. The front brake may be either drum or hydraulic disc depending on the model.

DRUM BRAKE

The rear brake is a single leading shoe type actuated by one brake lever. The front brake is equipped with dual leading shoes actuated by two brake levers, one on each shoe.

The dual leading shoe arrangement provides the increased braking power necessary for front brakes.

Disassembly/Assembly

1. Remove front or rear wheel as outlined in Chapter Eight or Chapter Nine.

2. Remove brake backing plate from drum. Refer to **Figure 1** for front brake (dual leading shoe) and **Figure 2** for rear brake (single leading shoe).

3. To remove the brake shoes, firmly grasp and spread shoes against the spring pressure (**Figure 3**) and lift shoes off backing plate.

4. Assembly is the reverse of these steps. Do not attempt to install brake shoes without first connecting shoes together with the 2 return springs. Ensure that shoes are firmly seated on the backing plate.

5. If new shoes were installed on the front wheels, adjust the brake cam lever rod as follows:

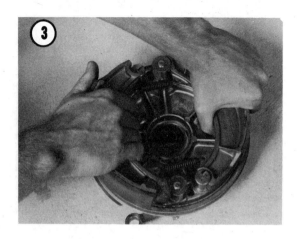

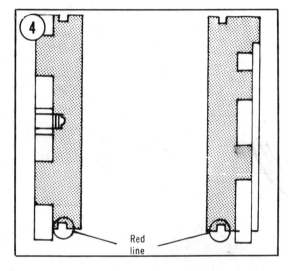

Red
line

a. Loosen locknut securing cam lever rod.
b. Lightly press brake lever until leading shoe contacts the brake drum, then turn cam lever rod until all free play is removed from the other brake lever and the trailing shoe just contacts the brake drum.
c. Tighten locknut securing cam lever rod.
d. Rotate cable adjuster nut on the front wheel until there is approximately 5 mm (3/16 in.) free play in the brake cable measured at the brake lever.
e. Spin the front wheel to make sure the brake shoes do not drag when the brakes are *not* applied.

Inspection

1. Check the brakes for wear and the presence of foreign matter. Grooves in the drum, deep enough to snag a fingernail, are an indication that the drum should be turned down on a lathe and new shoes fitted.
2. Examine the brake linings for oil, grease, or dirt. Oil-soaked linings cannot be satisfactorily rejuvenated; they should be replaced. Dirt imbedded in the lining may be removed with a wire brush.
3. Measure the thickness of the lining at its thinnest part. Replace both shoes when any portion of the lining is worn to about 1.5 mm (1/16 in.).
4. Check the brake shoe return springs for tension. If the springs are stretched and weak, they will not fully retract the shoes from the drum, resulting in a power-robbing drag on the drums and premature wear of the lining. In such a case, replace the springs.
5. During periodic inspection and when installing new shoes, lube the brake cam and pivot with high-temperature grease. Apply grease sparingly to prevent it from getting on the brake lining.

DISC BRAKE

The front disc brake caliper is actuated hydraulically by the front brake master cylinder lever. Master cylinder and caliper rebuilding and repair require special tools and expertise. These tasks should entrusted to your dealer.

Two types of front brake calipers are used. All 1979 and earlier models share one style, while all 1980 and later models are fitted with a "square pad" style caliper. All front calipers are single-piston units.

WARNING
If necessary to top off either master cylinder reservoir, only use brake fluid marked DOT 3 or DOT 4. All models use a glycol-based brake fluid. Mixing a glycol-based fluid with a petroleum-based or silicon-based fluid may cause brake component damage leading to brake failure.

Brake Pad Replacement (1979 and Earlier Models)

Replace both front pads as a set when they are worn down to the red line as shown in **Figure 4**.

10

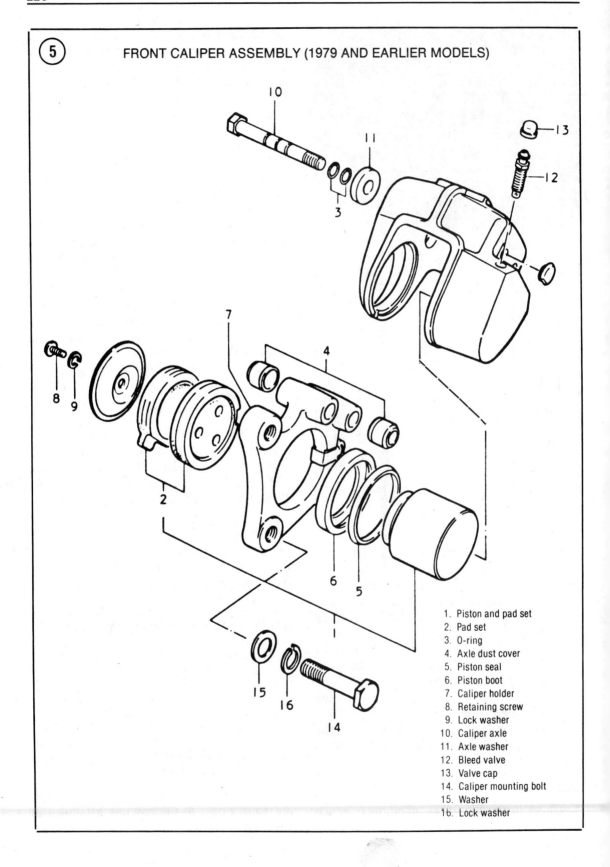

⑤ FRONT CALIPER ASSEMBLY (1979 AND EARLIER MODELS)

1. Piston and pad set
2. Pad set
3. O-ring
4. Axle dust cover
5. Piston seal
6. Piston boot
7. Caliper holder
8. Retaining screw
9. Lock washer
10. Caliper axle
11. Axle washer
12. Bleed valve
13. Valve cap
14. Caliper mounting bolt
15. Washer
16. Lock washer

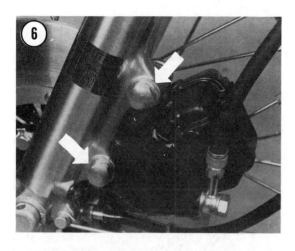

Refer to **Figure 5** for this procedure.

1. Remove the bolts securing the front caliper to the fork leg (**Figure 6**) and slide the caliper off the disc.

NOTE
Do not actuate the front brake lever while the caliper is removed or the caliper piston may be pushed completely out of the caliper body.

2. Remove the screw securing the pad lock plate (**Figure 7**) and remove the plate.
3. Press out and remove the stationary pad (**Figure 8**).
4. Pry up and remove the sliding pad (**Figure 9**).
5. Remove the cover from the front master cylinder reservoir. Wrap a rag around the reservoir to catch any brake fluid spills.
6. Slowly press the caliper piston back into the caliper as far as it will go.
7. Apply a *light* film of PBC brake pad grease (part No. 99000-25110) to the back of the sliding pad and to the surface of the caliper piston.

NOTE
Suzuki recommends a light film of PBC base (copper-colored) Brake Pad Grease (part No. 99000-25110) be applied between the pad and piston when new pads are installed. The grease then acts as a cushion and helps prevent "brake squeal" due to metal-to-metal contact.

10

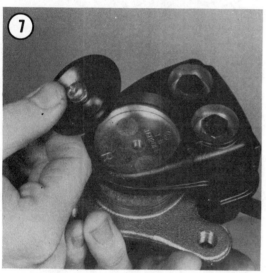

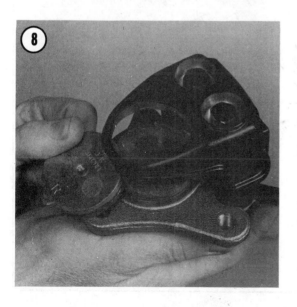

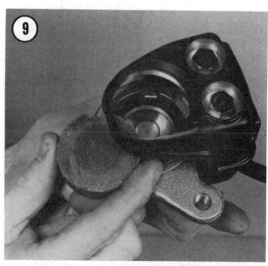

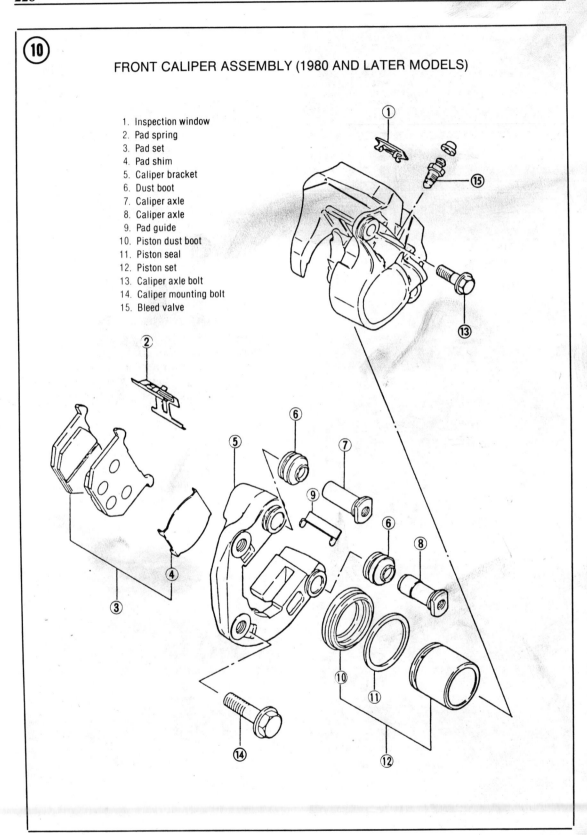

FRONT CALIPER ASSEMBLY (1980 AND LATER MODELS)

1. Inspection window
2. Pad spring
3. Pad set
4. Pad shim
5. Caliper bracket
6. Dust boot
7. Caliper axle
8. Caliper axle
9. Pad guide
10. Piston dust boot
11. Piston seal
12. Piston set
13. Caliper axle bolt
14. Caliper mounting bolt
15. Bleed valve

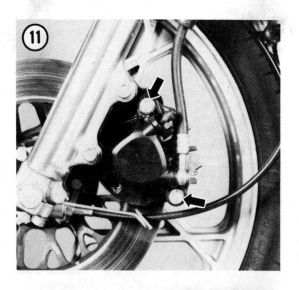

CAUTION
Do not allow any grease to get on the pad friction material or the pad will be ruined.

8. Install the sliding pad into the caliper body. Make sure that the notch in the pad engages the locating tab in the caliper.

9. Install the stationary pad and secure it with the pad lock plate.

10. Install the caliper. Torque the caliper mounting bolts to 2.5-4.0 mkg (18-29 ft.-lb.). Top up the master cylinder reservoir, if necessary.

11. Spin the front wheel and apply the front brakes a few times to ensure that the brakes operate properly and the pads adjust correctly.

Front Pad Replacement
(1980 and Later Models)

Refer to **Figure 10** for this procedure.

NOTE
Suzuki recommends the use of a small amount of silicon base (colorless) Caliper Axle Grease (part No. 99000-25100) on the caliper axles when the caliper is disassembled for pad replacement. Use the grease sparingly or pad and disc may become contaminated with grease, resulting in loss of braking power.

1. Remove the caliper axle bolts securing the outer caliper body to the caliper mounting bracket (**Figure 11**).

2. Carefully remove the caliper body from the fork leg (**Figure 12**).

3. Remove the outer brake pad (**Figure 13**). Note the metal backing plate on the pad.

4. Remove the inner brake pad as shown in **Figure 14**.

5. Use a clean rag and wipe the pad sliding surfaces on the caliper mounting bracket (**Figure 15**).

6. Install new inner and outer brake pads. Ensure that the outer plate is fitted with the metal backing plate.

7. Remove the cover from the front master cylinder reservoir. Wrap a rag around the reservoir to catch any brake fluid spills.

NOTE
If the reservoir is full, brake fluid may overflow slightly when the caliper piston is pushed completely back into the caliper.

8. Apply a *light* film of colorless Caliper Axle Grease (part No. 99000-25100) to the caliper axles (**Figure 16**).

CAUTION
Do not allow any grease to get on the pad friction material or the pad will be ruined.

9. Install the caliper axles with the "flats" on the axles positioned horizontally as shown in **Figure 17**.

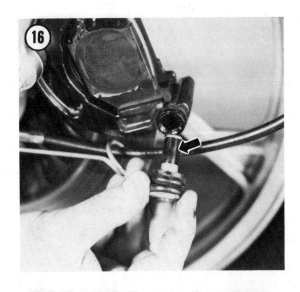

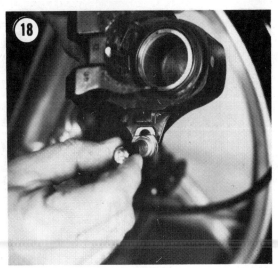

WARNING
*The caliper axles must be positioned correctly so the "flats" fit exactly in the notches in the caliper body or the brakes will not operate correctly. See **Figure 18**.*

10. Slowly press the caliper piston back into the caliper as far as it will go.

11. Ensure that the caliper springs are correctly positioned as shown in **Figure 19**.

12. Hold both pads in position and carefully slide the caliper body onto the caliper mounting bracket (**Figure 20**).

13. Torque the caliper axle bolts (A, **Figure 21**) to 1.5-2.0 mkg (11-15 ft.-lb.).

14. Top up the master cylinder reservoir with approved brake fluid, if necessary, and install the reservoir cap.

15. Spin the front wheel and apply the front brake a few times to ensure that the brakes operate properly and the pads adjust correctly.

Caliper Removal/Installation

1. Remove banjo bolt securing brake hose to caliper. Have a drain pan ready to catch the dripping brake fluid.

NOTE
If caliper is being removed for pad replacement, it is not necessary to remove the brake hose.

2. Remove 2 bolts (**B, Figure 21**) securing caliper to fork leg and remove the caliper.

3. Installation is the reverse of these steps. Bleed brakes if brake hose was removed. Torque caliper bolts to 2.5-4.0 mkg (18-29 ft.-lb.). Torque brake hose bolt to 1.5-2.5 mkg (11-18 ft.-lb.).

Master Cylinder Removal/Installation

1. Pull back rubber boot and remove banjo bolt securing brake hose to master cylinder. Have a drain pan or container ready to catch draining fluid.

CAUTION
Do not allow brake fluid to contact the fuel tank or frame, or the paint may be damaged.

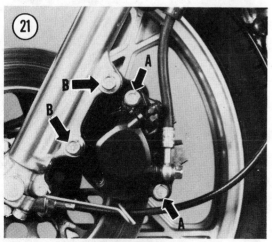

A. Caliper axle bolts
B. Caliper retaining bolts

10

2. Remove 2 bolts securing master cylinder to handlebar (**Figure 22**) and remove master cylinder.

3. Installation is the reverse of these steps. Refer master cylinder repair to a dealer. Torque brake hose bolt to 1.5-2.5 mkg (11-18 ft.-lb.). Torque master cylinder mounting bolts to 0.6-1.0 mkg (4-7 ft.-lb.). Bleed the brake system.

Disc Removal/Installation

Front disc removal and installation is described in *Front Wheel Disassembly*, Chapter Eight.

BLEEDING AND CHANGING BRAKE FLUID

Bleeding

The hydraulic brake system must be bled to remove all air and contamination. Bleeding the system is necessary any time a line or hose is disconnected, a cylinder or caliper is removed and disassembled, or when the brake "feel" in the lever or pedal is spongy, indicating the presence of air in the system.

1. Fill the master cylinder reservoir with fresh brake fluid to the upper line. Install the reservoir cap.

> *WARNING*
> *When adding brake fluid to the master cylinder reservoir, only use brake fluid marked DOT 3 or DOT 4. All models use a glycol-based brake fluid. Mixing a glycol-based fluid with any other type of fluid, whether petroleum-based or silicon-based, may cause brake component damage leading to brake failure.*

2. Refer to **Figure 23** and remove the dust cap from the bleeder valve. Connect a length of hose approximately 2 feet long to the bleed valve. Place the other end of the tubing in an empty can.

3. Pump the brake lever several times until resistance is felt. Hold the lever and open the bleeder valve about 1/4 turn. Continue to squeeze the lever until it reaches the limit of travel. Hold it in this position and close the bleeder valve.

4. Release the lever and repeat the previous step as many times as necessary until the fluid passing through the tubing is clean and free of air bubbles.

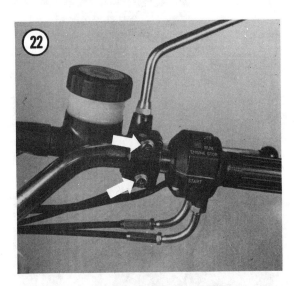

NOTE
Do not allow the reservoir to empty during the bleeding process or more air will be drawn into the system. Always keep the reservoir topped off.

5. When the brake fluid is clean and free of air, tighten the bleeder valve and remove the tubing. Replace the dust cap on the valve.

6. Top up the reservoir to the upper limit line. Hold the lever down and check all the brake line connections for leaks. Correct any leaks immediately.

Changing Fluid

Each time the reservoir cap is removed a small amount of contamination and moisture enters the reservoir. The same thing occurs if there is a leak or any part of the system is loosened or disconnected. Dirt can clog the system and moisture can lead to corrosion of internal brake components.

To keep the brake system as clean and free of contamination as possible, completely change the brake fluid at least every 2 years.

To change the fluid, perform *Bleeding* and continue adding new fluid until the fluid bled out is visibly clean and without air bubbles.

10

INDEX

11

1977-1978 GS400

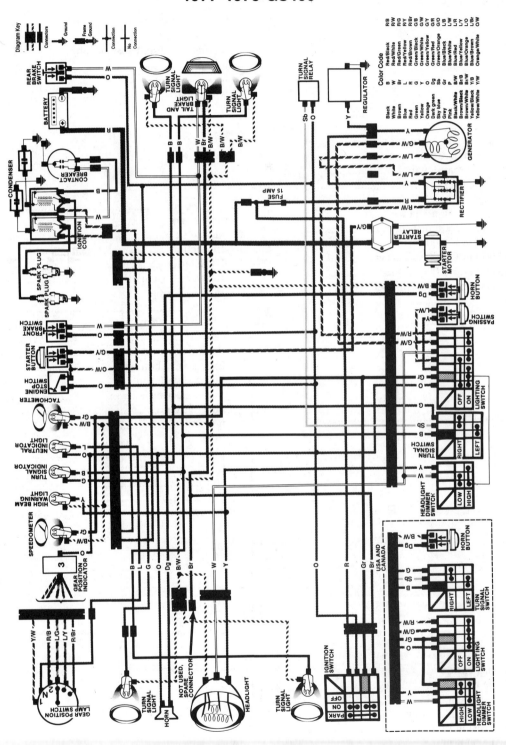

1979 GS425

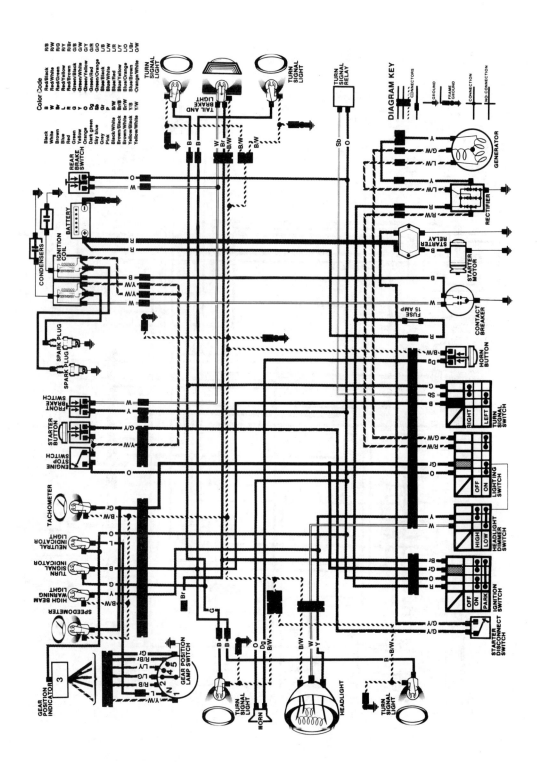

1980-1981 GS450ET, LT, ST, EX, SX

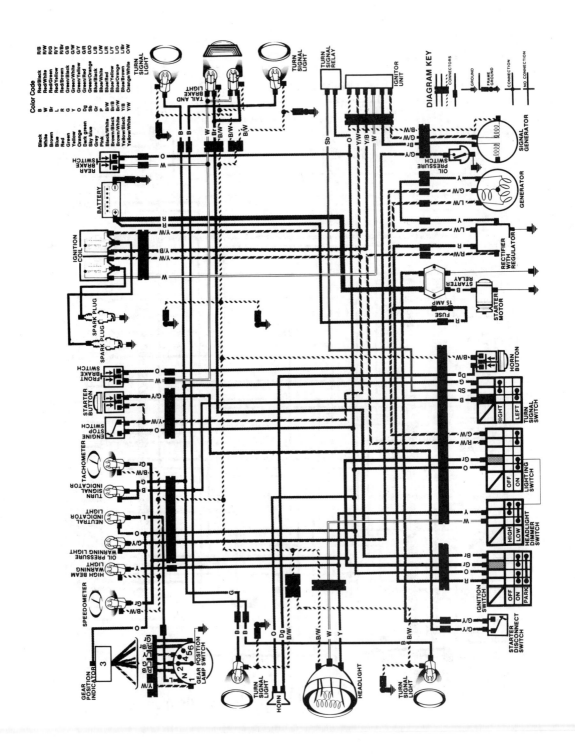

1981 GS450LX, TX

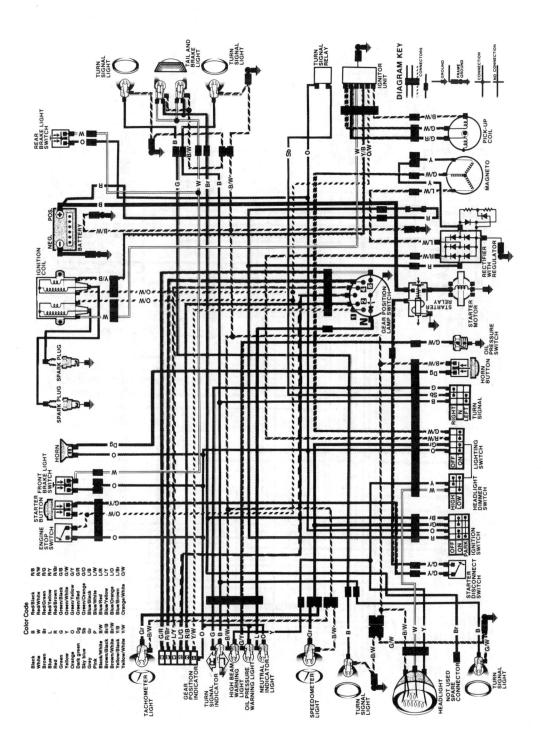

1982 GS450EZ, LZ, TZ, TXZ

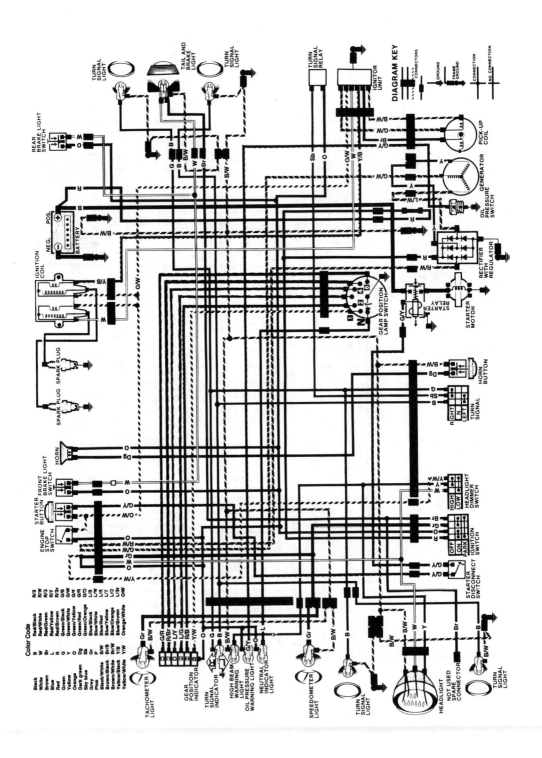

1983 GS450ED

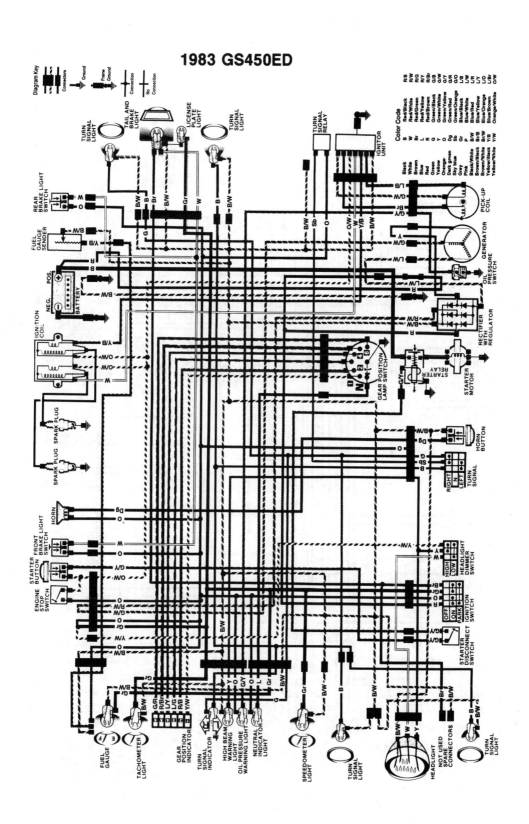

1983, 1985-1986 GS450LD, LF, LG

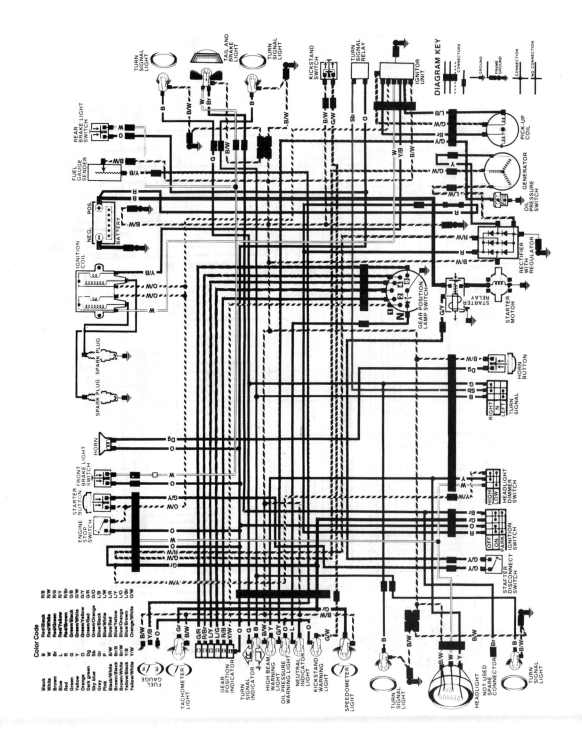

1983 GS450TXD

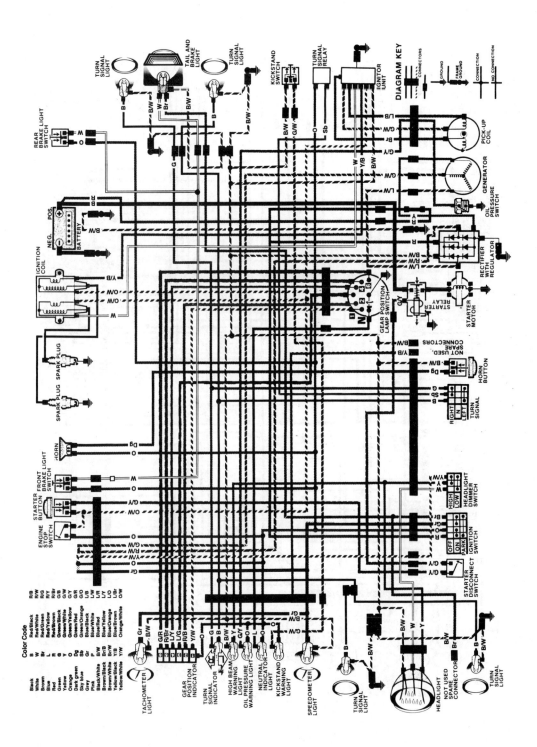

1987 GS450LH

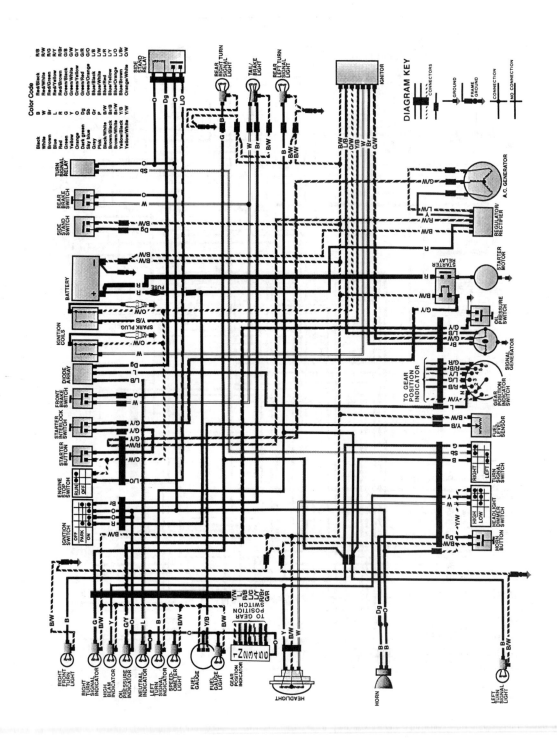

MAINTENANCE LOG

Date	Miles	Type of Service

BMW

M308	500 & 600cc Twins, 55-69
M502-3	BMW R50/5-R100GS PD, 70-96
M500-3	BMW K-Series, 85-97
M501-3	K1200RS, GT & LT, 98-10
M503-3	R850, R1100, R1150 & R1200C, 93-05
M309	F650, 1994-2000

HARLEY-DAVIDSON

M419	Sportsters, 59-85
M429-5	XL/XLH Sportster, 86-03
M427-3	XL Sportster, 04-11
M418	Panheads, 48-65
M420	Shovelheads,66-84
M421-3	FLS/FXS Evolution,84-99
M423-2	FLS/FXS Twin Cam, 00-05
M250	FLS/FXS/FXC Softail, 06-09
M422-3	FLH/FLT/FXR Evolution, 84-98
M430-4	FLH/FLT Twin Cam, 99-05
M252	FLH/FLT, 06-09
M426	VRSC Series, 02-07
M424-2	FXD Evolution, 91-98
M425-3	FXD Twin Cam, 99-05

HONDA

ATVs

M316	Odyssey FL250, 77-84
M311	ATC, TRX & Fourtrax 70-125, 70-87
M433	Fourtrax 90, 93-00
M326	ATC185 & 200, 80-86
M347	ATC200X & Fourtrax 200SX, 86-88
M455	ATC250 & Fourtrax 200/250, 84-87
M342	ATC250R, 81-84
M348	TRX250R/Fourtrax 250R & ATC250R, 85-89
M456-4	TRX250X 87-92; TRX300EX 93-06
M446-3	TRX250 Recon & Recon ES, 97-07
M215	TRX250EX, 01-05
M346-3	TRX300/Fourtrax 300 & TRX300FW/Fourtrax 4x4, 88-00
M200-2	TRX350 Rancher, 00-06
M459-3	TRX400 Foreman 95-03
M454-4	TRX400EX 99-07
M201	TRX450R & TRX450ER, 04-09
M205	TRX450 Foreman, 98-04
M210	TRX500 Rubicon, 01-04
M206	TRX500 Foreman, 05-11

Singles

M310-13	50-110cc OHC Singles, 65-99
M315	100-350cc OHC, 69-82
M317	125-250cc Elsinore, 73-80
M442	CR60-125R Pro-Link, 81-88
M431-2	CR80R, 89-95, CR125R, 89-91
M435	CR80R & CR80RB, 96-02
M457-2	CR125R, 92-97; CR250R, 92-96
M464	CR125R, 1998-2002
M443	CR250R-500R Pro-Link, 81-87
M432-3	CR250R, 88-91 & CR500R, 88-01
M437	CR250R, 97-01
M352	CRF250R, CRF250X, CRF450R & CRF450X, 02-05
M319-3	XR50R, CRF50F, XR70R & CRF70F, 97-09
M312-14	XL/XR75-100, 75-91
M222	XR80R, CRF80F, XR100R & CRF100F, 92-09
M318-4	XL/XR/TLR 125-200, 79-03
M328-4	XL/XR250, 78-00; XL/XR350R 83-85; XR200R, 84-85; XR250L, 91-96
M320-2	XR400R, 96-04
M221	XR600R, 91-07; XR650L, 93-07
M339-8	XL/XR 500-600, 79-90
M225	XR650R, 00-07

Twins

M321	125-200cc Twins, 65-78
M322	250-350cc Twins, 64-74
M323	250-360cc Twins, 74-77
M324-5	Twinstar, Rebel 250 & Nighthawk 250, 78-03
M334	400-450cc Twins, 78-87
M333	450 & 500cc Twins, 65-76
M335	CX & GL500/650, 78-83
M344	VT500, 83-88
M313	VT700 & 750, 83-87
M314-3	VT750 Shadow Chain Drive, 98-06
M440	VT1100C Shadow, 85-96
M460-4	VT1100 Series, 95-07
M230	VTX1800 Series, 02-08
M231	VTX1300 Series, 03-09

Fours

M332	CB350-550, SOHC, 71-78
M345	CB550 & 650, 83-85
M336	CB650,79-82
M341	CB750 SOHC, 69-78
M337	CB750 DOHC, 79-82
M436	CB750 Nighthawk, 91-93 & 95-99
M325	CB900, 1000 & 1100, 80-83
M439	600 Hurricane, 87-90
M441-2	CBR600F2 & F3, 91-98
M445-2	CBR600F4, 99-06
M220	CBR600RR, 03-06
M434-2	CBR900RR Fireblade, 93-99
M329	500cc V-Fours, 84-86
M349	700-1000cc Interceptor, 83-85
M458-2	VFR700F-750F, 86-97
M438	VFR800FI Interceptor, 98-00
M327	700-1100cc V-Fours, 82-88
M508	ST1100/Pan European, 90-02
M340	GL1000 & 1100, 75-83
M504	GL1200, 84-87

Sixes

M505	GL1500 Gold Wing, 88-92
M506-2	GL1500 Gold Wing, 93-00
M507-3	GL1800 Gold Wing, 01-10
M462-2	GL1500C Valkyrie, 97-03

KAWASAKI

ATVs

M465-3	Bayou KLF220 & KLF250, 88-10
M466-4	Bayou KLF300, 86-04
M467	Bayou KLF400, 93-99
M470	Lakota KEF300, 95-99
M385-2	Mojave KSF250, 87-04

Singles

M350-9	80-350cc Rotary Valve, 66-01
M444-2	KX60 83-02; KX80 83-90
M448-2	KX80, 91-00; KX85, 01-10 & KX100, 89-09
M351	KDX200, 83-88
M447-3	KX125 & KX250, 82-91; KX500, 83-04
M472-2	KX125, 92-00
M473-2	KX250, 92-00
M474-3	KLR650, 87-07
M240-2	KLR650, 08-12

Twins

M355	KZ400, KZ/Z440, EN450 & EN500, 74-95
M360-3	EX500, GPZ500S, & Ninja 500R, 87-02
M356-5	Vulcan 700 & 750, 85-06
M354-3	Vulcan 800 & Vulcan 800 Classic, 95-05
M357-2	Vulcan 1500, 87-99
M471-3	Vulcan 1500 Series, 96-08
M245	Vulcan 1600 Series, 03-08

Fours

M449	KZ500/550 & ZX550, 79-85
M450	KZ, Z & ZX750, 80-85
M358	KZ650, 77-83
M359-3	Z & KZ 900-1000cc, 73-81
M451-3	KZ, ZX & ZN 1000 &1100cc, 81-02
M452-3	ZX500 & Ninja ZX600, 85-97
M468-2	Ninja ZX-6, 90-04
M469	Ninja ZX-7, ZX7R & ZX7RR, 91-98
M453-3	Ninja ZX900, ZX1000 & ZX1100, 84-01
M409	Concours, 86-04

POLARIS

ATVs

M496	3-, 4- and 6-Wheel Models w/250-425cc Engines, 85-95
M362-2	Magnum & Big Boss, 96-99
M363	Scrambler 500 4X4, 97-00
M365-4	Sportsman/Xplorer, 96-10
M366	Sportsman 600/700/800 Twins, 02-10
M367	Predator 500, 03-07

SUZUKI

ATVs

M381	ALT/LT 125 & 185, 83-87
M475	LT230 & LT250, 85-90
M380-2	LT250R Quad Racer, 85-92
M483-2	LT-4WD, LT-F4WDX & LT-F250, 87-98
M270-2	LT-Z400, 03-08
M343-2	LT-F500F Quadrunner, 98-02

Singles

M369	125-400cc, 64-81
M371	RM50-400 Twin Shock, 75-81
M379	RM125-500 Single Shock, 81-88
M386	RM80-250, 89-95
M400	RM125, 96-00
M401	RM250, 96-02
M476	DR250-350, 90-94
M477-3	DR-Z400E, S & SM, 00-09
M384-4	LS650 Savage/S40, 86-07

Twins

M372	GS400-450 Chain Drive, 77-87
M484-3	GS500E Twins, 89-02
M361	SV650, 1999-2002
M481-5	VS700-800 Intruder/S50, 85-07
M261-2	1500 Intruder/C90, 98-09
M260-2	Volusia/Boulevard C50, 01-08
M482-3	VS1400 Intruder/S83, 87-07

Triple

M368	GT380, 550 & 750, 72-77

Fours

M373	GS550, 77-86
M364	GS650, 81-83
M370	GS750, 77-82
M376	GS850-1100 Shaft Drive, 79-84
M378	GS1100 Chain Drive, 80-81
M383-3	Katana 600, 88-96 GSX-R750-1100, 86-87
M331	GSX-R600, 97-00
M264	GSX-R600, 01-05
M478-2	GSX-R750, 88-92; GSX750F Katana, 89-96
M485	GSX-R750, 96-99
M377	GSX-R1000, 01-04
M266	GSX-R1000, 05-06
M265	GSX1300R Hayabusa, 99-07
M338	Bandit 600, 95-00
M353	GSF1200 Bandit, 96-03

YAMAHA

ATVs

M499-2	YFM80 Moto-4, Badger & Raptor, 85-08
M394	YTM200, 225 & YFM200, 83-86
M488-5	Blaster, 88-05
M489-2	Timberwolf, 89-00
M487-5	Warrior, 87-04
M486-6	Banshee, 87-06
M490-3	Moto-4 & Big Bear, 87-04
M493	Kodiak, 93-98
M287	YFZ450, 04-09
M285-2	Grizzly 660, 02-08
M280-2	Raptor 660R, 01-05
M290	Raptor 700R, 06-09

Singles

M492-2	PW50 & 80 Y-Zinger & BW80 Big Wheel 80, 81-02
M410	80-175 Piston Port, 68-76
M415	250-400 Piston Port, 68-76
M412	DT & MX Series, 77-83
M414	IT125-490, 76-86
M393	YZ50-80 Monoshock, 78-90
M413	YZ100-490 Monoshock, 76-84
M390	YZ125-250, 85-87 YZ490, 85-90
M391	YZ125-250, 88-93 & WR250Z, 91-93
M497-2	YZ125, 94-01
M498	YZ250, 94-98; WR250Z, 94-97
M406	YZ250F & WR250F, 01-03
M491-2	YZ400F, 98-99 & 426F, 00-02; WR400F, 98-00 & 426F, 00-01
M417	XT125-250, 80-84
M480-3	XT350, 85-00; TT350, 86-87
M405	XT/TT 500, 76-81
M416	XT/TT 600, 83-89

Twins

M403	650cc Twins, 70-82
M395-10	XV535-1100 Virago, 81-03
M495-6	V-Star 650, 98-09
M281-4	V-Star 1100, 99-09
M283	V-Star 1300, 07-10
M282-2	Road Star, 99-07

Triple

M404	XS750 & XS850, 77-81

Fours

M387	XJ550, XJ600 & FJ600, 81-92
M494	XJ600 Seca II/Diversion, 92-98
M388	YX600 Radian & FZ600, 86-90
M396	FZR600, 89-93
M392	FZ700-750 & Fazer, 85-87
M411	XS1100, 78-81
M461	YZF-R6, 99-04
M398	YZF-R1, 98-03
M399	FZ1, 01-05
M397	FJ1100 & 1200, 84-93
M375	V-Max, 85-03
M374-2	Royal Star, 96-10

VINTAGE MOTORCYCLES

Clymer® Collection Series

M330	Vintage British Street Bikes, BSA 350–650cc Unit Twins; Norton 750 & 850cc Commandos; Triumph 500-750cc Twins
M300	Vintage Dirt Bikes, V. 1 Bultaco, 125-370cc Singles; Montesa, 123-360cc Singles; Ossa, 125-250cc Singles
M305	Vintage Japanese Street Bikes Honda, 250 & 305cc Twins; Kawasaki, 250-750cc Triples; Kawasaki, 900 & 1000cc Fours